PARTING COMPANY

PARTING COMPANY

INNOVATIVE STRATEGIES TO

PLAN FOR SUCCESSION

MANAGE THE TRANSITION

SELL OR TRANSFER YOUR BUSINESS

ANDREW J. SHERMAN

KIPLINGER BOOKS
Washington, D.C.

Published by
The Kiplinger Washington Editors, Inc.
1729 H Street, N.W.
Washington, D.C. 20006

Library of Congress Cataloging-in-Publication Data

Sherman, Andrew J.
   Parting Company: innovative strategies to plan for succession, manage the transition, sell or transfer your business/Andrew J. Sherman.
     p. cm.
   Includes index.
   ISBN 0-938721-66-6 (cloth)
   1. Sale of business enterprises—United States—Planning. Sale of small businesses—United States—Planning. 3. Family-owned business enterprises—United States—Succession—Planning. 4. Business enterprises—Registration and transfer—United States—Planning. I. Title.
HD2746.6.S54 1999   99-37347
658.1'6—dc21   CIP

©1999 by The Kiplinger Washington Editors, Inc. All rights reserved. No part of this book may be reproduced or transmitted in any form or by any means, electronic or mechanical, including photocopying, recording or by an information storage and retrieval system, without the written permission of the Publisher, except where permitted by law.

This publication is intended to provide guidance in regard to the subject matter covered. It is sold with the understanding that the author and publisher are not herein engaged in rendering legal, accounting, tax or other professional services. If such services are required, professional assistance should be sought.

First edition. Printed in the United States of America.
9 8 7 6 5 4 3 2 1

"The Ultimate Test" reprinted by permission of FORBES Magazine © Forbes Inc., 1997.

Kiplinger publishes books and videos on a wide variety of personal finance and business management subjects. Check our Web site (www.kiplinger.com) for a complete list of titles, additional information and excerpts. Or write:
Cindy Greene
Kiplinger Books & Tapes
1729 H Street, NW
Washington, DC 20006
e-mail: cgreene@kiplinger.com
To order, call 800-280-7165; for information about volume discounts, call 202-887-6431.

Dedication

In loving memory of
family business owners
Samuel and Elsie Goldman

Acknowledgments

THIS BOOK WOULD NOT BE POSSIBLE WITHOUT the editorial and logistical support of Jennifer Robinson and David Harrison at Kiplinger Books. It has also benefited from Kevin McCormally's invaluable tax advice, Allison Leopold's skillful copy editing and Rosemary Neff's painstaking proofreading. And I tip my hat to Mary Pat Doherty and Heather Waugh for their work on the book's cover and interior, respectively.

Parting Company commences a series of books and resources for closely held and family businesses that will be published by Kiplinger over the next few years, and its timing is especially appropriate: Last year marked the 75th anniversary of *The Kiplinger Washington Letter*, which has been published by a business that has faced its own share of succession-planning and business-growth challenges. I began reading *The Letter* nearly 30 years ago, when my uncle, Gary Goldman, gave me his copy to read at age 9. I am truly honored to be the author of a book published by this excellent organization.

I also want to thank my partners at Katten Muchin & Zavis for their continuing support and encouragement, especially Michael Hartz for his willingness to review and edit Chapters 4, 5, 6 and 8, and Mark Weisberg for his careful review of Chapter 8. For the seventh book in a row, I turned to my friend and trusted colleague, Michele Woodfolk, for her organizational skills and word-processing magic.

Finally, my wife, Judy, and children, Matthew and Jennifer, again deserve much of the credit for putting up with me, chapter after chapter, and the many afternoons spent writing that we could have spent together as a family.

Table of Contents

Introduction xi
Foreword xv

SECTION ONE:
An Overview of Succession Planning and Transition Management

Chapter 1: Why You Need a Plan 1
The Basics of Succession Planning • The Differences Between Estate Planning and Succession Planning • The Succession-Planning Preparedness Quiz • Transition Management and Exit Strategies

Chapter 2: What's Your Company Worth? 15
The Valuation Challenge for a Small or Closely Held Company • Use of a Professional Business Appraiser • Determining Strategic Value • Categories of Valuation Methods • Selecting a Method

Chapter 3: The Importance of Insurance 29
Choosing the Right Product • Life Insurance and Taxes • How Much Do You Need? • Life Insurance for Your Spouse • Shopping for the Best Insurance Deal

SECTION TWO:
Succession Planning and the Family Business

Chapter 4: The Special Challenges of Dealing With Relatives 39
The Next Generation's Perspective • Setting the Stage for Seamless Succession

Chapter 5: Developing The Family Business Continuity Plan 49
The Pre-Planning Process • The Basics of Business and Financial Planning • The Family Business Continuity Plan

SECTION THREE: Succession Planning Strategies

Chapter 6: Keeping Your Business in the Family 67
Gifting • Trusts • Estate Freezes • Family Limited Partnerships

Chapter 7: Dealing With Non-Family Co-Owners 85
Why Have a Co-Founder? • Understanding the Buy-Sell Agreement • Valuation and Pricing Issues • The IRS and the Buy-Sell Agreement

Chapter 8: Selling to Your Employees 105
Selling to Your Staff: ESOPs as an Exit Strategy • Alternatives to the ESOP

Chapter 9: Selling to a Third Party 121
Will I Be Able to Find a Buyer? When is the Right Time to Sell? • Getting Your House in Order: Preparing to Sell Your Business • Common Preparation Mistakes Sellers Make • The Letter of Intent • Preparing the Work Schedule • Structuring the Deal

Chapter 10: Going Public 143
The Hidden Legal Costs • Selecting an Underwriter • The SEC's Small Business Initiatives • An Overview of the Registration Process • Ongoing Reporting and Disclosure Requirements

Chapter 11: Creative Exit Strategies 155
Business Format Franchising • Joint Ventures • Licensing

Resource Directory 175

Appendix 197
Legal Audit Checklist • Sample Shareholders' Agreement • Sample Stock Option Plan • Sample Letter of Intent

Index 247

Introduction

THE SUBJECT OF THIS BOOK—PLANNING FOR THE future of a closely held business—is one that is near and dear to my heart. That's because the Kiplinger publishing company is just such a business. It's also one of the small minority of family-run firms that have survived into the third generation.

The vast majority of closely held businesses don't continue under family ownership and management into even a second generation. Sometimes this results from a carefully considered plan by the founder to sell the firm to employees or outside interests. But too often, it's the result of happenstance—the absence of clear-headed succession planning.

The theme of this book is simple: There are many different scenarios that can end successfully for the business, its founders, their heirs and employees—but only if planning is begun early and intelligently. Sadly, many business owners and managers feel they are too busy with today's challenges to plan for tomorrow. Or they don't want to confront tough emotional issues.

Our company's founder, my grandfather W.M. Kiplinger, operated in an era before succession planning and family-business consulting had become the formal discipline it is today. But, as a journalist who followed business management issues, he was well-positioned to adopt—indeed, to pioneer—some of the strategies for family business preservation that would later become commonplace. He also embraced some practices—such as companywide profit-sharing and corporate philanthropy—that still haven't caught on with most closely held businesses today.

Foresightedly, W.M. Kiplinger created two classes of stock for his company—one with voting privileges, one without. Today, the non-voting, dividend-paying shares are broadly owned by three generations of family members, most of them not employed by the company. But voting stock isn't so dispersed. It's held by only three family members (my father, brother and me) who work in the company.

Long before ESOPs (employee stock ownership plans) became popular, my grandfather gave—not sold—nearly a third of the company's stock (non-voting shares) to his employees, to be held in a stock trust that functions like an ESOP. This gesture of great generosity also had the effect of reducing his taxable estate and thereby helping to keep the company in family control. Our employees benefit in three ways—from the company's annual profit-sharing contributions to the trust, from dividends paid on the shares owned by the trust, and most of all, from price appreciation on the shares. (W.M. Kiplinger also gave a big chunk of his Kiplinger stock to a private foundation he created—a charitable gift of a kind that was later limited by regrettable changes in federal tax law.)

All of these initiatives were smart estate planning moves, and they have helped keep our company independent through three generations. But they weren't succession plans—moves to transfer control of the company during his lifetime. Succession planning is about management more than ownership, and like many entrepreneurs, W.M. Kiplinger had a harder time giving up control than shares of stock. He didn't create a plan for passing control to anyone else during his lifetime (only at his death) or a timetable for his own retirement. He was still chairman of the board, with legal control of the company, when he died at the age of 76, after several years of declining health and waning involvement in the company.

But despite the lack of a formal plan, succession at the Kiplinger organization was never in doubt. The founder's son—my father Austin Kiplinger—had shown a great talent for both journalism and management, in jobs within and outside the company. After working with distinction in television news for ABC and NBC in the 1950s, Austin rejoined the Kiplinger organization, and as its president, he ran it very successfully for several years before his father's death.

This tradition of informal, rolling shifts in leadership continues at the company today. It works because of respect and trust among family members. Leadership is very collegial, and authority is delegated gradually, almost seamlessly, to younger executives, both family and non-family employees. My older brother, Todd, has worked in the firm his whole career, moving through several departments (editorial, subscription sales, etc.) before taking over management of the company's financial portfolio assets. I worked in newspaper journalism outside the company for 13 years, as a Washington reporter and bureau chief, before joining the company in 1983, to learn and eventually run the publishing operations.

Our father isn't retired, but he has gradually withdrawn from active management to devote more time to civic and philanthropic affairs. He is still chairman of our board, but unlike his father before him, he shares voting control with the next generation—Todd (vice chairman) and me (president). The three of us strive for agreement on major issues, but if we ever fail to agree, a majority of two would decide. Someday voting control will be shared equally by Todd and me, with tie-breaking power vested in a committee of our senior executives.

Our succession planning strategies aren't perfect, but we've got the big pieces in place. After all, we're still in business after nearly 80 years. And more important, we still get along as a family. We've accomplished this by doing over the years, consciously or unconsciously, the sorts of things recommended as "best practices" in this excellent new guide by attorney and business consultant Andrew J. Sherman.

For example, we commission biennial professional appraisals of the company's value, updated internally every four months. We try to maintain a modest dividend, to give non-employee family shareholders some current income. As the resources of the company permit, we offer to buy back shares of Kiplinger stock—at the appraised price—from family shareholders and from the employee stock trust. We communicate regularly with the numerous family shareholders who don't work in the business, telling them how it is doing and what challenges and opportunities it faces. We try to anticipate the big tax bills that lie ahead when family shareholders die, so the company will be prepared to buy stock from their estates. We family members try to deal professionally and courteously with each other at all times, to minimize the tensions that can surface in all family businesses.

Are there things we could do better? Sure. We should have regular, rather than occasional, family meetings focusing only on strategic planning issues. We should have more-formal succession and retirement plans. We should be constantly examining whether the ownership structure that has served us well for 80 years—the small privately held business—is still our best model for prospering in tomorrow's economy.

I learned a lot from studying the manuscript of this book as it moved through our editing process. I think you will too. Whether your goal is keeping your business in the family forever, selling to a partner or competitor, or taking it public, Andrew J. Sherman gives you a blueprint for pursuing it.

From all of us at Kiplinger, our best wishes for success and personal fulfillment along whatever road you take.

Knight Kiplinger

Knight Kiplinger
Editor, *The Kiplinger Letters*
President, The Kiplinger Washington Editors, Inc.

Foreword

THE TITLE OF THIS BOOK WAS CAREFULLY CHOSEN. Many books focus on succession planning, concentrating only on family-owned businesses, and detailing how the next generation takes over when the present owners are ready to retire. But retirement's not the only reason that a business owner needs to think about change in leadership. And not all small businesses are family owned. *Parting Company* broadens the lens. The subject is transition management—how small, closely held businesses (including family-owned enterprises) can prepare for and have an answer to the question they'll each ultimately face: Who will take over when the founder—or the current leadership team—is ready to step down?

The reasons *why* you (as the owner or part of the current leadership team) may be ready to depart must be taken into account and may affect *how* the transition will be managed (for example, which strategy might best facilitate a smooth transition). You'll have to consider a wide variety of factors, including:

- **your current and future financial needs;**
- **the tax implications** of the selected strategy;
- **the current and projected performance** or valuation of the business;
- **the third parties** (such as employees, customers, vendors, licensees, lenders, landlords and others) who might be directly or indirectly affected by the selected strategy;
- **the availability of "creative exit strategies"** such as franchising or an initial public offering, which would accomplish a partial rather than total transition;
- **the existence of any agreements,** such as shareholders' agreements, commercial-loan requirements or venture-capital investment agreements, that restrict or affect the range of choices available,

Strategies for Leaving Your Business

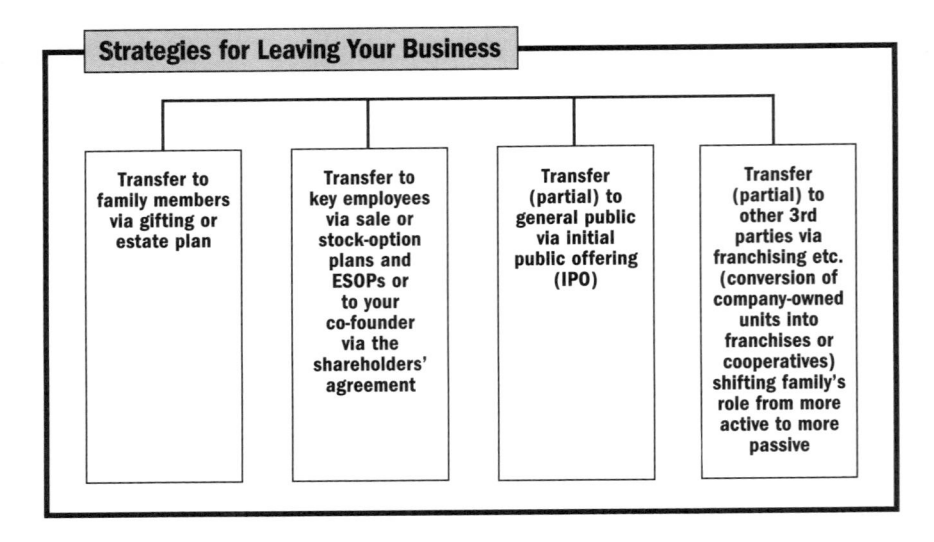

| Transfer to family members via gifting or estate plan | Transfer to key employees via sale or stock-option plans and ESOPs or to your co-founder via the shareholders' agreement | Transfer (partial) to general public via initial public offering (IPO) | Transfer (partial) to other 3rd parties via franchising etc. (conversion of company-owned units into franchises or cooperatives) shifting family's role from more active to more passive |

- **trends within the company's industry** (for example, consolidation or expansion); and
- **the overall health of the domestic** and international economy.

If you own a small business, you'll inevitably have to face these issues, so developing strategies for the transition of ownership isn't optional—it's *mandatory*. Despite Ponce de Leon's admirable efforts, you will not live forever and won't likely want to run or own your company forever. In fact, trends indicate just the opposite—owners of small and closely held businesses are looking for liquidity and exit strategies earlier than ever before, in order to enjoy retirement when they're younger and healthier. "Career entrepreneurs" are likely to search for an exit strategy so they can move on to their next venture. This book will look at *how* to get out, *when* to get out and your options for accomplishing these objectives. It is not a book about what to do with the money once you depart—there are more than enough books on estate- and financial-planning already on the market. It is also not a book on managing the challenges and conflicts of a family-owned business—there are plenty of great resources on that important topic as well.

Instead, I'll address what to do when it's time to go, whether your exit is voluntary, due to retirement, burn-out or the desire to move on to the next venture; involuntary due to death or poor health; or due to circumstances such as irreconcilable differences between two co-founders (a "business divorce") or market conditions that force a sale of your business. We'll look at both traditional and creative solutions to transition challenges.

Transition Management

For the purposes of this book, I define transition management as "the process of transitioning the leadership and the ownership of a closely held or family business to the next generation of leaders and owners." The issues I'll address include:

- **Why plan now?** (Factors leading to sale or retirement.)
- **What is my company worth?** (If you don't know the value of your business, you can't easily plan for its transfer.)
- **How and when will these decisions be made?**
- **What contingencies might affect my primary strategy** and do I have secondary strategies in place?
- **Who is affected directly and indirectly?**
- **What team of advisors and internal staff** will assist me in developing these plans?
- **What transition strategies are available?**

Failing to Plan is Planning to Fail

It's been estimated that as few as 20% of all small and closely held businesses in the U.S. have a formal succession or transition plan currently in place. But as the adage above makes clear, "failing to plan" is a recipe for disaster for the remaining 80%. Why do so many business owners fail to make this important task a priority? Here are just a few reasons:

- **Inability to accept one's own mortality** (the "Ponce de Leon" syndrome).
- **Family politics and infighting,** which prevent consensus building.

- **The inability to delegate** or give up control over the business.
- **The fear that getting good advice will be "too expensive."**
- **Confusion about succession-planning alternatives** (handing over the business to the next generation of sons, daughters, nephews or nieces isn't the only succession planning option).
- **Confusion or misunderstanding over the tax** and financial aspects of succession planning.
- **Classic "issue avoidance" or plain laziness.** ("This is a tough task, I'll get to it tomorrow.")
- **Fear that discussions of "succession" will scare away key employees** or somehow show weakness to competitors

Kiplinger Reached Out and the Readers Responded

In the November 21, 1997, edition of *The Kiplinger Washington Letter*, Knight Kiplinger asked readers to share their war stories about succession and transition planning in their companies. There were well over 100 responses, and I reviewed each one of them very carefully. Some were stories of success and some of failure. Some had gifted or sold their ownership to the next generation, and some had sold the business to employees or another third party. A few had considered going public, and others had explored the creative strategies, that are discussed later in the book.

The family-business stories were often the most interesting—tales of both family harmony and discord. Some business owners welcomed their sons- or daughters-in-law into the business with open arms, while others would have preferred extensive dental surgery. In a few cases, the owner of the company continued to employ an effective son- or daughter-in-law, even after a bitter divorce from the owner's child. There were tales of sibling rivalry—from mild cases to those that rivaled Cain and Abel.

The letters described plans that had been put in place for tax reasons, management reasons, strategic reasons, estate-planning reasons, financial reasons, psychological reasons, ego reasons—or combinations of these. There were plans that had been effectively implemented, plans that hadn't (and needed to be) and plans that were never implemented. I'll share some of these stories throughout the book.

Most of those who responded didn't have a plan at all, but wished they had when tragedy or some other circumstances beyond their control hit their company.

Before we jump into Chapter 1, consider the following two letters. One describes a situation that works, the other a situation that needs to be fixed.

> "We are a family farm of some 32,000 acres growing substantial amounts of cotton, processing tomatoes, garlic, onions, lettuce, alfalfa hay, grapes, almonds, pistachios and a few miscellaneous crops. We own a "controlling" interest with neighbors in a tomato-paste processing facility, cotton gins, and an almond-processing facility (we are the operators) plus an almond-tree nursery. Our annual sales are in the area of $150 million. My wife and I have two daughters, four sons and 19 grandchildren. Each member of the family owns 960 acres of land, plus, there's a grandchildren's trust that owns a substantial amount of land.
>
> Some 25 years ago, my wife and I created a corporate entity with our six children as sole stockholders, with a management agreement flowing to a board of directors. In addition to my wife and me, the board consists of our six children and four non-family members. Through the years most growth endeavors were placed in this entity. We had an agreement in place giving operating control in the early years to my wife and me. We also had terms regarding buying and selling if someone wanted out, and confirmation that the underlying land ownership would be retained by each owner. Land is leased to the first-mentioned entity—rentals paid less any payments that may be due—although all are receiving some annual cash over and above payments.
>
> Our third son, age 38, is now CEO and President. Four outside board members establish his compensation and bonus, as well as valuations to be used in the event a family member wishes to sell some of his or her interest. Land

cannot be sold except to the family business, or its nominee, and then on terms. Our fourth son, age 35, helps us run the family business; our second son is a practicing dentist but also manages our 1,100 acres of pistachios. Both men "report" to the CEO. All family members who wish to work in the family business must first work with another company for at least three years. Grandchildren must abide by the same rules—and then are employed only if they are qualified and if openings exist.

This has worked for us. Our six children are college graduates, plus a few have master's degrees. One son-in-law is an attorney and the other a banker; our daughters-in-law are college graduates. My wife and I have spent considerable time over the years explaining our hopes for and details of the business.

There are a few problems. Our oldest son was in top management in the business and saw his younger brother—who was blessed with talents communication, marketing, finance and management skills—"on the move," which was a difficult parental decision. Our oldest son left the family business, received a loan from a local lender, and runs his own citrus operation.

The CEO's "perks" are set by the non-family board members. From time to time a little sibling rivalry occurs, but the non-family board members have helped then, too.

My wife and I have been blessed with children who genuinely like one another. We take all of them on short vacations at our expense for hotels and meals. We believe the number-one item to help good feeling is to have some modest cash flow to each owner.

■■■

"I'm 57 years old and hope to step down from my business by at least age 65. I can offer you this:

Be very careful about committing yourself to children or employees.

I have two daughters I'd hoped would take over the business. Not so! Daughter number one married in 1994, but is now divorcing her husband—who happens to work for me!

Daughter number two has just married a gentleman I don't wish to <u>ever</u> bring into my business.

I really don't know what to do—should I sell the business and take what I can get? When should I do this? How should I do this? Many questions go unanswered."

Well, I welcomed the insights and planning from the first writer, and shared the frustrations of the second. This book is dedicated to learning from their successes and offering strategies to deal with their confusion.

In Chapter 1, I have included a general discussion of transition management and succession planning, which should be helpful regardless of the path you select. Chapter 2 focuses on valuation issues that affect all types of succession planning strategies. Chapter 3 discusses the role of life insurance in any succession plan. In Chapters 4 and 5, the emphasis is on the family business, with a focus on transition planning. Chapter 6 is a toolbox filled with some of the more common succession planning techniques that may be used by family-owned or closely held businesses. Chapter 7 looks at the dynamics of business co-ownership, with an emphasis on co-founder relationships and agreements among shareholders. An increasingly popular (but relatively nontraditional) succession-planning strategy—the transfer of ownership to employees, either through a stock-option plan (for key employees) or an employee stock ownership plan (for nearly all employees)—is covered in Chapter 8. The more common exit strategies (which also are a type of succession planning) of selling your business or taking your business public are dealt with in Chapters 9 and 10. I address nontraditional and creative transition-planning strategies such as franchising, licensing and joint ventures in Chapter 11. Finally, the Resource Directory provides referrals on topics and areas which pertain to the focus of this book.

When developing your transition plan, don't lose sight of the factors that helped you achieve your success. Your "harvest strategy" should be consistent with the history and culture of your organization. For example, if being a small and nimble company has driven your success, then an exit strategy which involves selling out to a much larger competitor may destroy the current value of your business. A well-developed plan will do the following:

- **maximize the present value** of the net liquid capital that you'll realize from the sale or transfer (thereby minimizing the tax consequences of the proposed transaction);
- **recognize that the future ownership** and management team must be trained, mentored and properly prepared well in advance of the actual transition; and
- **account for the impact on your employees,** your family and the surrounding community.

As you read, remember that the most successful transition plans are those that are: (a) seamless and painless to those who are affected; (b) mutually beneficial from an economic and psychological perspective to those who will participate in them; and (c) respectful of the organization's history by preserving its culture and values, honoring the legacy of the founder who is handing over the baton, and embracing the new leader who is accepting the baton.

An effective exit strategy shouldn't be driven by a founding entrepreneur's relentless quest for immortality. A transition plan governed by principles of fairness, open communication and financial security will be the most effective tool available to protect and preserve the value of the business. A transition plan that rewards talent, performance and productivity instead of nepotism, ego and greed will be the plan with the most integrity and the highest chance of success. The transition plan that evolves with changes in the marketplace, technology, or family circumstances and that acknowledges the company's mission statement while allowing for fresh perspectives is the plan that will endure over generations.

One note: For the sake of simplicity I'm assuming that you are the senior business owner, entrepreneur or founder who is planning your exit from the business. You'll notice that throughout the book I address you directly wherever possible, as if you were a client sitting across the desk from me.

PART ONE | PARTING COMPANY

An Overview of Succession Planning and Transition Management

CHAPTER ONE | PARTING COMPANY

Why You Need a Plan

MANY ENTREPRENEURS WHO HAVE FAMILY-OWNED or closely held businesses say that their most difficult challenges are deciding who will succeed the current generation and how to preserve and build the company's value by providing for a smooth transition of ownership and management. Statistics support their concerns: Only 35 percent of family businesses survive past the first generation of ownership. Only 20 percent survive to the third generation. Closely held businesses don't fare much better.

Yet, more than half of family-business owners don't have a written succession plan, and when there is a plan it's often inadequate, either because no family member wants—or is able—to manage the business, or because too many family members want to run the business.

The greatest intergenerational transfer of wealth in history will occur in this country over the next decade. An estimated $10 trillion is expected to change hands, and much of this wealth will be managed by second-generation entrepreneurs in the form of stock ownership. What this means for the almost 13 million family-controlled businesses remains to be seen. But one thing is certain: Second-generation entrepreneurs will hold the

CHAPTER ONE PARTING COMPANY

economy of this country in their hands for many years into the new millennium. They will inherit challenges—new technologies, increased competition and changes to the work force—more complicated than those you faced. And if you remain actively involved, the second generation's job of running a family business becomes monumental.

The Basics of Succession Planning

Estate- and succession-planning decisions involve complex questions of law, tax and business—decisions about the types of property to own, the form of ownership, and, for small-business owners, the organization and operation of the business and steps for passing it on to the next generation. The only way to find the plan that's best for you is to work closely with your lawyer and other specialists who can advise you properly throughout the planning process: tax accountants, appraisers, life insurance agents, bank trust officers and financial planners. You must make the final decision about the organization and disposition of your business, so it's essential that you be well informed about the choices that are available so that you can make the best decision for you and your family.

Succession planning is a *process*, not an *event*. And once the formal succession plan is in place, it must be an evolving document that's reviewed and updated from time to time to reflect changes in the marketplace, competitive conditions, or your health or capabilities. The process forces you to confront difficult issues, such as:

- **Choosing among several** capable successors.
- **Dealing with apathy among potential successors** (for example, if nobody in the family is really interested in or capable of taking over, what other exit strategies are available?)
- **What if your health is deteriorating** but you're unwilling to relinquish authority or ownership?
- **What are the estate- and gift-tax implications** of the proposed plan?
- **What is the impact of the plan on other "stakeholders"** in the com-

Why You Need a Plan

BOX 1-1 The Transition Management Flow Chart

```
                    ┌─────────────────────┐
                    │  Planning Your Exit │
                    └──────────┬──────────┘
                ┌──────────────┴──────────────┐
    ┌───────────────────────┐         ┌───────────────────────┐
    │ Sale or gift of       │         │ Sale of business to   │
    │ business to next      │         │ third parties         │
    │ generation (keeping   │         │ (considering          │
    │ it within the family) │         │ non-family ownership) │
    └───────────┬───────────┘         └───────────┬───────────┘
                │                         ┌───────┴────────┐
    ┌───────────────────────┐    ┌─────────────┐  ┌──────────────┐
    │  To whom? For how     │    │  Employees  │  │ Third-party  │
    │  much?                │    │             │  │ buyers       │
    └───────────┬───────────┘    └──────┬──────┘  └──────┬───────┘
                │                       │                │
    ┌───────────────────────┐    ┌─────────────┐  ┌──────────────┐
    │ Dealing with          │    │  Financing  │  │ Strategic    │
    │ non-participating     │    │  issues     │  │ vs. financial│
    │ family members        │    │             │  │ buyers       │
    └───────────┬───────────┘    └──────┬──────┘  └──────┬───────┘
                │                       │                │
    ┌───────────────────────┐    ┌─────────────┐  ┌──────────────┐
    │ Gift- and estate-tax  │    │ Structure   │  │ Getting your │
    │ considerations        │    │ of the deal │  │ house in     │
    │                       │    │             │  │ order/       │
    │                       │    │             │  │ Planning for │
    │                       │    │             │  │ the sale     │
    └───────────────────────┘    └──────┬──────┘  └──────┬───────┘
                                 ┌─────────────┐  ┌──────────────┐
                                 │ Estate-     │  │ Estate-      │
                                 │ planning    │  │ planning     │
                                 │considerations│ │considerations│
                                 └─────────────┘  └──────────────┘
```

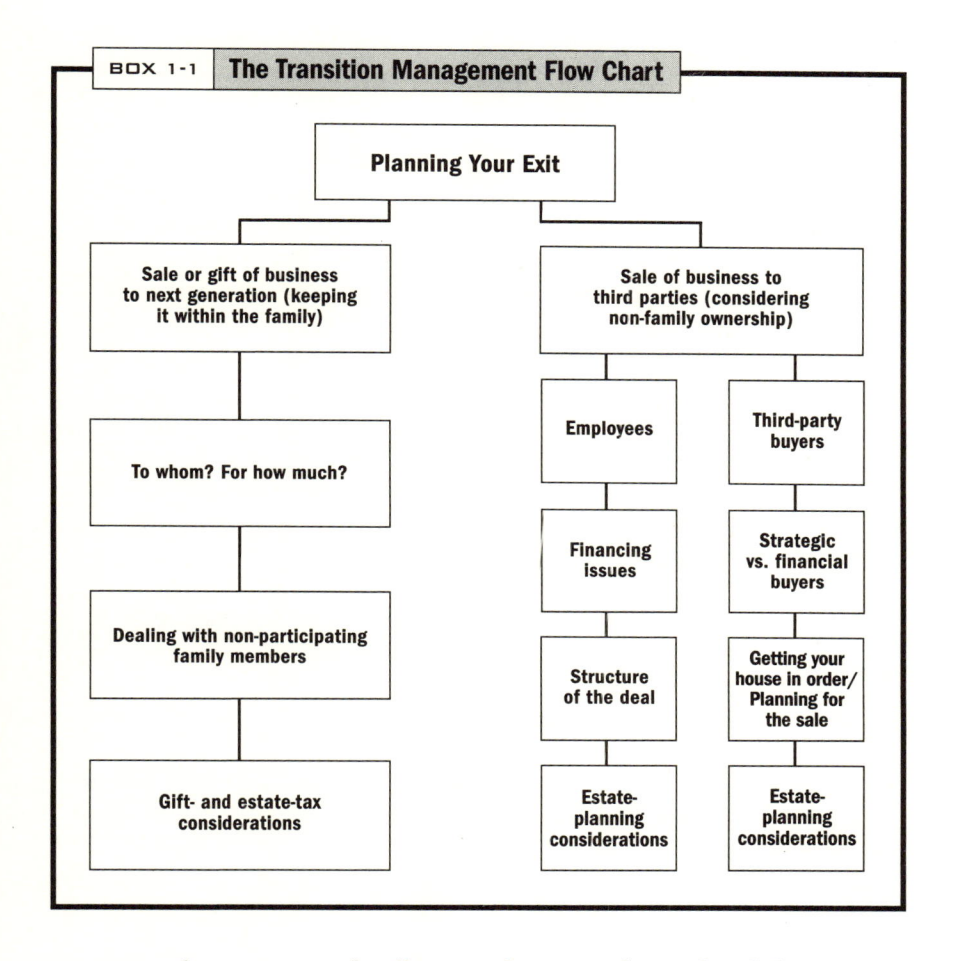

pany who are non-family members, such as loyal key employees, vendors or customers?

- **If the business will not or cannot be kept in the family,** then who are the likely buyers? Employees? Strategic buyers (competitors or companies in parallel lines of business)? Financial buyers (investors interested purely in the profits or financial potential of the business)?
- **How do intra-family feuds** and normal family pettiness affect changes to the succession plan, if at all?
- **Who should be included in the decision-making** and planning process? How will family advisory councils and boards of

CHAPTER ONE PARTING COMPANY

BOX 1-2 Elements of an Effective Succession Plan

AN EFFECTIVE succession plan must address the following concerns:

- **Diversification** of your financial resources so that you are not over-dependent on the assets of the business for support.
- **A secure retirement income** and a plan for the eventual loss of your spouse.
- **Incentives for your children** and in-laws to remain active in the company or to encourage non-active siblings to become involved.
- **Liquidity** that your estate can draw on in the event of your death to pay taxes and expenses relating to the business.
- **The transfer of stock** or assets in a tax-efficient manner.
- **A capital structure** or contractual rights that will guarantee you an income stream.
- **Acknowledgment** that treating all the children "equally" may not mean treating them all "fairly," especially if a few of the children have stronger business acumen than others and could build long-term value for the benefit of the owners.
- **What rewards** or special treatment will be given to children already active in the company and what considerations will be given to other children.
- **Provisions that allow a child who is active in** or who controls the business to buy out his non-active siblings, and a method for setting a fair price for this purchase.
- **Provisions that allow** noncontrolling children to require the controlling child to buy them out, again at fair value.
- **A plan for the continued growth** of the business in its current form, with consideration given to the timing of the proposed transfer for gift-tax purposes.
- **A fallback plan** should the family members prove incapable of running the business or if there is a change in the family situation (such as divorce, relocation, death of a child, career changes) or a change in the marketplace (such as market consolidation). Will it be sold to the employees (and if so, how) or to a third-party buyer?

---

directors (which should include some competent and objective outsiders) influence the final decision or changes to the plan over time? To be successful, the development of the succession plan must be truly a team effort with teamwide acceptance of the goals and objectives of the plan. If the affected parties fail to genuinely embrace the details of the plan, then implementation will lead only to more feuding and, eventually, to litigation.

Owners of closely held and family businesses are often too focused on day-to-day challenges, and they often fail to plan for the eventual transfer of the fruits of their labor to their families. In other words, they neglect succession and estate planning. In doing so, they jeopardize the future of their companies as well as the financial security of their families. Effective succession and estate planning establishes who will run the business after the owner (or a co-founder) retires or dies and how ownership will be transferred. The plan will include details as to how the owner will pass the wealth accumulated and held in the company to surviving family members. Once developed, the succession plan should be reviewed annually and modified periodically as circumstances change.

The succession plan should also seek to minimize estate and gift taxes, while providing the resources to pay these taxes and support the surviving spouse and dependents. Life insurance is often used to cover these obligations; wealth-transfer strategies, such as gifts, trusts and family partnerships, can be used during the owner's lifetime to transfer wealth (see Chapter 6).

If you're the family-business founder, you must be prepared to relinquish the helm without reluctance or regret. You must send a strong message to the next generation, the employees and the customers that this decision was made without duress or shame. You may or may not want to have some continuing role as an adviser to the management of the business. Sometimes it's better to make a "clean break" and refocus on either a relaxing retirement or some commitment to community or charitable activities. A successful transition plan will require you to choose a fixed departure date (and really stick to it), have a strong and independent team of advisers in place to support the new generation of leadership, resist the temptation to meddle or interfere, have a fallback plan or alternative exit strategy if (after a reasonable period of time) the new leadership fails, and have a set of rewarding and challenging activities to pursue after your departure.

The Differences Between Estate Planning and Succession Planning

Estate planning consists in part of deciding how property should be distributed at death. Succession planning focuses on decisions about the form of ownership and the organization and operation of the business, including the eventual transfer of the business to the next generation, third-party buyer or group of employees. Don't confuse the role and value of a will with the importance of effective succession planning. A will is not an effective substitute for a well-written succession plan.

Another distinction (that we'll explore in more detail in Chapter 5) is the difference between *ownership succession* and *management succession*. The first letter that I included in the Foreword demonstrated that these two important concepts *are* different and can be separated for the purposes of succession and transition planning. Agreements can be put in place which separate how the stock or assets of the business will be owned, which is different from how the stock or assets will be managed. Ownership involves the property rights inherent in being an equity holder in the business, such as voting on major decisions and receiving a pro rata share of dividends and distributions. However, day-to-day operation, control and accountability for the management of the business can be delegated by contract to those most capable of understanding and running the business.

The Succession-Planning Preparedness Quiz

Effective succession planning involves building the value of the business during your period of ownership and management, and having a plan in place when you are ready to step down. It means that management authority and control are delegated responsibly. Finally, it means that the benefits of ownership are fairly distributed to those who are entitled to them. It begins with an analysis of your answers to the following questions:

> **BOX 1-3** | **Tips for Effective Succession Planning**
>
> - **Realize that life will not last forever** and that, if properly managed, your business has the potential to easily outlive you. Nobody enjoys discussing his or her mortality, but an effective succession plan establishes the ground rules for what will happen when you are no longer around or no longer capable of managing the company's affairs.
> - **Be prepared to appoint members** to your company's board of directors who are objective and outside the circle of family owners.
> - **Have regular strategic-planning meetings** that include both family members (particularly those who will succeed you) and key non-family employees.
> - **Select and communicate regularly** with a team of outside advisers, including lawyers and accountants who have experience with closely held businesses, complex corporate matters and estate planning. Such advisers can also be a source of insight, continuity and strength during an unexpected family crisis.
> - **As you contemplate successors,** be honest with yourself when analyzing the strengths and weaknesses of various family members. Try to separate issues of love and fairness from issues of business acumen and strategic management.
> - **Prepare for the unexpected.** Many small and closely held family businesses suffer a loss of leadership when the owner suddenly dies or becomes disabled, leaving behind a spouse or a child who is too young or inexperienced to effectively manage the business. What would be your plan for the "following Monday morning"? Who would run the company?
> - **Invest the time and money** needed to properly train the next generation of leadership, whether it's your spouse, children, other family members or key employees.

- **How old are you?** How is your health? How and when do you plan to retire?
- **How old are your children?** What exposure have they had to the business? How would you rate their business acumen and leadership skills?
- **Do you want to keep the business** in your family?
- **If not, then what is your exit strategy?** What estate-planning steps have you taken to manage the proceeds of an eventual sale?

BOX 1-4 Multiple Views on Transition and Succession Planning

THE FOLLOWING interviews appeared in a *Forbes* article, "The Ultimate Test."

Peter Georgescu
Chairman & CEO, Young & Rubicam Inc.
I was in my job for just a couple of months, and already one of my key advisors, Tom Moser, was on my case: "Peter you gotta be prepared. If, God forbid, something happens to you, who is going to sit at the head of the table?" he nagged. I said, "C'mon, I just got on the job." But no, he was aggressively after me, so I wrote down a recommendation to the board about how they should go about electing the next chief executive and gave it to our general counsel. Now you may not recall, but Tom Moser, sadly, is the fellow who was killed by the Unabomber. It happened nine months after he badgered me into writing the note. If it wasn't for Tom, I'm not sure I would have faced the decision as carefully as he made me do it. And now, even without Tom here—or maybe because of it—I have continued to work on that note.

Marshall Carter
CEO, State Street Corp. (a diversified financial services and investment company)
When I was 26, on my first tour of duty in Vietnam, I commanded Marines. And on one of our big operations, out of 175 we took into combat, we had 36 killed or wounded in just six hours, including 2 of the 3 lieutenants and 6 of the 9 sergeants. In Vietnam contin-gency planning was a natural event for us. That's the same thing we've done here. This company has to continue because it's 205 years old and has 15,000 employees. We have a document called the contingency plan for the unplanned loss of the chairman and the chief executive. It's held in a sealed envelope by the general counsel and the head of the executive compensation committee. If I fall in front of a subway, they pull this out, open it up and review it with the executive compensation committee. It was my idea. I took it to the board.

James F. Conway III
CEO, Courier Corp. (printer/book manufacturer)
I don't think about death. I'm 45. Anyway, all these succession plans in bigger organizations—no one really knows until the plan is executed whether it's a good one.

Virginia Harris
Chairman, Christian Science Church
The founder of the Christian Science Church, Mary Baker Eddy, faced the issue of her death and succession over 100 years ago. In 1892, she set up the first five-person board of directors and established the succession plan. The five us who serve on the board of directors function as one in the sense of one full-time chief executive officer, but each of us has our own area of the organization we head up. We serve for life. If I were to die today, the four would meet and pray that they choose

the best candidate. Because we are a self-perpetuating board, I see our leadership as about perpetuating the vision, rather than about a personal style or about myself.

George Schad
CEO, Intergram International (a telecommunications services company)
We just raised additional funding, and the investor group required me to come up with a transition plan. This includes the hiring of a strong number-two person who could take over the company from me. And then they have taken out a $3 million life insurance policy to fund short-term cash infusion, should I not—should I die—might as well say it that way. If they did have to recruit a new chief executive, there would be search fees and relocation expenses, quite a large sum of money. It's scary to think I'm worth more dead than alive. But they've got millions and millions of dollars invested in my life, and I owe it to them to transcend my fear and come up with a plan. I'm in my mid 40s, so it's probably an age when I should be doing it anyway.

John L. Ridihalgh
CEO, Neoprobe Corp. (a biotechnology research and product development company)
We're in the cancer business. We see death every day, and we see its consequences. It can't be too far out of one's mind. You learn that every day is a great day. You learn not to worry. I don't fear death. It's a natural thing.

We have a fairly natural succession plan. Our president and chief operating officer, David Bupp, would slip into my role. It's actually very satisfying to see somebody take control of the operations and set himself up as my successor whether I die or go off to something else.

Victor Fink
Founder and President, Club Getaway (sports resort)
I'm 52. If I have a heart attack tomorrow, there's not a written succession script. You get busy in your day-to-day operation, you don't spend time thinking about death. I like to think of myself as the positive life force behind the club. I need another 10 years, hopefully longer. My son is 10 years old, and he's a dynamic guy who might have the spirit and fever to take over, but I have to give him some time to decide. In the interim, I have a dynamic group of people who love the place as much as I do. I think they would take over by committee.

C. Dean Metropoulos
CEO, C. Dean Metropoulos & Co. (acquisitions firm)
We don't have a succession document for the company. I have two young boys, 14 and 16. I would like to have them run the business down the road. But if something happens to me before that, the same senior executives who can manage the companies we acquire can also step into my shoes and manage our company.

CHAPTER ONE PARTING COMPANY

- **If the business *is* to stay in the family,** then which family member(s) would you select to control it? Are they truly committed to the long-term business objectives of the company?
- **Is there a need for transition management** involving key non-family employees?
- **If you sell the business to your children** or other family members (or even to your employees), how will they finance the purchase? How will you get the liquidity or proceeds that you need to live comfortably during retirement or to meet your estate-planning objectives?
- **If you choose to transfer the business as a gift** (or at a price below fair market value), how can you be fair to "non-active" children and protect the business from their demands?
- **What continuing role,** if any, do you envision for yourself?
- **Will your withdrawal be partial** or complete, and what will your timetable be?

The bottom line is that succession planning is a process that involves many steps, including (1) acceptance of the task; (2) building consensus; (3) choosing the proper candidates, options and strategies; (4) clearly defining roles; and (5) monitoring the plan to ensure its effectiveness. And as you will see in the chapters ahead, there are several ways you can achieve a smooth and orderly transition. Among your options:

- **Transferring ownership to your children** or other family members (Chapter 6);
- **Sale of your equity** to remaining co-founder(s) (Chapter 7);
- **Sale of some or all of your equity** to some or all of your employees (Chapter 8);
- **Sale of some or all of your company** (either a portion of the equity or a spin-off of a particular operating division of your business) to a competitor, strategic buyer or investor (Chapter 9);
- **Sale of a significant portion of your company** to the general public through an initial public offering (Chapter 10);
- **Implementation of a creative growth-and-transition strategy,** such as franchising, licensing or joint ventures (Chapter 11).

Why You Need a Plan

How do you choose which strategy (or which combination of strategies, because certain strategies are not mutually exclusive) is best for your business? Many factors will influence your decision, such as:

- **Your business strategy** and personal financial objectives and retirement needs;
- **The availability** of a viable family successor;
- **The presence of co-founders** or minority shareholders in the company;
- **The pool of key employees** who might be interested, capable and financially qualified for ownership;
- **Trends** within your industry;
- **The valuation of your company,** and the status of the financial markets. These and other factors that will be discussed in greater detail throughout the book will also affect your leave-taking strategy.

Transition Management and Exit Strategies

Traditional succession planning—passing the torch from one generation of the family to the next—isn't your only option when passing on your business. As you'll see in the following chapters, "succession planning" is really a broad topic that involves many approaches to transition management and strategies for exit. And whether you're ready to accept it or not, we all must exit our companies at some point and in some fashion.

The need to deal with transition challenges is not limited to small and closely held family businesses. Companies of all types and sizes must deal with transition issues. As Peter Drucker once observed, "The final test of greatness in a CEO is how well he chooses a successor and whether he can step aside and let his successor run the company." We've seen leadership changes in recent years at many, if not most, of our nation's most well recognized companies. We saw Steve Jobs leave Apple Computer

CHAPTER ONE PARTING COMPANY

in the early 1990s, and watched the company suffer, only to be revitalized when he returned in 1997 (albeit with a little help from some strategic partners, such as Microsoft). We have seen companies spend years planning and grooming their CEO's successor while others are forced to implement a plan promptly due to to sudden loss of leadership, such as the unexpected death of Robert Goizueta at Coca-Cola. Coca-Cola's stock and the overall stability of the company has actually *risen* since Goizueta's demise, primarily because he had a succession plan in place. A new era of transition is under way in corporate America, spurred by an increase in mergers and acquisitions, the aging of today's top CEOs (more than 44% are over 60), legal actions against management brought by disgruntled shareholders, and a trend toward earlier retirement. The challenges faced by companies like AT&T, which spent years looking for a successor to Robert Allen, are evidence of how difficult the task of succession can be. And if companies as large and wealthy as AT&T, Disney, IBM, General Motors and Apple can have problems with the process, then so can you. The well-publicized family feuds at smaller companies such as the DartGroup (the Haft family), and the confusion over succession and ownership of the Washington Redskins in the Cooke family, are examples of what can go very wrong.

It's helpful to look at the successful team approaches to transition taken at companies such as Corning Glass Works, Merck & Co. and the modern-day General Electric. Rather than relying on old-fashioned internal competition ("winner take all") or the designated CEO-in-waiting (the "crown prince" approach), these companies built consensus and developed advisory teams that helped provide for a smooth and effective transition. In many cases that meant a transition from family control of the company (together with the public shareholders) to non-family management.

As you can see from the box on pages 8-9, avoiding the issue is not an effective solution. The problem won't just magically disappear if you ignore it long enough. Unlike a fine wine, the problem—the lack of a plan—only gets worse as you and your company grow older.

Some owners of family and closely held businesses seem to believe that it's easier to go from day to day with the mystery, confusion and ambiguity of not knowing how or when the next generation of leadership will be designated. But avoiding the issue allows the rumor mill to run rampant, which causes more ruffled feathers and frustration than no communication at all. Remember that apathy or silence won't prevent family members, key employees or even your competitors from reaching their own conclusions as to how the pie should be divided from a management, control, compensation and ownership perspective, or about what the future might bring for the company. A carefully structured, well-researched, written succession plan that is communicated to all affected parties well before the proverbial "eleventh hour" will stop the rumors in their tracks. That in turn will allow the company and its leadership to focus on what is really important—serving the needs of customers, increasing market share and profitability, and building value.

CHAPTER TWO | PARTING COMPANY

What's Your Company Worth?

BEFORE YOU CAN BEGIN TO PLAN YOUR EXIT, YOU need to understand the basics of business valuation. The ability to determine your company's fair market value will help you get your arms around what you have and the financial, tax and estate-planning implications for the future.

Business valuation will also help you determine how much and what kind of advice you'll need to formulate a succession plan. For example, if you are the sole owner of a professional-services business in a shrinking industry, and an appraisal of your company yields a valuation of $100,000, then you probably shouldn't spend $25,000 in legal and accounting fees to develop a complex succession plan. On the other hand, if your business has several offices, dozens of employees and a balance sheet rich with real estate, equipment and inventory, and you haven't had the business appraised in the past ten years, then you may not realize what you *really* have. It's nearly impossible to develop an effective transition-management strategy if you don't know the true value of your business.

The valuation dilemma (in the context of succession planning) is how to set a value that offsets the impact of federal taxes while simultaneously balancing your financial (and retirement) needs with the capital the company needs to remain viable and healthy for the next generation.

This process is more often driven by a "balanced budget" approach than by applying the IRS guidelines of "fair market value"—what a ready and willing buyer would pay for the business, which may or may not be relevant to the current owner's goals or circumstances.

Although the business valuation is a vital component of an effective succession plan, it's important to realize that valuation isn't an exact science, especially for small, closely held or family-owned businesses. There are numerous acceptable valuation methods that may be used and, in most situations, each method will result in a different price. All methods should, in theory, yield the same result, but rarely does that happen; market conditions, the industry in which the company operates, and the type and nature of the business can all affect the outcome of the valuation. I'll cover the three main methods of valuation used for succession planning, but keep in mind that no one method will provide a valuation safe from questioning by a disgruntled family member or a third-party buyer. The methods are useful in that they supply a range of reasonable and justifiable values and provide a starting point for the succession- and estate-planning process.

The valuation of your business by a trained and independent appraiser (or other professional who is familiar with your industry) is an effective financial exercise even outside the context of a succession plan. The valuation report can influence the viability of a wide range of exit strategies, including the sale of your company to a third party, an initial public offering (IPO) or the adoption of an employee stock-ownership plan (ESOP). It can also help you pinpoint operational or strategic problems that can be resolved before the next generation of owners takes the helm, such as over-dependence on a single customer, the expiration of patents or over-reliance on certain key employees.

But the impact of an appraisal report on the succession-planning process can be a two-edged sword. If the valuation is too high, it may complicate a long-term gifting program, which may be the centerpiece of the succession plan (see Chapter 6). But if the valuation is too low, would-be buyers may walk away unless they are able to see an intrinsic or strategic value of the company between the lines of the appraisal report. An artificially low valuation for estate- and gift-tax purposes could be a ticking time bomb that could blow up your estate plan if the Internal Revenue Service challenges the claimed taxable value of your gifted stock. In a gift-tax dispute with the IRS, the government's opening position will be that the stock in your company is worth the highest possible amount unless you can demonstrate otherwise. And it's always a quandary for a proud entrepreneur and business owner to have to argue how little his life's effort is worth. As the saying goes, "No self-respecting farmer works all year in hopes of a bad harvest."

For these reasons, the valuation of a business in the context of the development of a succession plan will often focus on a measurement of the company's fair market value. Fair market value is commonly defined by financial consultants, the IRS and the courts as the amount at which property would change hands between a willing seller and a willing buyer when neither is under compulsion to buy or sell and both have reasonable knowledge of the relevant facts.

The Valuation Challenge for a Small or Closely Held Company

The focus of this book is on small and closely held companies, which traditionally are more difficult to value because of the "information risks" inherent in their size. These information challenges, which often result in lower valuations, include:

- **Lack of externally generated information,** including analyst coverage, resulting in a lack of business forecasts.
- **Lack of adequate press coverage** and other avenues for disseminating company information.
- **Lack of internal controls.**
- **Possible lack of internal reporting.**

In addition, many small and closely held companies are more

difficult to value for reasons specific to their businesses, such as:

- **Inability to obtain reasonably priced financing** or *any* financing.
- **Lack of diversification**—product, industry, and geographic.
- **Inability to expand** into new markets.
- **Lack of management expertise.**
- **Higher sensitivity** to macro- and microeconomic movements.
- **Lack of dividend history.**
- **More sensitivity to business risks,** supply squeezes and demand lulls.
- **Inability to control or influence** regulatory activity and union activity.
- **Lack of efficiency** in labor or plant costs.
- **Lack of access** to distribution channels.
- **Lack of long-term** and diversified relationships with suppliers and customers.
- **Lack of product differentiation** or brand-name recognition.
- **Lack of deep pockets** necessary for staying power.

Often the true value of the business must be separated into three critical components for estate- or succession-planning purposes: the right to control, the right to appreciation and the right to income. Every share of stock in the business embodies these three rights, which can be separated for succession-planning purposes through corporate recapitalization and restructuring techniques discussed in Chapter 6. Separating the value of these rights and allocating them accordingly can often solve complex succession-planning issues or resolve questions of fairness among your heirs.

Use of a Professional Business Appraiser

There are several ways to arrive at a valuation for a small or closely held company, such as a self-evaluation or a study of comparable companies, but the most widely accepted method is through the use of a professional business appraiser. An appraiser will ensure that the initial valuation used as the starting point of the succession plan is a valid one.

An appraiser is trained to look objectively at a company and its assets, management, employees, financials and future projections, and turn this assessment into a range of values that are valid for determining the company's worth. In order for the appraiser to arrive at a realistic range of values, cooperation on the part of the company's owners is critical. The company's founder may feel threatened by the appraiser's scrutiny of every aspect of operations and management, but this thoroughness is important to the appraiser's ability to arrive at a fair valuation. An appraiser probably will request access to various offices or work sites run by the company as well as approval to interview key personnel from both management and employee ranks. And, of course, the appraiser will need to see complete financial records from recent years.

Some General Guidelines

To avoid problems down the road, discuss your succession planning and strategic objectives with the professional business appraiser you hire. Be sure to define the terms under which the appraiser will be working when he or she is initially hired. Set forth in advance the expected time frame for completion of the appraisal—and be reasonable. Don't expect to hire an appraiser on Monday and receive a complete report on Wednesday. A proper appraisal will take a minimum of several weeks to complete, and you should state clearly your due date and desired format before the work begins. Valuations related to the development of a succession plan should be presented in writing, followed by a meeting with the appraiser to iron out any misunderstandings and address any questions that may have been raised by the report's findings. Finally, be careful to define the fee structure for the appraisal and when that fee will be paid. Beware of fee structures that could be subject to a conflict of interest. For example, don't hire an appraiser who pushes for his or her fee to be a percentage of the company's final valuation or an appraiser who'll accept payment only upon completion of a merger or acquisition transaction, especially if you haven't yet chosen your exit strategy. In both cases, the appraiser has compromised his or her objectivity by creating an incentive to tailor the value of the company to fit his or her best interests. Such appraisals lack credibility as negotiating tools.

Determining Strategic Value

If the sale of your business is your strongest exit strategy, a veteran appraiser will create a set of financial projections that will predict the performance of your business as if it had already merged with a prospective buyer's company. The first step is to prepare a cash-flow projection for the entities as if they had been combined already. Next, the appraiser examines several "what-if" scenarios to determine how specific line items would change under various circumstances. This exercise allows the appraiser to identify a range of strategic values based on the projected earnings stream of your company under its proposed new ownership. The higher this earnings stream, the higher the purchase price you can command. (However, if gifting is the centerpiece of your succession plan, high earnings is the opposite of what you'd want in an appraisal. That's why it is critical to discuss your strategic objectives at the outset.)

To arrive at this "strategic value," the appraiser will obtain large amounts of financial data and general information on many aspects of your business, such as the quality of management and the company's reputation. The appraiser will attempt to assess how your company's value will be affected by any changes to the operations or foundation of the company as a result of the proposed transaction, such as a loss of key customers or managers.

The appraiser should also examine your "intangible assets" when determining strategic value. Intangible assets include customer relationships, intellectual property, patents, license and distributorship agreements, regulatory approvals, leasehold interests, and employment contracts. The better you can describe the value that these intangible assets would have for a prospective buyer, the better the chances that the appraiser will give the assets the credit they deserve in the final valuation report.

Finally, the appraiser will analyze your financial and

> **BOX 2-1 | Different Definitions of Value**
>
> THE TERM "VALUE" has many different meanings in the context of a business valuation, depending on the valuation's purpose. It is therefore important to be aware of these distinctions.
>
> **Book Value (or Net Worth)**—Assets minus liabilities equals book value, or net worth. Book value usually has a weak relationship to fair market value.
>
> **Appraised Value**—Value, determined by an appraisal, of the cost of replicating the business from scratch, minus the applicable depreciation.
>
> **Conditional Value**—The value that will result if a particular event occurs.
>
> **Expected Value**—A weighted value that combines all the conditional values. Each conditional value is weighted by its probability.
>
> **Fair Market Value (IRS definition)**—The price at which a willing buyer will buy and a willing seller will sell a certain item of property, neither being under any compulsion to buy or sell and both having a reasonable knowledge of all the relevant facts.
>
> **Going Concern Value**—Value as determined by intangible elements such as having a trained work force, trademarks and copyrights, operation manuals, and a loyal customer base.
>
> **Liquidation Value**—The value that would result from selling all the assets of a business. This is used when no buyer is willing to buy the business in its present form or when the value of the assets sold separately is higher than if sold as a unit.

accounting practices and evaluate how accurate and appropriate they are. Your company's credit rating, reputation in the business community, future plans and projections will all be taken into account by the appraiser in estimating the future value of the firm.

Categories of Valuation Methods

A professional business appraiser typically will apply a few different methods of valuation (outlined below), and use the knowledge gained from these exercises to pick one or two methods best suited for the valuation's purpose. Remember that the application of just one method will not necessarily provide a credible statement of value. Several factors influence the valuation of a company, some of which cannot be predicted in advance. The appraiser must take these factors into account when deciding on the appropriate mix of methods to use. The appraiser must consider the relevant market conditions at the time that he or she performs the valuation, as well as the availability and quality of pertinent data. If you familiarize yourself with the following methods—comparable worth, asset valuation, and financial performance—you'll have a strong foundation for understanding what is involved in your company's valuation.

The Comparable-Worth Method

The comparable-worth method uses the performance and potential selling prices of comparable publicly and privately held companies to arrive at a value. The appraiser examines publicly held companies operating in the same or similar industry providing the same or similar products and services. The assumption is that potential buyers will not pay more for your company than they would for a similar company that trades publicly. Care must be taken when choosing publicly held companies to use for comparison. The companies should be as similar to yours as possible, particularly in regard to their location and relationship to suppliers.

Because it won't be possible to find companies similar to yours in all respects, it's important for the appraiser to use the available data as creatively as possible. For example, if the firms' sales volumes differ, it will be more useful to compare the ratio of sales to costs rather than one sales amount to another. This will provide a clearer picture of your company's relative strengths and weaknesses compared with others in its industry. Once the appraiser has reached some preliminary range of valuations based on this method, he must adjust the prices to reflect situations particular to your company. If, for example, your company has profits that are consistently above industry averages due to an unusually low cost structure, then your company's value must be adjusted upward to account for that competitive advantage.

This method can present some difficulties when used to value a closely held company. The goals of financial reporting for a publicly held company are quite different from those of a closely held company. A publicly held company's management strives to show high earnings on its financial reports in order to attract investors and therefore to improve its price-earnings ratio. On the other hand, a closely held company's that is managed by a sole entrepreneur or small group may wish to minimize the earnings shown on its financial reports in order to minimize its tax burden. Both goals are legitimate, but for an appraiser trying to compare the financial ratios of your company with those of a similar publicly held company, the difference can be confusing.

The Asset-Valuation Method

If your company has a large portion of its value wrapped up in fixed assets, an appraiser may lean toward some type of asset valuation in attempting to price the company. The assumption, again, is that a prospective buyer wouldn't pay more for your company's assets than for a comparable set of assets (or "substitute" assets) elsewhere. With this in mind, the appraiser then chooses how to value the substitute assets, using either the "cost of reproduction" (what it would cost to construct a substitute asset using the same materials as the original, at current prices) or the "cost of replacement" (the cost to replace the original asset at current prices, adhering to modern standards and using modern materials). The appraiser also considers how much time is required to get the substitute assets in place, in a usable condition.

When using the asset-valuation method, the appraiser examines every asset held by your company, including tangible assets such as machinery and equipment, real estate, vehicles, office furniture and fixtures, land and inventory, and intangibles such as patents and customer lists. Intangibles are often referred to as the company's goodwill (that is, the difference in value between the company's hard assets alone and the true value of the company as a whole). It generally will be in your best interest to supply the business appraiser with as much specific detail about your company's intangibles as possible. The greater the value of the goodwill that can be attributed to specific, well-defined intangibles, the higher the company valuation is likely to be. For example, rather than lumping all patents held by the company as a single item under the intangible goodwill category, list the patents as separate assets and include specific information on each one, such as the patent's date of expiration and how it benefits the company's operations.

The Financial-Performance Methods

Perhaps the most common approach to business valuation for the purpose of succession planning is to apply a set of methods that measure financial performance. These methods attempt to measure historical as well as future performance and are typically used when the most likely exit strategy is the sale of the business as opposed to a long-term gifting program. Financial performance methods measure: net present value (NPV), internal rate of return (IRR), or return on investment (ROI).

NET PRESENT VALUE ANALYSIS. NPV is perhaps the most common method of financial-performance analysis used by appraisers in a pre-acquisition valuation. NPV is a capital-budgeting model that compares the present value of the proposed transaction's benefits with the present value of its costs. The difference between benefits and costs is the net present value of the proposed deal. A positive NPV means that the benefits of the deal exceed the costs, and the decision to go forward would increase the value of the buyer (and consequently its shareholders' wealth). A negative NPV means the opposite: Costs exceed benefits, and the decision to undertake the proposed deal would decrease the value of the buyer and its shareholder wealth. An NPV of zero means that benefits equal costs, with no effect on the value of the buyer or the wealth of its shareholders.

To conduct an accurate NPV analysis, the appraiser gathers financial data and evaluates projections of cash flow based on the perceived level of risk and length of time considered. It is the appraiser's job to review all financial documents and search for mistakes, inconsistencies and areas of disagreement (such as future-earnings claims). This type of painstaking examination is not easy for a company to endure, but is vital to a successful appraisal.

INTERNAL RATE OF RETURN ANALYSIS. The internal rate of return is a capital-budgeting model represented by the discount rate that equates the price with the anticipated profits from the proposed transaction. The business appraiser must take two steps to evaluate the seller's business based on this method: (1) calculating the IRR, and (2) comparing the IRR with the required rate of return. Acceptable proposed transactions are those whose IRR is greater than the required return. Proposed transactions should be rejected if the IRR is less than the required rate of return.

RETURN-ON-INVESTMENT RATIO. In certain cases, the professional business appraiser may use the return on investment (ROI) ratio in valuing the seller's business from the buyer's perspective. Taken as an average of the seller's recent years' earnings to net equity and long-term debt, the ROI can be an important benchmark for determining the value of the business. The process of evaluating a company's financial health and future-growth prospects is a very involved process in which the appraiser must educate the potential seller about the factors that the buyer will take under consideration.

Selecting a Method

Your appraiser shouldn't rely on a single method to arrive at a final valuation without first considering other methods or other factors that may affect the business. One method may overlook aspects of the business that another method would uncover. For example, if the appraiser uses a number of methods and consistently arrives at a range of $2.2 million to $2.6 million, then an asset valuation that yields a result of only $1.5 million can reasonably be eliminated. Because other valuation methods were used, the appraiser knows that the value of assets alone is not a fair approximation of the company's value; intangibles or other market or com-

> **BOX 2-2 IRS Views on Valuation**
>
> THE IRS provided guidelines for the valuation of stock in a closely held business for estate- or gift-tax purposes in Revenue Ruling 59-60. These factors should be considered in valuing any company—whether a corporation or an unincorporated entity—or valuing a partial ownership interest in a company. Under "Factors to Consider," the ruling states that the following are fundamental and require careful analysis in each case:
>
> **(a) the nature of the business** and the history of the enterprise from its inception;
> **(b) the economic outlook** in general, and the condition and outlook of the specific industry;
> **(c) the book value** of the stock and the financial condition of the business;
> **(d) the earning capacity** of the company;
> **(e) the dividend-paying capacity;**
> **(f) whether the enterprise** has goodwill or other intangible value;
> **(g) sales of stock** and the size of the block of stock to be valued; and
> **(h) the market price of stocks** of corporations engaged in the same or a similar line of business having their stocks actively traded in a free and open market, either on an exchange or over the counter.
>
> These factors are critical elements of a business appraisal; they should be combined with common sense, informed judgment and reason in arriving at a value.

petitive trackers must also be taken into account. Had the appraiser relied solely on the asset-valuation method, the company would have been underpriced dramatically.

For merger and acquisition transactions, a valuation method that appears to be too simple probably is, although simple methods are often used for other purposes (and are actually prescribed by law in some cases). These simple methods include many that are common to the business world, such as "industry multipliers" or "rules of thumb," that most likely were valid at one time in a particular market but may no longer hold true. For example, it may be commonly accepted that in Industry X, the price to pay for a business is five times the company's annual earnings or amount of goodwill. But you'll likely find it quite difficult to convince a well-informed potential buyer to purchase a company for a price defined only by convention, or persuade the IRS that this rule of thumb (without any other analysis) yielded the correct result in a gift-tax audit. And how is the seller to know that his or her company is not worth more than the amount yielded by a simple formula? In fairness to both parties, the appraiser should not take the easy way out of this task. Better to invest a bit more time and effort up front than to experience remorse after the deal has been consummated.

Final Valuation Report

At the end of the appraiser's analysis, he or she will produce a report detailing the range of values for your business. But while the detailed methods of valuation can provide a solid starting point, often that is all they provide. The ultimate value of the business can vary widely and is dependent on diverse factors, including market conditions, the timing of negotiations and the valuation date, the internal motivation and goals of both the buyer and seller, the operating synergies that result from the transaction, the structure of the transaction, and other factors that may not be explicit.

CHAPTER THREE | PARTING COMPANY

The Importance of Insurance

MANY BUSINESS OWNERS' ESTATES INCLUDE AS A primary asset life insurance (or disability) policies that name the company or the family members (or both) as the beneficiaries.

Life insurance can play an important role in the overall strategic-planning process. In the context of a long-term gifting strategy (as discussed in Chapter 6), life insurance proceeds can be used to "equalize" legacies among active and non-active members of the next generation. Let's say a small business worth $3 million will be gifted over time to a daughter who has been very active in the business. This could be offset by a life insurance policy in the same amount on the founder, naming as the main or sole beneficiary the son who practices dentistry thousands of miles away. This "equalizes" the legacy when the founder passes away. Most family-business experts agree that this is not only a fair solution but also is in the best long-term interests of the business, rather than vesting one-half of the ownership and control in a child who has not stepped inside the company's doors since he was a teenager.

As good as it may sound at first, equalization is not a panacea because valuation can be a moving target. For example, do you adjust the amount of the policy for the son with each new appraisal of the business? If yes, why should the non-active son continue to get a windfall for the efforts of the daughter whose hard work has helped build the value of the business? But in fairness to the son (given the time value of money and assets), why should his sister get a "gift" each year when he must wait until his parents' deaths for his share? This is the dilemma when life insurance is used as the equalization tool instead of cash or a periodic distribution of other assets in the estate.

As discussed in Chapter 7 in the context of a buy-sell agreement among co-owners of a business (or among family members), life insurance proceeds can be used to fund the purchase of shares under the buyout clause in the shareholders agreement, and therefore plays yet another important role in the context of succession planning. A buy-sell arrangement for co-owners to purchase each other's business property is often suggested for closely held businesses; upon the death of an owner, the mechanism is in place for an orderly transfer of ownership to the remaining owners. Buy-sell arrangements typically include details concerning who has the option to buy from a seller (including an estate), how the sales price is established and how the transfer may be financed. If the buy-sell agreement is written for the death of an owner, then life insurance becomes a financing option.

Both life insurance and heir or third-party financing can be used to transfer the business to a continuing operator upon the property owner's death. A child who operates a business owned by a parent can purchase life insurance on the parent to finance the property purchase from non-business heirs. Life insurance proceeds can similarly fund a partnership or corporate buy-sell arrangement.

Insurance premiums aren't tax-deductible, but the proceeds are free from federal and state income tax. Since the decedent never owned the policy, the proceeds are not included in his estate. Life insurance premiums begin when the policy is purchased and cease at death (or sooner) when the insurance proceeds are used to purchase the business. In contrast, the cost of heir or third-party financing will not begin until death and will continue until payments are completed.

Choosing the Right Product

The wide array of life insurance products that are available can be confusing at first, but it really boils down to two basic choices:

- **Do you want life insurance,** pure and simple, without any complicated investment or tax-deferred-savings features attached? If so, your choice should be "term" life.
- **Do you want your life coverage to double** as a retirement-savings vehicle that offers the advantage of tax-deferred money growth over the long term? If so, and you have the money to spend on this higher-cost coverage, a "cash value" or "whole life" policy may be the direction to go.

Both routes have advantages and disadvantages, and financial-planning experts are forever debating which is better. The one you choose depends on the amount of money you have available, your age, the level of coverage you need and the confidence you have in your own investment abilities.

There are variations of these two basic types, as well as other types of policies designed to meet the special needs of business owners.

Term life insurance covers the insured for a limited time period, or term. It has no cash value or savings feature. It cannot be borrowed against, cashed in or used to provide retirement income. Because term insurance provides coverage for only a stated period of time, a new term policy can cost less than a new whole-life insurance policy yet provide the same amount of death benefits. Because of this, term insurance is often recommended for younger small-business owners and entrepreneurs who need a large amount of income protection for their dependents but who do not have a large amount of money to purchase life insurance.

Whole-life, or cash-value, insurance provides coverage for the remainder of the insured's life. The premiums paid in the early period of a whole-life policy are greater than what is necessary to provide for the policy's stated death benefits. The excess amount accumulates and is known as the "cash value" of the policy. Later in the insured's life, when the premiums paid are less than what is necessary to provide the stated death benefits, the accumulated cash value is used to help pay the cost. Whole-life policies can be purchased with various payment plans. Many are paid up when the insured reaches age 65.

The cash value of a whole-life policy can be borrowed against, at an interest rate that is stated in the policy. Policies that have been in existence for a long time may have extremely low interest rates. New policies have higher interest rates. If you borrow against your policy, the death benefit is reduced while the loan is outstanding. The cash value of the policy also may be received as cash if you terminate your policy.

Life Insurance and Taxes

Life insurance premiums are generally not tax-deductible as a business or personal expense except when a corporation provides life insurance for its employees. Life insurance death benefits also are not normally subject to income tax.

Death benefits paid to a beneficiary usually are exempt from income tax. If the benefits are paid in a lump sum at the time of death, the amount of the payment to the beneficiary is free from income tax. If the benefits are paid in installments, only the additional interest earned on the death benefits is subject to income tax. The spouse of the insured (if he or she is the beneficiary), however, has a $1,000 annual exclusion for interest earned from installment payments. If only interest is paid from the proceeds, then the $1,000 annual exclusion is not available.

Life insurance proceeds are subject to estate tax if the deceased owned the policy. But insurance proceeds paid to the surviving spouse qualifies for the marital deduction and thus would not be taxed. (The marital deduction allows any amount of property to go from one spouse to the other—via lifetime gifts or bequests—free of federal gift or estate taxes.) If someone other than the person insured owns the policy, and the benefits are not paid to the estate, then the proceeds are not subject to estate tax.

Life Insurance in a Partnership, Corporation or Limited-Liability Company

Life insurance can be used in a partnership to help transfer one partner's interest to the remaining partners upon his or her death. Various arrangements can be used for this purpose. In a cross-purchase agreement, each partner owns a policy on each of the other partners, pays the premiums, and names himself or herself as beneficiary. When a partner dies, the remaining partners together will have sufficient funds to purchase the deceased partner's share of the business. With a buyout agreement, the partnership itself owns the policy, pays the premium and names itself as the beneficiary. In either case, the premiums are not tax-deductible and the proceeds are free from income tax. If the partnership owns the policy, part of the proceeds may be included in the taxable estate of the deceased.

Cross-purchase and buyout agreements can be used for a corporation or limited-liability company with the same results. These companies can also provide life insurance for their employees and deduct the premiums as a business expense. The amount of coverage is limited when the premiums are deductible expenses.

How Much Do You Need?

Rules of thumb often are used to recommend the amount of life insurance a family should carry. A common rule is that the death benefits should be at least six to ten times the yearly income of the family. This works for wage earners but not for business owners who derive income from property ownership. Rather than use rules of thumb to set insurance amounts, business owners should use a more systematic approach. You should prepare an income-requirement and income-source budget that estimates your family's income needs in your absence. The estimate depends on the number of dependents and their ages, the age of your surviving spouse, whether he or she will be able to work, and whether a college education is planned for your children.

It is important to consider that different types of businesses produce different types of revenue streams, which have varying degrees of dependence on the founder. For example, a real estate management business may be driven by rental income, which could easily continue after the founder dies, but a consulting business probably relies heavily on the founder's presence to continue to earn revenues.

Life Insurance for Your Spouse

Life insurance can't replace a lost husband or wife. It can, however, help replace the income or other economic value that is lost with the death of a spouse. It's usually much easier to measure the expected economic loss when a wage earner or head of household dies than to do so for a non-salaried participant in a family business.

Determining how much life insurance is enough to cover the spouse of a business owner depends on the survivors' needs and the degree to which the spouse participates in operating the business. If the spouse is active in the business, it might be wise to buy enough life insurance to cover the expenses of hiring someone to perform his or her duties. If the spouse is employed outside the business, his or her life might be insured to reflect the loss of income to the family.

Insuring a parent who is not employed outside the home is a more subjective process because there are few standard measures of the economic value of a homemaker. There should be enough life insurance to pay for the care of young children and for the housekeeping services provided by a homemaker if there is no one else in the family who can step in to take over these important functions.

Shopping for the Best Insurance Deal

Pay attention to the ratings of insurers. It's crucial to pick an insurer that won't die before you do. That means buying only from companies that earn the highest ratings from independent evaluators. Ask your insurance agent to provide the latest ratings for any company you're considering.

A.M. BEST has been rating insurers about half a century longer than anyone else, and Best's ratings are the industry standard. Buy only from insurance companies that have achieved an A rating or better from Best. You can check a Best rating yourself by calling the company (908-439-2200) or checking its Web site (www.ambest.com). The cost is $4.95 for each Best's Rating or $19.95 for each *Best Company Report*.

WEISS RESEARCH also rates insurance companies. You can obtain an oral report over the phone (800-289-9222) for $15 per company.

THREE OTHER COMPANIES that follow the insurance industry—Moody's Investors Service (212-553-0377), Standard & Poor's (212-438-2400) and Duff & Phelps (312-368-3157)—will each give you a single rating over the phone at no cost.

For help in evaluating cash-value policies, you can tap a service offered by the Consumer Federation of America (CFA) Insurance Group. A detailed evaluation costs $45 for the first policy, then $35 for each additional policy requested at the same time. For more information, contact CFA, 1424 16th Street, N.W., Suite 604, Washington, DC 20036; 202-387-6121.

PART TWO | PARTING COMPANY

Succession Planning and the Family Business

CHAPTER FOUR | PARTING COMPANY

The Special Challenges of Dealing with Relatives

SUCCESSION PLANNING HAS DIFFERENT GOALS DEPENDing on the structure of your business. In a closely held business, the focus is usually to find a strategy that provides the owner with sufficient proceeds for his or her retirement and estate-planning needs (or even future entrepreneurial or business plans). In a family business, the objective is usually to keep the business in the family and provide an income stream for the founder. The next three chapters focus on the family business and how to accomplish its succession-planning objectives. This chapter provides a brief overview of the special succession-planning challenges facing a family business. Chapter 5 introduces the family business continuity plan (FBCP), and Chapter 6 examines tools and techniques to implement that plan—and keep the business in the family.

From there, we'll move on to exit strategies that can be considered by all types of closely held companies, including family businesses. Chapter 7 introduces the dynamic of one or more co-founders, to whom you may not be related. The co-founder issue requires an understanding of shareholders' agreements among co-founders (and subsequent owners) and how to resolve co-founder disputes. The balance of the book examines various types of exit strategies, such as mergers and acquisitions, employee stock ownership plans (ESOPs) and initial public offerings (IPOs)—again, strategies used by both family and non-family businesses to meet the financial and retirement objectives of their owners.

When you decide to pass the baton to the next generation, you'll naturally have to confront questions of *how*, *when* and *to whom*. You may find it difficult and emotionally taxing to answer these questions—and the answers themselves are often complex. There are a host of talented and nationally renowned family-business consultants who have written volumes of text on the psychological, cultural, emotional and organizational dynamics of succession planning issues within a family business. I highly recommend virtually anything written by family-business consultants Leon Danco, John Ward, Craig Aronoff, Paul Karofsky, Sharon Nelton or James Lea. Many of their works are available on the Internet on sites hosted by family-business resource centers, such as the Northeastern University Center for Family Business, Arthur Andersen and the Family Enterprise Center at Kennesaw State University (see the Resource Directory for a more comprehensive list). You may also wish to read *You Can't Fire Me—I'm Your Father*, by Neil Koenig (Kiplinger Books). Rather than attempt to boil down thousands of pages of research, case studies and practical advice on this subject into one chapter, I refer you to these complementary resources.

The focus of this book is the legal and strategic aspects of various transition-management and exit strategies, and this chapter will introduce basic tenets and tips for the smooth transition from one generation to the next in a family business. A survey reported in the February 1998 *ABA Journal* suggests that the need for the leaders of family-owned businesses to focus on these issues is greater than ever. Consider the following as presented in the *Journal* article:

- **43% anticipate a management change** within the next five years, particularly the retirement or semi-retirement of a chief executive officer.
- **43% of CEOs ages 56 to 60 who expect to retire** within five years have selected a successor.

- **33% of CEOs 61 and older who expect to retire** within five years have selected a successor.
- **87% of companies have selected a family member** to succeed the current CEO as head of the business.
- **25% are not sure how they will divide ownership** among members of succeeding generations.

As discussed in the Foreword and in Chapter 1, perhaps the most commonly selected succession-planning strategy for the owner of a closely held business is to provide for the eventual transfer of the business to a family member, such as a son or daughter. As simple as this may sound, it raises difficult planning issues and challenges, especially if you have several children with varying degrees of interest, business acumen and financial needs or objectives.

The dynamic of succession planning in a family business is complex because each family member may feel that he or she has a vested interest in the company's future. Each may have spent after-school hours working in the business, or experienced their parents missing special events like school plays and Little League games because of business demands. Most would like some involvement in the business, even if their roles aren't full-time.

Each family member may envision a different type of participation that may or may not be feasible depending on the company's performance or future needs. For example, if two of your three children move away to pursue careers outside the company, yet fully expect to have a one-third ownership interest when you step down, will the remaining one-third interest be enough to entice the third child to take over the business? What's fair? To what degree are the first two children "penalized" for moving away?

There are no easy answers to these kinds of questions. The *challenge*, then, is to select the child, children, or other relatives who will ensure the continuation of the business as a family business, provide participating roles for the remainder of the family, and accomplish all this while maintaining family harmony.

You should address these issues in the preparation of the

family business continuity plan, which is discussed in Chapter 5. The key objectives of the Plan will be to provide smooth and seamless transition of the ownership and control of the business, provide liquidity for the "retiring" generation, minimize estate taxes, preserve capital in the company for future growth, and, where possible, to maintain family harmony.

The Next Generation's Perspective

When you're working on your transition plan, you may have to separate issues of ownership and wealth from issues of management and control. Keep in mind that the next generation will often have multiple perspectives: as children who enter the business, as siblings who don't enter the business, as your children's spouses and as your employees. For each of these groups there are issues of career and financial planning, career opportunity and career satisfaction, fairness of treatment, family relations, and old-fashioned politics and greed.

The issues surrounding the group of likely "business heirs" are complex and challenging to manage. These issues may be further complicated by deep-seated psychological problems, sibling jealousy and rivalry, marital problems among the children, in-laws who don't get along, and so on. The group of business heirs must view their inheritance not so much as a gift as a responsibility to you and to future generations. The family-wide preservation of wealth is in the *continuity* of the business, not in its demise due to infighting. In order to transfer ownership without conflict, the business heirs must be flexible, respect the decisions you make and accept the guidance of your professional advisers.

The mix of management, financial, family and psychological factors affecting the selection of the next-generation leadership triggers the need for expertise beyond that occurring in the typical family business. The next generation can be helped greatly by a diverse external advisory committee as well as individual consultants who will all play a role in the preparation of the family business continuity plan.

Setting the Stage for Seamless Succession

Family-business consultants Craig Aronoff and John Ward are often credited with the following quote: "The well-planned family-business succession is neither random nor choreographed." My experience leads me to agree wholeheartedly. Succession planning in a family business should be neither so rigid that it ignores the fact that circumstances can and will change, nor so flexible that it leaves planning for the last minute, turning the business over on a whim to whichever relative is standing closest to Uncle Fred when he dies. There are several key steps that you can take today to set the stage for a smooth transition. These steps recognize that any successful transition is a process, not an event, and that now is the time to begin that process by implementing the following:

PREPARE AN ORGANIZATION CHART WITH DEFINED POSITION DESCRIPTIONS. Determine *now* which family members (and non-family members) will hold which positions, with clear statements of duties and responsibilities as well as the performance goals to which they will be held accountable. In assigning positions, be guided by merit, education, passion and commitment, not by love or nepotism.

TRAIN, TRAIN, TRAIN. Set up a training, coaching and formal mentoring system so that you can begin to impart knowledge, experience and trade secrets to the next generation. The training shouldn't be ad hoc, but should be structured as a mix of formal classroom training, field experience, and informal training at social or family events. *Start now* before you are unable due to death or disability. *Start now* before you lose the next generation of leadership to a competing company, career or other life circumstance. *Start now* so that key lessons can be repeated and reinforced, not "dumped" all at once a month before your retirement. *Start now* so that you'll be able to enjoy your retirement without six phone calls a day from your son or niece!

GET GOOD ADVICE. One of the keys to a smooth transition will be the quality of the advice that you get from your professional

> **BOX 4-1** | **Family Business Council Policies & Procedures**
>
> THE FAMILY Business Council should develop a written statement of policies and procedures, essentially a set of operational by-laws. These should include the following topics:
>
> - **Statement of mission** and values of the family and the business
> - **Rights and responsibilities** of ownership
> - **Overview of long-term** corporate strategy and positioning
> - **Governance mechanisms**—composition of the family board of directors and membership criteria
> - **Executive-team succession** issues
> - **Training and mentoring** of the next generation
> - **Dividend** and distribution policy
> - **Executive-team salaries** and bonuses
> - **Methods** for resolving disputes among family members
> - **The establishment** and recruitment of an outside board of advisers
> - **Building trust** through knowledge—distribution of periodic reports

advisers, such as accountants and attorneys, who should be experienced with the succession-planning and transition-management needs of closely held and family-owned businesses. You will also need an objective and experienced board of advisers, made up of outside business leaders and professional advisers who can help the company with difficult transition-management decisions as well as with the implementation of the transition-management plan.

ESTABLISH GOVERNANCE AND COMMUNICATION STRUCTURES. Many well-run family businesses anticipate succession issues well in advance and create a culture of genuine interest and involvement early on by creating a family council (or even a family assembly, depending on the size of the family). These non-traditional governance and communications groups may have certain protocols or bylaws that leave key decisions to be discussed and voted on by affected family members in a manner that augments and supersedes the traditional decision-making structure set forth in typical state corporate laws. These group-developed core principles will assist in the selection of the next generation of leadership. For example, once the vision for the family business is articulated, the Family Council has a better idea of the types of future leaders that it needs to begin to develop today.

ESTABLISH CRITERIA TO ELIMINATE SURPRISES. You should establish clearly communicated criteria for ownership and management candidates in the upcoming generation to remove the element of surprise when the successors are selected. The criteria can be objective—such as education, performance and experience—but could also include some subjective factors, such as passion, commitment, and respect and trust by family members and employees. Establishing these criteria and then sticking to them will not only eliminate the element of surprise but also mitigate the risk of anger, dissent and even litigation.

COMMUNICATE EARLY AND COMMUNICATE OFTEN. You must constantly communicate with the next generation—sharing information and imparting knowledge not only to build trust but also to "take the pulse" of its members' goals, circumstances and general mood. Establish and keep open the communication channels through periodic reports, quarterly meetings, one-on-one mentoring and other forums to keep the next generation interested in the family business and poised for transition. These channels will help ensure that the proverbial baton is not dropped on the track during the hand-off.

PRESENT SUCCESSION AS AN OPPORTUNITY, NOT A DUTY. You won't get very far if the next generation views a future in the business as some type of moral and family obligation as opposed to a viable business opportunity. When succession is presented as a duty rather than as a potentially lucrative economic and career opportunity, the results are likely to be disappointing. The next generation should view succession with enthusiasm, not reluctance. An organizational culture should be built around principles of stewardship—instilling the notion that the upcoming owners should regard themselves as stewards of a family legacy and that the ability to step into the shoes of leadership is a privilege to be earned, not a birthright. A lack of enthusiasm and interest is a clear signal that you should seriously consider an alternative exit strategy, such as those discussed in Chapters 8 through 11.

SUPPORT (AND EVEN ENCOURAGE) EMPLOYMENT OUTSIDE THE FAMILY BUSINESS FIRST. The traditional approach of grooming the next generation when they are teenagers—forcing them to work their way up the ladder and eventually retire as family-business employees—is in many ways a dead paradigm. The more enlightened approach is to support and encourage a career track that includes employment outside the family business, either within or outside the industry, with the hope and expectation that these designated leaders will return to the family business at the appropriate time to take the helm. The obvious risk is that they will not want to leave their current situations or professions. Despite that risk, it's likely that working outside the family business will develop more confident and balanced leaders who have proved that they can succeed in other circumstances without the shadows of nepotism. This also allows for more gradual transition to new management because the next generation isn't just sitting around waiting for you to step down, but rather gaining experience (and making mistakes) elsewhere until the time is right. Naturally, the next generation should not be invited to return only days before the baton is passed; a several-year training and phase-in period prior to the transition should be built into the plan.

BREAKING THE MYTH OF THE "ONE" LEADER. For many years, the primary dilemma of family-business succession planning was determining how to select only *one* leader from each generation when there may be several qualified siblings or cousins. The new model seems to offer some interesting alternatives, including multiple chiefs. Such is the structure at family-owned Nordstrom, where six fourth-generation leaders share the title of co-president. This "collective management" concept isn't unique and is growing more common in second- and third-generation family businesses. For example, the 50-year-old Magid Glove and Safety Manufacturing Co., based in Chicago, has an eight-member management committee representing

The Special Challenges of Dealing with Relatives

> **BOX 4-2** | **Succession in the Family Business is a Process**
>
> 1. **Facing reality**
> 2. **Assembling an advisory team**
> 3. **Communicating**
> 4. **Gathering data**
> 5. **Research**
> 6. **Performing tax** and financial analyses and evaluations
> 7. **Developing primary** and fallback strategies (including selection of successors and family/non-family team)
> 8. **Building consensus** (family participation)
> 9. **Implementation** (including training and development of the next generation (Succession Development Plan)
> 10. **Monitoring** (including flexibility to implement fallback plan in the event of a change in circumstances)
> 11. **Repeat the process** for the next generation, anticipating the next round of change

three different generations, and *no* CEO or president. Family members from the third generation who aren't yet eligible to serve on the committee participate in family-council meetings where goals and objectives, the conditions for participating in ownership, and other family-business matters are discussed. Another option, discussed in detail in Chapter 6, is restructuring the company to allow each qualified member of the next generation to be the leader of a strategic business unit—essentially creating a separate kingdom for each qualified candidate. You should also consider the disadvantages of having multiple leaders—confusion, deadlock and feuding among co-presidents. You don't want to end up with a compromise that serves no one.

WHEN YOU STEP DOWN, YOU SHOULD *REALLY* STEP DOWN. Although it's well accepted in law and religion that you *cannot* "manage from the grave," it seems to be less understood that you *should not* manage from the golf course or local community center. When the time comes for you to let go, you should truly let go, provided that all of the training and mentoring have been accomplished before the transition. One key to building a platform for effective family-business succession is for you, the departing owner, to have an activity or series of activities that are truly meaningful and that require enough of your time to prevent post-transition meddling and micromanagement of the incoming generation of leadership.

CHAPTER FIVE | **PARTING COMPANY**

Developing the Family Business Continuity Plan

THE FAMILY BUSINESS CONTINUITY PLAN (FBCP) IS a written document that establishes a primary plan as well as a series of fallback plans for ensuring that your business continues. By "continues," I mean operating in some capacity, serving customers and creating revenues and profits for your estate (and your successors) long after you retire, die, are disabled or otherwise leave the business.

The Pre-Planning Process

The planning prior to the actual preparation of the FBCP is an important exercise that considers all possible exit strategies, including:

- **Transferring the business to your children** or other family members (through one of the methods described in Chapter 6);
- **Selling the business** (or your portion of the business) to co-owners, where applicable, or to key employees or all employees (Chapters 7 and 8);
- **Selling the business to a third party** (Chapter 9);

49

CHAPTER FIVE PARTING COMPANY

- **Selling a significant portion** of the company to the general public through a public offering (Chapter 10);
- **Choosing among other creative exit strategies** described in Chapter 11.

This pre-planning process considers key factors and long-term objectives such as:

- **your financial needs** and goals,
- **the future** of the business,
- **the valuation** of the company,
- **the availability** of qualified family successors,
- **trends** within your industry, and
- **the degree of risk** you're willing to assume and control you wish to exercise over the company *after* the transfer or exit strategy has been implemented.

It's important to understand that each strategy will have a different impact on risk/control analysis, which you and your advisers should carefully weigh prior to ranking the exit strategies and selecting the one you will pursue.

This chapter assumes that your primary strategy is to keep ownership and control of the business within your family (even though other strategies may be equally or even more attractive from a financial perspective). However, your FBCP might still include some strategies for *partial* transfer of ownership and control, such as through an initial public offering, or the sale of a portion of the company to an employee stock ownership plan (ESOP).

Flexibility is also a critical component of the pre-planning process. The conditions and circumstances present when you draft the FBCP may be ideal for today but disastrous two years from now. The FBCP must be flexible enough to respond to changes within the family or within the marketplace. Alternatively, the FBCP may be based on certain assumptions or conditions about the future that may not come to fruition. For example, you might base your FBCP on an assumption that the number of new stores you'll open each year will grow by 20%, without being able to assess the impact of e-commerce on your business model. Therefore, the FBCP must be flexible enough to accommodate inevitable changes ; it has to be an evolving document that can and *must* be promptly amended when change occurs or assumptions about the future aren't realized.

A shortsighted reader at this point may be thinking, "Changes, what changes? I have one child and I'm certain that she'll get this business when I'm ready to step aside!" Sounds simple, right? Wrong. The pre-planning process anticipates the many factors down the road that might trigger a need for a change to the FBCP, even when there's only one child, such as:

- **She finds her calling** as a social worker in Nepal and has no interest in the family business.
- **She loves the family business** but lacks any business acumen despite your best efforts to train her.
- **She marries a gentlemen** whose idea of hard work is three rounds of golf in one day and who is eyeing your business as a means of keeping his golf habit going.
- **She bears you three grandchildren,** two of whom show a genuine interest in and understanding of the business, which opens up additional possibilities (and complications).
- **The value of the business grows** to such a significant level that you feel the need to "share the wealth," either with philanthropic organizations, other family members or even key employees who helped build the value.
- **A niece or nephew shows interest** in the business, is doing an excellent job and shows leadership potential.
- **Industry trends dictate** that the sale to a third party will fetch a significant valuation that you can't (or shouldn't) resist.
- **Your cash or savings position diminishes** to the point where "gifting" the business is no longer viable or attractive from a retirement-planning perspective.

So, even what appears to be a simple and straightforward FBCP that assumes you want to keep the business in the family with just one child can get complicated. So imagine the additional issues when there are several family members involved and each has his or her own view as to how the busi-

CHAPTER FIVE PARTING COMPANY

> **BOX 5-1 Where Do I Start?**
>
> - **Assemble** your team
> - **Consider** all the possibilities
> - **Build** consensus/Seek input
> - **Gather** data
> - **Analyze** options and strategies
> - **Select** primary objective
> - **Develop** FBCP (driven by your primary objective)
> - **Be ready** to implement

ness should be divided and how management and control should be allocated. All the more reason to have a definite plan in place.

You must also consider how the reasons for your exit will affect your choice of primary strategy. For example, you may feel differently about who should step into your shoes in the event of an unexpected death versus a gradual and voluntary retirement. In the latter scenario, you'll have time to phase out your role and responsibilities and train your hand-picked successor. Unfortunately, a sudden death will not afford you those luxuries. A transitional advisory board, which would provide support to your successor, should be included in the plan in the event of your unexpected death. Depending on your age, there are many health and relationship contingencies to provide for. And with our nation's divorce rate at nearly 50%, the possibility of divorce, remarriage, stepchildren and children-in-law can really muddy the waters in choosing among potential successors and heirs. Many of these family-relationship contingencies can be dealt with in your estate plan (which is not the focus of this book, but the estate plan may be affected by strategies set forth in the family business continuity plan).

During the pre-planning process, don't let complex emotional and family-political issues cloud your judgment or allow you to lose sight of the key objectives of any FBCP, namely:

- **To preserve and protect the value** of the company that you have worked so hard to build.

- **To provide a primary strategy** and fallback strategies to convert that value into the resources that you need for retirement and estate-planning goals.
- **To provide an orderly transition** of the ownership and control of the business to the next generation of owners—family or non-family—while protecting the interests of the company's various stakeholders. Remember that *ownership succession* is not the same as *management succession*. Plans could be made to begin the transition of management without directly linking the transfer of ownership, which could be delayed or tied to certain performance goals for the new management team.

Key Steps in the Pre-Planning Process

The steps that lead up to the actual preparation of the FBCP include goal-setting, consensus-building and financial-analysis exercises that will help ensure that your FBCP truly meets your objectives. These steps include:

DETERMINE YOUR LIFE PLAN AND TIMETABLE. Naturally, your age, health, retirement horizon and whether you view this business as your "last hurrah" will all dictate the strategies in your FBCP. If you're a "career entrepreneur"—essentially in the business of starting, building and exiting businesses—you may not view your current venture as your last. You would therefore want exit strategies that work not only for your investors but also for yourself.

DETERMINE THE CURRENT AND FUTURE VALUE OF WHAT YOU HAVE BUILT. Again, the number of options available to you will be driven in part by what your business is currently worth or what it may be worth to future owners. See Chapter 2 for methods of valuing your business. The ultimate value will also be a key factor in the next analysis.

DETERMINE YOUR RETIREMENT AND ESTATE-PLANNING NEEDS. Your personal financial goals and needs will also steer you to a strategy. For example, if you've accumulated all the wealth that you'll need to retire and provide for your estate, then money may not be as important to you as keeping the business in the family. If, like most small-business owners, your company is still the primary asset on your personal balance sheet, then your FBCP will need to provide the assets and income that you will need to retire (and provide for your estate). Such a need may preclude traditional "gifting" to the next generation (because you'll need to derive income from the transfer of the ownership of the business) unless the gifting is coupled with employment contracts, consulting agreements or other means of generating income.

CONDUCT A LEGAL AUDIT. In a legal audit, the company's management team meets with corporate counsel in order to: (1) discuss strategic plans and objectives, (2) review key documents and records, and (3) identify and analyze current and projected legal needs of the company. The audit also lays the groundwork for establishing an ongoing compliance and prevention program to ensure that the company's goals, structure and ongoing operations are consistent with the latest developments. Finally, the audit helps managers identify and address the legal issues that are triggered by changes in strategies, goals or objectives. (See the Legal Audit Checklist on page 197 of the Appendix.)

FOCUS ON CORPORATE STRUCTURE AND REORGANIZATION. In addition to all the other benefits of a legal audit discussed above, the audit process should focus on how your current ownership structure will affect the strategies available under the FBCP. For example, does the current structure inhibit or restrict in any way, either by contract or by charter, the options that would otherwise be available? Unless there is a valid legal, tax or financial reason to do so, you may want to consider restructuring to allow for maximum flexibility. On a related issue, does the current structure provide for "creative" solutions to the implementation of the FBCP? For example, if your children have different talents and interests—or, worse, are feuding—do you have the option to transfer different components of the business to different children? Let's say one of your two sons has an engineering background and the other is in sales and marketing; despite the different backgrounds, there is a potential for conflict in the event of co-ownership. Perhaps you could restructure the company now to set up separate ownership of the manufacturing and distribution functions of the business, which allows these separate business units to evolve before your exit.

GATHER DATA AND BUILD CONSENSUS. Don't prepare your FBCP in a vacuum. You need to seek input from your advisory team (lawyers, accountants and consultants), those parties targeted as the next owners (family and non-family) and affected stakeholders, to make sure that the FBCP will be well-received and smoothly implemented.

You may be surprised to learn how people really feel and how they react to the primary strategy that you've selected in the draft of the FBCP. You can't please all the people all the time, but you don't want to make the mistake of pleasing no one by drafting a plan that's based on false assumptions. You're the only one who'll decide whether these people will have a vote or merely a voice. While some business owners want to retain the final veto for themselves, others are open to a more democratic process (though, depending on the players, not all votes need to count equally). The key is to make all affected parties feel as if they are part of the process, which is hard to do if you merely present the FBCP to them in final form. If your exit is due to a voluntary and gradual retirement, you'll have fewer sleepless nights if you allow affected family members to participate in the process and voice their views and concerns.

Okay, we have established what a family business continuity plan is, why you need one and the steps to take as part of the pre-drafting process. We now understand that even an apparently simple situation can be very complex, and that the most effective final plans are usually the result of a limited democratic and participatory process, rather than an act of despotism. The next step is to understand business and financial planning.

The Basics of Business and Financial Planning

Effective business and financial planning is critical to a company's long-term success and viability, and much has been written by bankers, accountants, consultants and academics on the preparation of a business plan. Yet it seems the more information there is, the more confused the entrepreneurial community becomes, not only with respect to the proper preparation and use of a business plan but also as to what information to include. There's no one "right answer." A business plan should tell a story, make an argument and conservatively predict the future, and all companies have different stories to tell, different arguments to make and different futures to predict.

Business plans are often prepared to assist in the development of a family business continuity plan. Some of the questions that must be addressed in the plan will be financial in nature, such as:

- **What is our business model,** and how is it likely to evolve over the next five to ten years?
- **What market problems** and financial opportunities have been identified?
- **What services, products and projects** are planned to exploit these opportunities or solve these problems?
- **How much capital will be needed** to acquire the resources necessary to bring these projects to fruition?
- **How will the capital be allocated?** How will this infusion of capital increase sales, profits and the company's overall value?
- **How will the company meet its obligations** under commercial loans or leases or provide a meaningful return on investment to its investors and lenders?

There are also certain business-planning questions that will have a direct impact on the development of an effective succession plan:

- **Where do we expect the business to be** in the next five to ten years, and how will this affect today's decisions regarding

management and control?
- **How old are members of the current management team** and what are their retirement plans?
- **What expectations do the company's employees** have with respect to ownership? Have any promises been made to them?
- **How will the company's projected capital needs** affect your ability to maintain control?
- **What type of leadership is required** to keep the company competitive over the next five to ten years?

A comprehensive business plan should precede, or at the very least be incorporated into, the final family business continuity plan. Knowing what you have and where it's going will help determine what you want to do with it as you near retirement.

A well-written business plan serves as a management tool and a road map for growth; a realistic self-appraisal of the company's progress to date, as well as future goals and objectives; and a foundation for the development of a more detailed strategic and succession management plan.

Here is an outline of a typical business plan:

I. EXECUTIVE SUMMARY
  A. Brief history
  B. Overview of products and services
  C. Background of management team (summary)
  D. Mission statement (Why are we in this business?)
  E. Summary of financial performance
  F. Key features of the market

II. THE COMPANY—AN OVERVIEW
  A. Organizational and management structure
  B. Operational and management policies
  C. Description of products and services offered (both current and anticipated)
  D. Overview of trends in the industry and marketplace in which the company competes (or plans to compete)
  E. Key strengths and weaknesses of the company

III. PRODUCTS AND SERVICES OFFERED—AN EXTENDED DISCUSSION
  A. Key products and services offered
  B. Proprietary features, strengths and weaknesses of each product and service
  C. Anticipated products and services to be offered (explain how these plans will be affected by the financing sought)

IV. ANALYSIS OF THE MARKETPLACE
  A. Extended description of the markets in which the company competes (size, trends, growth, etc.)
  B. Analysis of major competitors
  C. Description and analysis of key customers or clients (current and anticipated)
  D. Market research (to support current and anticipated lines of products and services)

V. MARKETING AND ADVERTISING STRATEGY
  A. Strategies for reaching current and anticipated customers or clients
  B. Pricing policies and strategies
  C. Advertising and public relations plans and strategies

VI. FINANCIAL PLAN AND STRATEGIES
  A. Summary of financial performance for the past three to five years
  B. Current financial condition (include recent income statements and balance sheets as attachments)
  C. Projected financial condition (forecasts for three to five years)
  D. Extended discussion of budgets and anticipated allocation of proceeds

VII. SUGGESTED EXHIBITS AND ATTACHMENTS
  A. Current and projected financial statements (with detailed footnotes and assumptions)
  B. Resumes of key members of the management team
  C. Timetables for completion of key goals and objectives
  D. Organizational chart for management of the company
  E. Copies of key documents and contracts
  F. Copies of recent media coverage

G. Pictures of key products or advertising materials for services offered

H. List of customer and professional references

Preparing a business plan can be a challenging and energizing exercise that puts your company on a path for which the plan serves as a road map. But developing a successful plan hinges on anticipating and managing the roadblocks that come with family ownership.

Barbara Shomaker, president of Accord Limited, a Chicago consulting firm, has developed a detailed written framework for family-business leaders wanting to develop strategic plans, paying special attention to the challenges of developing plans for businesses that are family-run. This framework includes the following steps:

SEEK THE RIGHT GROUP OF CORE PLANNERS. Involve individuals who understand the business and how to make it grow, including one person who understands the economics of the company, a second who understands sales and marketing, and a third who understands manufacturing and distribution.

AGREE ON CRITICAL OWNER STRATEGIES. It's important for you to hold family meetings about issues that will influence the final plan, including requirements to enter or stay in the business, roles of inactive family shareholders, stock ownership for non-family members and in-laws, family compensation, performance and dividend expectations, retirement decisions, and leadership succession. Once there is consensus on these areas, you're ready to move on to the most critical issues—the ultimate objective of your company and its future business strategies.

SEEK TO MERGE OWNER STRATEGIES AND BUSINESS STRATEGIES. You must recognize that there's likely to be more than one set of realities floating around. Owners who are actively managing the business, as well as inactive owners, will have definite—but potentially conflicting—views on the organization's ideal direction. Gather input from active owners to develop an ultimate business objective. During family meetings, educate inactive owners about the vision, and steer them toward a common strategic ground. The process should be participatory but not necessarily democratic.

GATHER INPUT FROM THE OLDEST GENERATION. The most senior active owners (assuming they're more senior than you) are the linchpins of the planning process. It's a mistake not to include them in the process, even if a leadership transition is about to occur. Their input creates the context for making critical decisions.

BASE DECISIONS ON CONCRETE DATA. It's important to collect enough advance information about the external trends and factors affecting the future of your company so that you can make the right decisions during the internal planning process. Gather research and other materials that address the needs of major stakeholders; industry, market and technological trends; and current internal performance. Require participants to study the materials in advance so that they can hit the ground running at your meeting.

CONDUCT A SWOT ANALYSIS. Use your meeting to conduct a soul-searching analysis of your company's strengths, weaknesses, opportunities and threats (SWOT). Address such questions as: "How do we know that our *perceived* strengths are our *genuine* strengths? Who says they are?" "What weaknesses are shooting us in the foot and preventing our growth?" The plan itself will describe your mission, vision, goals, tasks and systems for monitoring results. Draft an initial plan, give the planners two weeks to mull it over, and then meet for one more day to put it into final form.

The Family Business Continuity Plan

With a business plan in place and the pre-planning process completed, the family business continuity plan can be developed and implemented. The FBCP should always include:

- **a vision for the business** and the family;
- **a family mission statement;**
- **strategic summary of the company's position** in the marketplace (for example, its strengths, weaknesses, opportunities and threats);
- **a set of projected revenues,** earnings and net worth for the next three to five years; and, most important,
- **a plan for the transition** of ownership and control to designated family members, which includes a clearly defined timetable, statements of responsibility and authority, and an organizational structure.

Preparing the plan may involve seeking the input of an advisory board or forming a succession-planning task force. Gathering all the details appropriate for the FBCP is emotionally hard work because it demands much discussion and documentation, and sometimes even requires the consent of third parties such as lenders, customers or suppliers (to the extent that your company's success depends on these relationships). So begin early, allow several years for its total design and implementation, and update it as people and conditions change.

The FBCP should address more than just *who* will be your successors; it should be a comprehensive transition plan that covers *why* and *how* they were selected—usually based on a combination of passion and skill. It should establish a game plan for educating and training the new generation of leaders, which will provide for a seamless transition over a certain timetable. The details of the FBCP should be communicated to all affected stakeholders in the company over a definite time frame and in a clear, consistent manner to prevent rumors or hurt feelings.

The legal impact of the implementation of the FBCP should also be addressed. These issues may include:

- **Who is eligible to participate** in the next generation of ownership, and when?
- **Are there existing shareholder** and buy-sell agreements (or any other legal documents affecting the company's ownership and control) that will need to be amended as a result of the

implementation of the family business continuity plan? Do you need to create new documents?

- **Will the company's charter need to be amended** to create multiple classes of stock, or to distinguish between voting and non-voting stock?
- **Are there any other key agreements** with vendors or customers that will be affected by the development and implementation of the family business continuity plan?

Some Final Thoughts on Preparing the Family Business Continuity Plan

FOUNDERS USUALLY WANT TO PASS OWNERSHIP on to their family to provide security for future generations, leave behind a legacy and keep the family together. Yet, if succession is poorly planned and managed, the opposite may happen. Poor planning could lead to taxes that cut deeply into the family's financial security, politics and anger that cut into the family's legacy, and disagreements that stir up discontent.

IT'S CRITICAL TO CONSIDER the emotional and social ramifications of the choices you make regarding future leadership. You may have to take steps to avoid a loss of face for those family members who are passed over, particularly to maintain family harmony. Even if your own child accepts your decision not to include her as a leader of the company, don't underestimate the power and importance of jealous in-laws. Say, for instance, that one child—whose spouse has expectations about future ownership—has worked hard in the business but doesn't have the skills to be a CEO. Meanwhile, another child, who does have leadership skills, will need to be lured away from a current career with a very attractive salary and benefits package. Such a scenario could turn up the heat on simmering family resentments.

INDENTURED SERVITUDE has been illegal for many years. It does not make personal or business sense to try to attach a "ball and chain" to a family member who doesn't really want to stay on to manage the business. In such cases, nobody wins, and ultimately employees and customers suffer. If the child you've selected isn't interested and others don't qualify, consider an alternative exit strategy.

FAMILY-BUSINESS OWNERS often feel that the next generation doesn't give them the respect and recognition they deserve. Succession planning is not about building shrines and worshipping idols—it's about preserving and building your family's financial net worth.

PART THREE | PARTING COMPANY

Succession Planning Strategies

CHAPTER SIX | PARTING COMPANY

Keeping Your Business in the Family

THE FAMILY BUSINESS CONTINUITY PLAN THAT WAS discussed in Chapter 5 addressed *who* gets *what,* and *when.* Next comes the *how,* and that depends on whether you'll be selling or transferring the business. If you're selling the business, you'll follow a process much like that described in Chapter 9. This chapter outlines how to transfer ownership, and do so smoothly. The *how* is important because how you transfer the business will greatly affect how much estate tax you—or, rather, your heirs—will have to pay. And if you fail to plan for the potential estate-tax liability, your family could be forced to give up control. Even if your heirs plan to sell, they might have to accept a fire-sale price in the scramble to pay the tax.

The following discussion provides simplified explanations of some of the more common and effective strategies you could use to reduce the tax bite. These strategies include gifting programs, trusts, stock recapitalizations, estate freezes and family limited partnerships. Some depend on the structure of your business (such as "regular" corporation, "S" corporation, limited-liability company, or partnership). If your business is a sole proprietorship, you'll have to convert to a more formal busi-

CHAPTER SIX PARTING COMPANY

ness structure to employ these strategies. Fortunately, you can probably accomplish this tax-free if it's part of a succession plan. Such plans can get complicated and are best left to a competent estate attorney to implement.

Let's see what the tax law would do to your estate—including your business—if you did no planning whatsoever.

First, a quick (and very simplified) lesson on the federal estate tax. Really, it's the gift and estate tax, a unified system designed to avoid a loophole that would let people dodge the estate tax by giving away their property before death. So, the law taxes gifts you make during your life as well as assets you own when you die. The same tax rates apply, and the law ignores the first several hundred thousand dollars worth of gifts and bequests. The protected amount is increasing each year, as the table on page 73 shows, and there are efforts in Congress to cut back death taxes even more. But at the time we went to press in the fall of 1999, the exempt amounts were those shown in the table. (The law also allows tax-free gifts of up to $10,000 annually to any number of people, as discussed later.)

Actually, there is no gift-and-estate-tax exemption, although that's what everyone calls it. It's really a tax credit big enough to pay the tax bill on the protected amount shown in the table. And, there's a big difference between a credit and an exemption. An exemption removes dollars from the highest tax bracket—which for estate-tax purposes can be as high as 55%. The credit, on the other hand, pays the tax bill on the first part of your taxable estate, the part that falls in the lowest tax brackets (rates start at 18%).

This distinction is particularly important to owners of family businesses because a new estate-tax break—first available in 1998—gives estates of qualifying owners the right to exempt up to $675,000 of the value of the business from the estate tax. Since this is an exemption, it applies in the highest bracket your estate faces and, thus, increases in value along with the value of your total taxable estate.

Alas, there's a catch. If your business qualifies for this special break (there are all sorts of requirements and restrictions, of course; your attorney or accountant can tell you whether you qualify) and you use the full $675,000 deduction, you're

Keeping Your Business in the Family

stuck with a stunted credit that won't protect as much of your estate as suggested in our table on page 73. You see, Congress decreed that, together, the credit and the special family-business exemption can't protect more than $1.3 million of your estate. If you use the $675,000 family-business exemption, then the maximum estate-tax credit available is the amount to protect $625,000. If, on the other hand, you claim only a $625,000 family-business exemption, the estate-tax credit protects $675,000 of your remaining estate.

Now, to our example: Assume that you die in 2005, that your business is worth $3 million and that you have other assets (a car, home, investments, life insurance, etc.) valued at $1 million.

The estate tax on $4 million would be $1,840,000 (see the tax-rate table on page 71). But you'd owe much less. Assuming your business qualifies for the $675,000 family-business exemption, your taxable estate would be just $3,325,000. The tax on that amount would be $1,469,550. Subtracting the $202,050 credit that protects the first $625,000, brings the bill down to $1,267,500.

That's still a painful bite; the point of planning is to make sure more of your estate goes to your true heirs...and less to Uncle Sam.

Gifting

The tax law actually encourages you to begin giving family members common stock in the business (or the equity equivalent, such as a membership interest in a limited-liability company) as soon as possible. As will be discussed later in the chapter, you can create and give voting stock to family members who will be active participants in the business and non-voting stock to those relatives to whom you want to give part of the business but who will not be taking part in its operation.

Giving stock in the business early reduces your estate two ways. First, you've given some of it away tax-free; second, you've given it away while the value of the business is presumably lower than it will be years later when you die.

This strategy takes advantage of provisions in the tax law

CHAPTER SIX PARTING COMPANY

that permit tax-free giving, or "gifting." Done properly, it can reduce—or even eliminate—the estate tax. Let's look at some examples.

Tax-Free Annual Gifting

In addition to the estate-and-gift-tax credit, the law permits you to give $10,000 a year annually to as many people as you wish without triggering what's called a gift tax. (To counter the eroding effects of inflation, this "gift tax annual exclusion" will increase periodically in $1,000 increments.)

Let's say you have three children to whom you want to leave your business. If you give each one $10,000 worth of the business annually for five years, you'll reduce your estate's value by $150,000.

You might be able to do even more with tax-free gifting. If your children are married, you can give each spouse $10,000 tax-free annually, doubling the five-year gift to $300,000. And if you are married, you can double the annual gift to $20,000 so long as your spouse doesn't give any of his or her own assets to the recipients of your gifts in the same year. That results in a potential tax-free gift (over five years) of $600,000. That would bring the taxable estate in our example on page 69down to $3.4 million. Subtracting the $675,000 family-business exemption knocks the amount down to $2,725,000. The tax on that amount is $1,145,050; and subtracting the $202,050 credit brings the tab down to $943,000. That means this tax-free gifting program would save your heirs $324,500. Not a bad return on your generosity.

Keep in mind that the IRS may question your valuation of the stock. While the IRS considers a $10,000 gift of cash as a $10,000 gift, what you consider $10,000 worth of stock may not be considered worth that by the IRS, which ultimately determines the value of the gift.

Tax-Free Annual Gifting Plus Accelerated Taxable Gifting

You can drive down the taxable estate still further by gifting

Keeping Your Business in the Family

BOX 6-1 | Gift and Estate-Tax Rate Schedule

TAXABLE AMOUNT	TAX BEFORE CREDIT
Up to $10,000	18%
$10,001 to $20,000	$1,800 plus 20% of amount over $10,000
$20,001 to $40,000	$3,800 plus 22% of amount over $20,000
$40,001 to $60,000	$8,200 plus 24% of amount over $40,000
$60,001 to $80,000	$13,000 plus 26% of amount over $60,000
$80,001 to $100,000	$18,200 plus 28% of amount over $80,000
$100,001 to $150,000	$23,800 plus 30% of amount over $100,000
$150,001 to $250,000	$38,800 plus 32% of amount over $150,000
$250,001 to $500,000	$70,800 plus 34% of amount over $250,000
$500,001 to $750,000	$155,800 plus 37% of amount over $500,000
$750,001 to $1,000,000	$248,300 plus 39% of amount over $750,000
$1,000,001 to $1,250,000	$345,800 plus 41% of amount over $1,000,000
$1,250,001 to $1,500,000	$448,300 plus 43% of amount over $1,250,000
$1,500,001 to $2,000,000	$555,800 plus 45% of amount over $1,500,000
$2,000,001 to $2,500,000	$780,800 plus 49% of amount over $2,000,000
$2,500,001 to $3,000,000	$1,025,800 plus 53% of amount over $2,500,000
Over $3,000,000	$1,290,800 plus 55%* of amount over $3,000,000

*A 5% surcharge applies to taxable estates over $10 million, making the effective rate 60%. The surcharge is Congress's way of taking back the benefit of the graduated rates so that big estates are hit with a flat 55% tax. The surtax stops at $17,184,000.

more than the annual allowable amount. While the additional gift is taxable, you can use the estate-and-gift-tax credit to make some or all of these gifts tax-free as well. While the amount of the credit is the same whether you use it during your lifetime or as an estate-tax credit, it is probably worth more in life because, as we've already noted, you'll be giving more of the business to your heirs while it has a lower value than presumably it will have in the future. Here's how that works.

Say you decide to give each of your three children $50,000 worth of stock in the business each year for five consecutive years. Let's say that only the first $10,000 gift each year is protected by the annual exclusion. The additional $40,000 is charged against the estate-and-gift-tax credit, gradually using it up rather than having it available to offset the estate tax after you die. Each year, you would report the $120,000 taxable portion and figure what the tax would be. That amount is not paid

CHAPTER SIX PARTING COMPANY

as tax; instead, it is the amount by which your estate-and-gift-tax credit is gradually reduced. Here's how it works:

- **In the first year,** using the schedule on page 71, the tax on the first $120,000 is $29,800, meaning that your estate-and-gift-tax credit is reduced by $29,800.
- **In the second year,** you add the new $120,000 taxable gift to the previous year's $120,000 and find the tax on $240,000—$67,600. From that amount you subtract the $29,800 from the first gift. So the tax—or credit reduction—on the second gift is $37,800.
- **In the third year,** you again add the new $120,000 to the $240,000 of taxable gifts given in previous years. Find the tax on $360,000, which is $108,200, and subtract that combined $67,600 tax on the previous gifts. The tax-credit reduction on your third gift is $40,600.
- **In the fourth year,** you add the $120,000 to the gifts you've previously given. Calculate the tax on $480,000—$149,000—and subtract the $108,200 by which your credit has already been reduced. In the fourth year you're reducing the credit by $40,800.
- **For the fifth and final year,** you again add your $120,000 gift to previous gifts, and your total is $600,000. The tax on that amount would be $192,800, from which you subtract the $149,000 from the four previous years. Your tax for the fifth gift of $120,000 would be $43,800, meaning you've reduced the estate-and-gift-tax credit by that amount, or a total of $192,800 over the five years

The point of adding in the previous gifts is to force you to march steadily up the graduated estate-tax rate schedule; even though the gifts given were the same size each year, the tax rises as the tax rate increases. Our example assumes that these gifts are the only ones you've made so far, so no tax would actually have to be paid. If you had made the same $600,000 taxable gifts in the same year, you would have had the same $192,800 tax bill and your estate-and-gift-tax credit would have been reduced by $192,800. Assuming your business qualifies for, and your estate claims, the $675,000 exemption—so your maximum credit is

BOX 6-2 — Tax Credits and the Family-Business Exemption

THE LAW ALLOWS you to make tax-free gifts of up to $10,000 annually to any number of people. If you're married—and your spouse agrees not to give any of his or her assets to the same person—you can give up to $20,000 tax-free each year to any number of people. As noted in this chapter, a multi-year gifting program can allow you to transfer a sizable portion of your business to family members tax-free. In addition to the annual exclusion, almost everyone gets an estate-and-gift-tax credit that covers the bill on the first several hundred thousand dollars of taxable gifts and/or the amount in your taxable estate when you die. The amount of that credit—and, accordingly, the amount of lifetime gifts and bequests that can be passed to the next generation tax-free (the exemption equivalent)—is rising gradually so that in 2006 and later years, up to $1 million can be transferred tax-free. There is also a special break designed to help families keep a business in the family after the owner's death. The family-business exemption allows estates to deduct up to $675,000 of the value of a qualifying business.

When the family-business break was created—it was first available in 1998—Congress declared that the maximum combined amount that could be protected by the credit and the exemption was $1.3 million. Therefore, as the credit increased over the years, it was assumed that the family-business exemption would effectively fall. That would be detrimental because while the exemption protects value that falls in the highest estate-tax brackets (they go as high as 55%), the credit applies to amounts that fall in the lowest brackets (rates start at 18%). To prevent a dilution of the value of the exemption, the law was changed to set the family-business exemption at a maximum of $675,000. If your estate qualifies for and opts to deduct the full amount, however, it will not get the benefit of the rising credit amount. Instead, the exemption equivalent will be stalled at $625,000—for a maximum $1.3 million. If you claim a smaller family-business exemption, however, you may deserve a bigger credit equivalent—as long as the combined total doesn't exceed $1.3 million.

ESTATE- AND GIFT-TAX YEAR	EXEMPTION EQUIVALENT*
1999	$650,000
2000	$675,000
2001	$675,000
2002–2003	$700,000
2004	$850,000
2005	$950,000
2006 and after	$1,000,000

*This is the amount protected by the estate-tax credit; as noted above, if your estate qualifies for and claims the maximum $675,000 family-business exemption, the exemption equivalent is $625,000 for each year.

CHAPTER SIX PARTING COMPANY

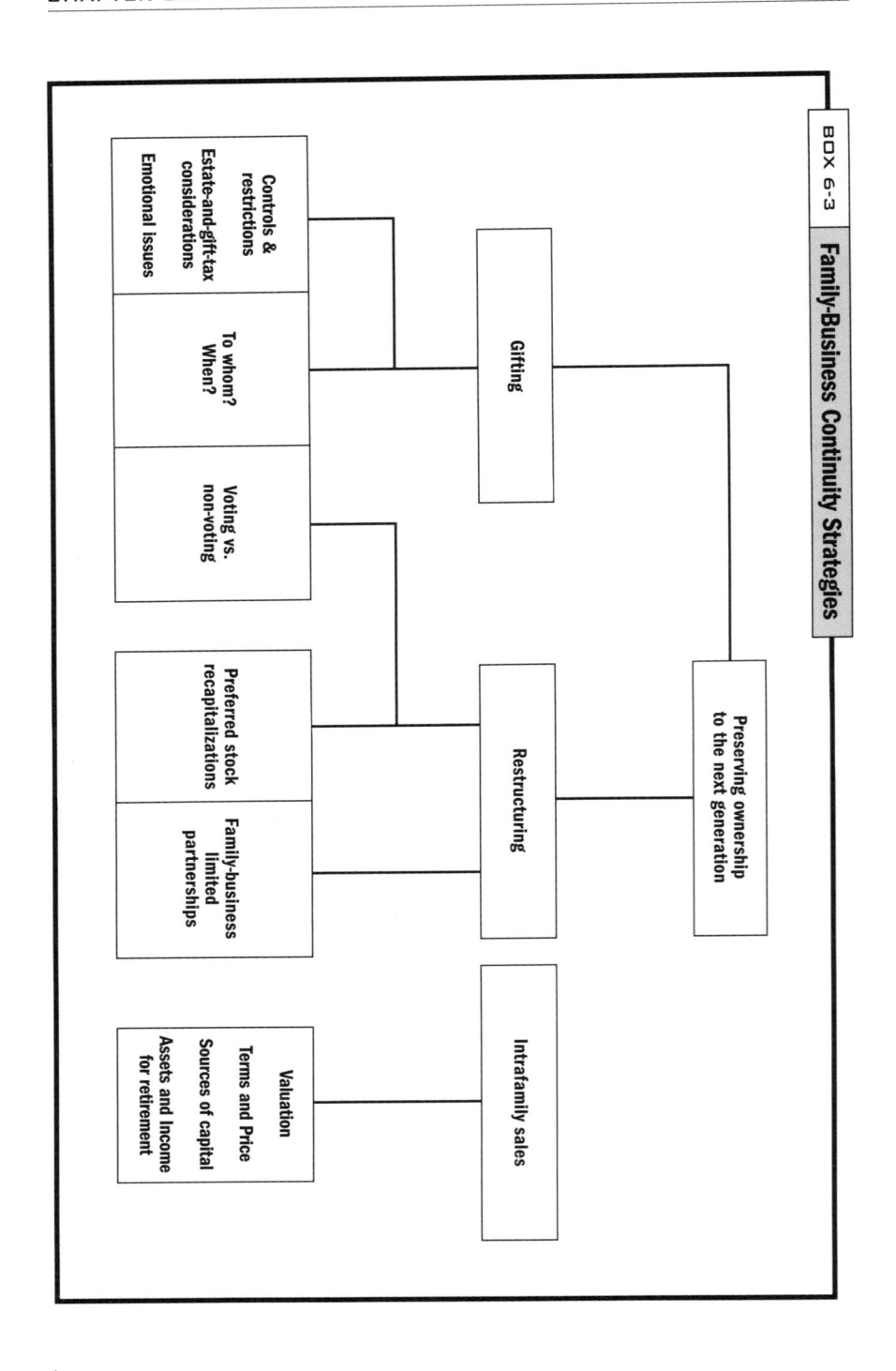

BOX 6-3 Family-Business Continuity Strategies

Preserving ownership to the next generation
- Gifting
  - Controls & restrictions
    - Estate-and-gift-tax considerations
    - Emotional issues
  - To whom? When?
  - Voting vs. non-voting
- Restructuring
  - Preferred stock recapitalizations
  - Family-business limited partnerships
- Intrafamily sales
  - Valuation
  - Terms and Price
  - Sources of capital
  - Assets and Income for retirement

74

$202,050—you'd have just $9,250 left to offset estate taxes.

Over those five years, you would have gifted $750,000 worth of your business. Let's say that during that period the value of your business increased from $2 million to $3 million—but your share would have remained at about $2 million because you gave away not only the shares but also their future appreciation. Your total estate would be about $3 million, about $1 million less than it would have been had you done nothing. Subtracting the $675,000 family-business exclusion would leave a taxable amount of $2,325,000. The tax on that amount is $940,050 (see the table on page 71). Subtracting the remaining $9,250 of the estate-tax credit brings the bill down to $930,800—$336,700 less than if you had done no gifting. And if you had made more of the gifts in tax-excluded $10,000 annual gifts, you would have had even more of the estate-and-gift-tax credit available to drive down the taxable amount of your estate even further.

It's almost always better to make the gifts during your lifetime, even if you use up the estate-and-gift-tax credit and have to pay tax on the gift. That's because your business will probably increase in value over the years, so you're better off giving it away while it's worth less. This can work in your favor because it offers the chance to push more future appreciation out of your estate. You'll need to work with your attorney or accountant to determine whether it makes sense to pay tax sooner rather than later, though. A key factor in that decision is how much appreciation you expect and, therefore, how much tax a gifting program could save.

Other Factors to Consider When Gifting

The distinction between voting and non voting shares may be critical if some of the next generation will be active owners and managers of the business while others will be passive. It's also important if you want to defer a shift in control by initially transferring non voting shares (transferring ownership but not necessarily control) and waiting to transfer the voting stock until you're closer to the date when you plan on leaving the company. There should, of course, be restrictions on resale,

CHAPTER SIX PARTING COMPANY

and other controls such as you'd find in a shareholders' agreement, voting trust or proxy transfer.

If your business is a regular corporation and its charter provides for only a single class of common stock, you may need to file articles of amendment or reorganization to create and authorize the issuance of non voting shares for the inactive members of the next generation. If your business is a subchapter S corporation, the rules do allow you (under certain circumstances) to create a class of both voting and non voting stock, which creates additional planning opportunities for closely held companies. Provisions for exchange, redemptions, conditional puts (the right of the company to redeem shares at its option upon notification to its shareholders) and calls (the right of the shareholders to tender the shares for mandatory purchase), and other repurchase rights should be built into the shareholders' agreement to deal with changing circumstances (for example, active members who lose interest in the business or passive members who become more involved).

Gifts can't be taken back; nor will they provide you with retirement income. As a result, you may conclude that *selling* the business to the next generation or to a third party (as discussed in Chapter 9) will provide you with enough money for retirement. If your children *buy* the business, they'll probably appreciate it more and work harder to build it up for *their* successors. If a third party buys the business, you can still look after your children through estate planning and gifting of the cash or stock proceeds that you receive from the sale. In cases where the next generation isn't really ready to take over the business or there is feuding, it may be wiser to sell to a third party than to watch the next generation run the business into the ground.

There's always the chance that your gifting-driven succession plan will take an unexpected turn. For example, one of your children might divorce a spouse who is a part of the family business continuity plan or may marry someone you distrust. Or you might die or become disabled halfway through the gifting process.

The bad divorce or shaky marriage scenario can usually be dealt with in a well-crafted shareholders' agreement or irrevocable trust that ensures that the shares will remain in the family, provided that certain state-law requirements are met. Take steps to ensure that your child's stock does not wind up as dividable community property and that a former son- or daughter-in-law does not wind up as a shareholder.

To be certain that your wishes are carried out even if you die or become disabled part of the way through the gifting program, make sure your attorney includes a "completion clause" in your plan. In the absence of this clause, the remaining ungifted shares might be governed by the estate plan and be divided equally among *all* family members, defeating the purpose of the plan. So make sure that the estate plan is designed to carry out the objectives of the gifting program.

Trusts

In many cases, it's wise to consider using trusts as the recipients of your gifts, as trusts can provide many tax (and nontax) advantages. Trusts can receive $10,000 gift-tax annual-exclusion gifts. While regular corporations, partnerships and limited partnerships can use any form of trust, S corporations can use only certain types (listed below). You can design a trust so that the assets it owns are free from the claims of the beneficiary's personal creditors, whether they are business creditors or, say, a spouse in a divorce settlement. (With a properly structured trust you'll have many of the benefits of a premarital agreement without the difficulties and complications of negotiating one.) Income generated by the trust that the beneficiary doesn't need can accumulate within the trust and continue to be protected from creditors.

A trust can also take advantage of another tax break: the generation-skipping tax exemption, which allows assets to pass to your grandchildren without the future value of those assets being subject to a 55% transfer tax. Used properly, a generation-skipping tax-exempt trust provides you with substantial tax savings. The rules governing the generation-skipping exemption are complex; your attorney can explain it fully to you and determine whether your business qualifies.

CHAPTER SIX PARTING COMPANY

Although as a general rule a trust cannot be a shareholder of S-corporation stock, there are three types of trusts that are qualified to hold this stock: a *grantor* trust, a *qualified subchapter S* trust (often referred to as a QSST), and an *electing small business* trust (often referred to as an ESBT). Each has different tax consequences; carefully review these differences with your attorney and accountant, who can help you decide which trust, if any, to establish.

There are many other types of trusts that you can use, depending on your business- and estate-planning objectives. Consider the following:

ALTHOUGH LIFE INSURANCE PROCEEDS are generally received *income-tax* free, they are not always *estate-tax* free. If you own your insurance policy or you have the right to designate the beneficiary, the IRS will include the policy's proceeds in your taxable estate. In addition to transferring life insurance to a family limited partnership (as discussed earlier), think about establishing an irrevocable life insurance trust (the "user friendly" type) and transfer the policy into the trust. Assuming you survive the policy's transfer by three years (an IRS requirement), the life insurance proceeds will be excluded from your taxable estate and your spouse's taxable estate. Presumably, your spouse and family will be the beneficiaries of the life insurance trust, enabling them to have access to the insurance proceeds just as if they had been named the direct beneficiaries. They can use proceeds from the life insurance trust to help pay any remaining estate tax, making it easier to keep the business in the family. Beneficiaries can also use proceeds to buy out family members who may not want to continue in the business. Irrevocable life insurance trusts can also be used to own second-to-die life insurance.

A CHARITABLE LEAD TRUST involves the transfer of assets (either personal assets or shares in the business) to a trust that provides for the payment of an annuity to charity for a preset time period (or for your lifetime). The present value of the annuity payable to charity qualifies as a gift-tax charitable deduction, leaving only the present value of the remaining interest (for example, the value of the assets put into the trust

Keeping Your Business in the Family

> **BOX 6-4 | The Role of a Trustee**
>
> GENERALLY, a trustee performs two major functions: He or she makes discretionary decisions regarding the distribution of income and principal to the beneficiary of the trust, and makes investment decisions regarding the trust's assets. You may design a trust so that the trustee's functions are divided, leaving the trustee with sole responsibility for making discretionary-distribution decisions, but providing for a separate investment committee to decide how to manage and invest the assets. This can be particularly important when the assets of the trust comprise ownership interests in the family business. A specific individual (or committee of individuals) that you designate would have the responsibility for voting the ownership interests in the family business. This is a good idea when the desired trustee doesn't have the acumen to make business decisions but is the ideal person to handle distributions to the beneficiary. Dividing the traditional trustee responsibilities can also help if you want to make gifts of interests in the family business equally among all of your children—not just those in the business. Let's say that interests in the family business are given in trust for the benefit of children who are not active in the business. The trust can provide that only those children who are active in the business will have the right to vote the business interests. This allows the economics of the business (dividends and capital appreciation) to be divided equally among all children while consolidating the control over the business (the vote) in the hands of those children who are active.

reduced by present value of the charitable annuity) as the taxable gift. Upon the termination of the charitable lead trust, the entire value of the trust estate will be distributed to your heirs without incurring any additional gift or estate tax. The designated beneficiaries of the charitable lead trust can be any public charity or a private family foundation. (Please note that if you create the charitable lead trust during your lifetime and the annuity is payable to your private family foundation, you shouldn't have any responsibility with regard to the distribution of the annuity by the foundation.) A charitable lead trust provides a creative alternative to meeting your twin objectives of making a charitable bequest and leaving assets for your heirs.

CHAPTER SIX PARTING COMPANY

SO-CALLED "DYNASTY" TRUSTS are designed to combine the use of your generation-skipping tax exemption with the transfer of assets to a trust that will not be required to terminate, unless otherwise required by applicable state law. Although your children and grandchildren can enjoy the economic benefits of the trust, no estate tax or generation-skipping tax (at a 55% tax rate) is incurred, regardless of the future value of the trust's assets. An interest in the family business is generally an ideal asset to place in a generation-skipping tax-exempt trust, because the value of the transferred interest can be discounted (due to the lack-of-marketability discount and the minority-interest discount) and because the rate of return on the value of the discounted business interest will generally be greater than the rate of return on undiscounted marketable securities. The mere fact that the future value of the family-business interest won't be subject to estate taxes for several generations easily translates into significant transfer-tax savings for your family.

Estate Freezes

Another way to keep the business in the family is an estate freeze in which the fair market value of the senior generation's interest in the business is "frozen" and future appreciation is shifted to the next generation. There are many ways to accomplish this, including preferred-stock recapitalizations and strategic reorganization.

Preferred-stock recapitalization is a reorganization of the corporation that creates both common and preferred classes of stock. (Preferred-stock recapitalizations are not permitted with S corporations.) The idea is that you allocate a significant portion of the company's value to the preferred stock, which you will retain. You can then gift the common stock to family members at little or no gift-tax cost. Because the terms of the preferred stock are fixed, the value of the preferred stock is frozen and all future appreciation in the company's value is reflected in the value of the common stock. This approach can substantially reduce your estate-tax liability and encourage younger generations to work for the company's continued profitability. Although the preferred stock doesn't share in the future growth of the business, it *does* have a stated dividend that must be paid to the holder of the preferred stock; if unpaid, the dividend will accrue and compound for the holder's benefit. The amount of the dividend depends on many factors, and typically a qualified appraiser is hired to determine the applicable dividend rate. Preferred-stock recapitalization can be a successful wealth-shifting tool if the company's profitability far exceeds the dividend payout. If the company is doing just marginally well, the dividend on the preferred stock may soak up a significant portion of the profits and not shift any meaningful wealth to owners of common stock.

This type of corporate restructuring will allow you to achieve many of your objectives. By using the gifting strategy discussed earlier in the chapter, you could give voting common stock to children active in management at the same time that you transfer non-voting common stock to children who are not active. You may choose to gift only non-voting stock prior to your death, which allows you to reduce the value of your estate without affecting your control. By making gifts of common stock, you ensure that the growth in value of that portion of the business will occur in the hands of the next generation. This will have the effect of reducing, if not "freezing," the value of your interest in the company as the stock appreciates after the date of the gift.

Another type of estate freeze is a "strategic reorganization," which is effective when a company is growing rapidly and estate- and-gift-tax exemptions will be of minimal assistance. A strategic restructuring breaks the current company into separate incorporated strategic units—divided by either function or region— and spins off different components to different heirs. This strategy meets certain tax-planning needs and may also be an effective solution (though tough to implement) for resolving disputes and accommodating different interest levels or diverse talents among the next generation. There are a number of ways these decentralized businesses can be held together. Your attorney can explain how agreements such as shareholders' and cross-purchase agreements, management agreements, licensing and joint-venture agreements work.

Strategic reorganization can work well if the company has several lines of business that are just plugging along and several

CHAPTER SIX PARTING COMPANY

> **BOX 6-5 Additional Succession Planning Alternatives**
>
> THERE ARE MANY non-traditional succession-planning strategies that are beyond the scope of this book. All of these strategies may have adverse tax consequences and should be reviewed carefully by your counsel. They include:
>
> - **Installment sales** between family members
> - **Private annuities**
> - **Self-canceling installment notes**
> - **Upgraded pension** and retirement benefits
> - **Increases in compensation** or bonuses
> - **Deferred-compensation plans**—both unsecured and secured—(may be secured with a Rabbi Trust, which segregates the funds needed to make the deferred payments from other assets)
> - **Redemption of your shares** directly by the company, which by definition increases the ownership of the remaining shareholders; limited to cash-rich companies
> - **Post-employment-termination payments** for consulting or as consideration for non-competes
> - **Renewal payments on real estate** or equipment that may be used by the business but is owned individually by the outgoing generation (or other types of passive income via royalties on intellectual property, director's fees, equipment leasing, etc.)
> - **Use of your underperforming assets** to create a tax-absorbing charitable deduction or to create a charitable trust

new "hot" or rapidly growing lines. Where appropriate, the hot businesses can be spun off, allowing you to "freeze" the hot businesses rather than the whole company. Having enough profit to achieve a significant shift of wealth will be easier because of the dynamics of a rapidly growing line of business.

Family Limited Partnerships

Historically, most businesses have operated in the corporate form, whether as "regular" corporations or as S corporations. The primary advantage of corporations over a sole proprietorship is that you, as the shareholder, are generally not liable for the debts and judgments of the corporation (unless you have pledged your personal assets to cover obligations of the company). Corporate liabilities generally don't reach beyond the corporation's assets. However, two income taxes will be incurred whenever a "regular" corporation pays dividends to its shareholders. And while S corporations were created to alleviate the double-tax scenario, there are many restrictions associated with them.

To avoid this double taxation and the limits of the S corporation, limited partnerships and, more recently, limited-liability companies (LLCs) began to gain in popularity as operating forms for family businesses. Limited partnerships and LLCs are "flow through" entities (that is, they're subject only to one level of taxation), yet can have multi-tiered capital structures and no limitations on the type or number of owners (as is the case with S corporations).

Family limited partnerships can also be set up to purchase and own life insurance policies, the proceeds of which will cover estate taxes or allow the members of the next generation to purchase your equity. Under this scenario, you—the insured—serve as the general partner and your heirs as limited partners. If the proceeds from the life insurance are payable to the partnership, then they are *not* considered part of your estate, even if you manage the partnership. Upon your death, only your equity interest in the partnership is included in your gross estate.

The IRS views some family limited partnerships as tax-avoidance devices and disregards them for estate-planning valuation purposes in certain limited circumstances. It has ruled against those partnerships that it determined were established in contemplation of death where the donor was terminally ill and died shortly after the partnership was created. The IRS has also ruled that, in general, transferred limited-partnership interests must be valued without regard to any restrictions on the right to sell or use the property. There is an exception, however, for a restriction that (1) is a bona fide business arrangement, (2) is not a device to transfer property to family members for less than full price, and (3) has terms that are comparable to similar "arm's-length" arrangements. In short, you must identify and document legitimate business reasons for forming a family limited partnership; intra-family transfer of partnership interests to

CHAPTER SIX PARTING COMPANY

avoid taxes will not be allowed.

Family limited partnerships that hold marketable securities will have the hardest time establishing a non-tax-related purpose. Reasons commonly cited for holding securities include consolidation of investment management, protection against creditors, and the ability to transfer interests to younger family members without transferring specific securities. Nevertheless, the IRS may view such arrangements as suspect, and they should be reviewed carefully by your tax advisers. Note that the new limited-liability company (LLC) structure may also be an effective vehicle for achieving these objectives, but it will be subject to the same degree of IRS scrutiny.

CHAPTER SEVEN | PARTING COMPANY

Dealing With Non-Family Co-Owners

THE PRESENCE OF ONE OR MORE NON-FAMILY CO-founders may have a significant impact on your available transition-management options. This is especially so if there is a shareholders' or buy-sell agreement already in place that directly addresses the retirement, disability or death of a given co-founder, which may or may not be consistent with your *individual* succession-planning or estate-planning goals. (Shareholders' and buy-sell agreements are also very common in family-owned businesses among family-business shareholders. However, for the purposes of this chapter, the focus is on the relationship between non-family co-founders or co-owners,)

Why Have a Co-Founder?

It's natural for small-business owners to look to others when starting new ventures. You probably took up with another person for such reasons as:

- **friendship and having a "sounding board"** for discussing ideas and strategies,

- **augmenting technical expertise** with capital or other resources in which one co-founder may be deficient, and
- **sharing and mitigating risk.**

It doesn't matter why you were brought together; as in any business "marriage," there will inevitably be bumps along the road. The causes may be internal, such as lack of communication, jealousy or differing objectives. Or they may be external, such as the influence of a spouse or key customer, competitive conditions or changes in technology or the marketplace.

Planning Issues for Co-Founders

When a company is started by several people, it's not uncommon to have written agreements or understandings in place that restrict the ability of any co-founder to pass his or her shares (and thereby ownership and control rights) on to a spouse or children. There's usually a mechanism for redeeming these shares and providing the surviving spouse or estate with either a lump-sum payment or installment payments. How and where the proceeds from this redemption will be directed are governed by the person's will or trust, making the matter at that point an issue of estate planning rather than succession planning. If you are a co-founder of a business, make sure that you've considered the following issues with your co-founders:

IS THERE A PLAN OR AGREEMENT in place that determines (or controls) the ownership of the shares upon death? How will things be different in case of disability or retirement?

HOW WILL YOU DEAL WITH THESE ISSUES in case of a dispute that leads to a co-founder's departure from the company, such as a breach of a non-compete clause, embezzlement or failure to perform key responsibilities?

WHAT FORMULA OR PERIODIC VALUATION technique will be used to determine the fair value of these shares upon redemption?

HOW AND WHEN will the proceeds be paid?

IF YOU ARE ALL ROUGHLY THE SAME AGE and the agreement provides for mandatory redemption upon death, who will eventually assume control of the business? If it's the last surviving co-founder (and then his or her estate), have you unintentionally created a "survival of the fittest" policy?

IF YOUR AGREEMENT (or lack of an agreement) provides that the shares of each co-founder may be passed on to a spouse or heirs, can you get along with them on a long-term basis? Do you want to separate ownership from control?

You'll find a sample shareholders' agreement on page 204 in the Appendix.

Understanding the Buy-Sell Agreement

The buy-sell agreement is a legal document that specifies how a company or its owners will redistribute ownership shares after one of the owners dies, becomes disabled, retires or otherwise leaves. The basis for the agreement is a contractual covenant by each owner (or the company) to redeem the stake of any owner who departs, eliminating many of the complications of having a surviving spouse (or even the entire family) at the ownership table. The primary goal is to avoid conflict and confusion by keeping ownership and control in the hands of those individuals who will be responsible for managing the operations of the business.

The ability of the remaining owners (or the company) to purchase the departing owner's shares must be provided for in some manner. This is typically accomplished through the purchase of a series of "key person" life insurance policies or some other reliable source, such as investment accounts specially designated for these purposes to ensure that cash will be available when the "triggering event" occurs. A triggering event may be death, disability, voluntary or involuntary termination (with or without cause), retirement, reaching a certain age, divorce, an acquisition or initial public offering, or some other change in personal, business or family circumstances.

The buy-sell agreement will also dictate, among other things, when an owner can transfer his or her shares and under what circumstances shares must be offered first to other shareholders or owners (or to the company)—known as "rights of first refusal." The agreement includes the procedures for doing so, payment terms or payment mechanism (lump-sum versus deferred or installment) to the departing owner, and procedures for resolving any disputes over valuation or non-payment. In a family-owned business, the restrictions on ownership and transfer of the shares can be very strict and in some cases may provide that only the lineal family members can be shareholders, either by initial issuance or upon transfer. You should consider the impact of a divorce or prenuptial agreement when you prepare these ownership-restriction provisions.

To ensure that the departing owner or survivors receive full value upon redemption, the agreement should spell out how the departing owner's shares will be valued, or direct that one or more outside appraisals be obtained when a triggering event occurs. (Chapter 2 describes various business-valuation methods and the role of business appraisers.) Your buy-sell agreement should provide for periodic mandatory valuations, using whatever method proves best for your type of business. But remember that while valuation of your business is a vital component of an effective succession plan, it's not an exact science, especially for small, closely held businesses.

When your business was first organized, you and your co-founders agreed how the business would be structured—as a partnership, corporation or other entity. You might have agreed on basic decision-making and governance procedures, although these procedures may well have changed after a few years as conditions changed. There might also have been some discussion as to how and when to dissolve the business or what would happen if one of you died or left the company. If these discussions weren't properly documented, you may be headed for frustration, disappointment and strained relationships unless you correct the situation as soon as possible. If you don't have a written agreement in place, or it's incomplete, use the following guide-

Dealing With Non-Family Co-Owners

> **BOX 7-1** | **Advantages of a Buy-Sell Agreement**
>
> A BUY-SELL agreement has numerous advantages for the business itself, the owners and the surviving family of a deceased owner.
>
> **ADVANTAGES FOR THE BUSINESS:**
> **1. Continuity.** A buy-sell agreement helps ensure the continuation of the business. This security produces confidence and peace of mind not only for the firm's owners but also the firm's employees, customers, suppliers and creditors.
>
> **2. No unintentional ownership.** A buy-sell agreement eliminates the problem of unintentional owners. Survivors usually are unqualified to help run the business. They can even interfere in its operation.
>
> **3. Smooth redistribution of ownership.** Because each owner joins in making the agreement, the plan can provide a built-in guarantee that each owner and his or her estate will be treated equitably regardless of who dies or leaves the business, or when.
>
> **ADVANTAGES FOR THE SURVIVING FAMILY MEMBERS:**
> **1. Liquidation of the ownership interest.** A buy-sell agreement can provide the surviving family members with what they need most: a ready "market" for selling the estate's ownership interest. The survivors need the ownership shares converted into liquid funds to provide an income, to pay estate taxes and costs, or to meet other needs. A buy-sell agreement is by far the most efficient way to convert ownership into cash.
>
> **2. Establishment of a fair price.** Through "arm's length" negotiation in making a buy-sell agreement, the owners determine the value or price of the shares to be purchased or redeemed from their estates. This is the best way to arrive at a fair price for each owner because no one knows who will leave or die first, and each owner can think of himself or herself as either the buyer or the seller. Negotiating a price after the fact takes away that balance and makes adversaries of the surviving owners and the decedent's estate.

---

lines as a starting point and consult with your corporate attorney to draft one. Even if you *do* have a comprehensive agreement, this is a good time to review its provisions. You may find the document needs updating due to a change in circumstances, the growth of the business or developments in your industry.

There are three basic types of buy-sell agreements:

CROSS-PURCHASE AGREEMENTS are ideal for partnerships and corporations with up to three owners. The remaining owners directly purchase the departing owner's interest in the business, rather than doing it through the company.

STOCK-REDEMPTION AGREEMENTS are simpler and easier to structure than cross-purchase agreements. This makes them best suited for corporations with four or more shareholders. The corporation redeems the shares of the departing owner through direct purchases; and the remaining owners see an increase in the *value* of their shares, not the *number* of their shares, as in a cross purchase.

HYBRIDS are combination arrangements that usually put the priority for redemption with the corporation, but give shareholders the option of directly redeeming a deceased owner's shares if the corporation is unwilling or unable to do so.

Valuation and Pricing Issues

Subject to the IRS guidelines described on page 91, the buy-sell agreement will also specify a method or a formula for arriving at the value of the shares to be transferred upon the triggering event. Chapter 2 addresses valuation issues in general; however, in the context of the buy-sell agreement, there are usually specific provisions that will determine how the ownership interests will be valued.

Generally, a buy-sell agreement either sets forth a formula price felt to be indicative of a company's appropriate value, or directs that one or more outside appraisals be obtained when a triggering event occurs. Common formulas for purchase prices include: book value, book value adjusted to the fair market value of certain assets and liabilities, a multiple of earnings, a multiple of weighted earnings over a period of time, or a combination of book value and a multiple of weighted earnings.

The appropriateness of any of these formulas is determined by the nature of the business. For example, book value of a pure service or technology business may be totally inappropriate—while the fixed assets of the business are relatively small or intangible, the assets may be generating substantial income. Where a formula purchase price is to be used, it is always advisable to consult with an appraisal firm or valuation expert to assist in the development of a formula that will truly reflect your company's continuing value and be consistent with trends in your industry.

In addition, the reason a co-founder leaves the business is important because it determines the procedure used to transfer ownership, how the interest is valued, and how the transfer is financed. You should consider including in the buy-sell agreement provisions to cover each type of triggering event. For example, at retirement a co-founder may be willing (or prefer) to receive payments for his or her shares over a number of years. At death, it may be more desirable to pay a lump sum. If the triggering event is a termination "for cause," you may want to penalize the shareholder for his breach of duties or obligations.

The IRS and the Buy-Sell Agreement

Although a key benefit of the buy-sell agreement is that it can often be used to establish the value of stock for gift and estate-tax purposes, tax-law changes in 1990 created certain new obstacles for closely held businesses. A buy-sell agreement entered into or "substantially modified" after October 8, 1990, cannot be used to fix the value of transferred stock unless the following requirements are met:

- **The buy-sell agreement** is entered into for bona fide business purposes;
- **The agreement is not a device** for transferring property to one's family for less than fair market value; and
- **The agreement's terms are comparable** to similar arrangements entered into at arm's length.

The fairness of the price as judged by the IRS is measured when the agreement is signed by the parties, not when the

CHAPTER SEVEN PARTING COMPANY

> **CASE STUDY** — **Fred Kelleher and Tanya Watson**

THE SITUATION—PART I
IN 1982, Fred Kelleher, 31, and Tanya Watson, 29, started LearnPro International, a computer-training company. For the first few years, sales were modest, but as more businesses turned to complex hardware and software solutions in the mid 1980s, business began to boom.

The Solution
In 1986, Fred, married to Sarah, and Tanya, unmarried, entered into a co-founders' agreement that provided that each would have the right to purchase the other's shares in the event of death. The purchase would be primarily funded by a key-person life insurance policy in the amount of $500,000 on each co-owner. If the policy would not be sufficient to cover the fair market value of the deceased co-owner's shares, the surviving co-owner would need to come up with the balance of the funds.

The Result
In 1989, Tanya married Tex Schaeffer. He disliked Fred and was jealous of the time and passion that Tanya devoted to LearnPro. In 1994, Tanya was diagnosed with ovarian cancer; she died six months later. Tex's resentment toward Fred and LearnPro was worse than ever; recognizing this, Fred exercised his option to purchase Tanya's shares from her estate. A business appraisal valued the company at $1.3 million, and Fred worked hard to raise the $150,000 needed above the proceeds from the key-person life insurance policy within the 60-day option that the buy-sell agreement provided to purchase Tanya's shares.

THE SITUATION—PART II
Two years later, after nearly 15 years of stress from growing the business and still upset by Tanya's death, Fred turned his attention to his own succession-planning issues. Two key employees, who had been with LearnPro since 1985, were threatening to leave unless some type of employee ownership or stock-option plan was put into place. Fred's son, Jason, was finishing his last year at MIT and had expressed an interest in joining LearnPro. Fred's daughter, Cindy, had no interest in joining the company, but did expect that she would somehow share in the wealth in the event of a sale or transfer of LearnPro.

The Solution
Fred worked out a succession plan in which he would offer 10% of the business to each key employee in the form of stock options over a five-year period. After Jason graduated, Fred would bring him into the business, show him how it operated and see how well he'd do managing it. If all went well, Fred would then give the remaining shares to his children, with Jason receiving 51% and Cindy the remaining 29% but with an assignment of her voting rights to Jason.

shares are ultimately transferred. If a buy-sell agreement uses a formula or otherwise sets a purchase price that is unreasonably low, bear in mind that it could be rejected by the IRS. This would have an adverse impact on the selling shareholder's estate because more taxes will need to be paid on proceeds which were never received!

The buy-sell agreement must also satisfy the following pre-1990 requirements:

- **the agreement must be valid** and enforceable;
- **the agreement must grant an option to purchase,** or require a transfer at a specific price on the shareholder's death and prohibit transfers at a higher price during the shareholder's lifetime; and
- **the agreement must provide for a fixed** and determinable price. Generally, to satisfy the third requirement, the price should approximate fair market value. One of the best ways to establish fair market value is to have the stock appraised by a professional appraiser using the accepted appraisal methodologies discussed in Chapter 2.

The Role of Key-Person Insurance in the Buy-Sell Agreement

As mentioned earlier in this chapter as well as in Chapter 2, insurance products can be a key piece of the puzzle in preparing a buy-sell agreement as well as in determining the procedures for cross-purchase or redemption of the departing shareholder's stake if a triggering event occurs. For example, in a cross-purchase agreement, each co-owner owns policies on each of the other co-owners, pays the premiums, and names himself or herself as beneficiary. The face value of the policies on each co-owner should be enough for the remaining co-owners together to buy the deceased co-owner's shares. With a redemption agreement, the company owns the policies, pays the premiums, and names itself as the beneficiary. The proceeds upon death are then used by the company to redeem the shares from the decedent's estate. As the value of the com-

> **BOX 7-2 | The Big "D" Path to Business Divorce**
>
> Distrust ▶ Dissension ▶ Disagreement ▶ Deadlock ▶ Destruction ▶ Divorce ▶ DISSOLUTION

pany increases, the amount of coverage should also be increased. Note that in the case study on page 92, the partners failed to increase the face value of the key-person policies, and Fred had to raise a substantial amount of money to buy out his partner. The premiums paid by the company may be deductible, although there are limitations to the amount of coverage when the premiums are deducted.

Managing Disputes and Problems Among Co-Founders

Perhaps one of the most challenging hurdles for a growing company to face is a dispute among its co-founders. Virtually every company, as it achieves various stages of growth, will confront disagreements and problems among its co-founders. The most common problems are disagreements over the company's future direction, a lack of communication, a breakdown of mutual trust and evolving personality differences. Some of these scenarios involve a third party or outside circumstance that none of the co-founders can control, but that clearly has a direct impact on the ability of each co-founder to continue growing the business. Although buy-sell agreements can be a helpful tool in resolving co-founder disputes, contracts are not enough; these agreements must be supplemented with sound management and business practices, a sensitivity to psychological and ego issues, and a clear strategic development plan.

In my experiences working with a wide variety of small and growing companies, I have encountered many of the most common types of partnerships and the problems that are specific to each relationship. Here are the top ten.

1. THE "HIGH SCHOOL BEST FRIEND/COLLEGE ROOMMATE" PARTNER. Many growing businesses are founded by former college roommates or high school friends. The mix of a personal friendship with a business conflict—and the partners' inability to separate personal and business issues—can make dispute resolution especially complex.

2. THE "OBSOLETE" PARTNER. Often as a business grows, one or more of the co-founders is unable to keep pace with the level of sophistication or business acumen that the company now requires. He or she is no longer making a significant contribution to the business and in essence has become "obsolete." It's even harder when the obsolete partner is a close friend or family member. In this case, you need to ask: Will the obsolete co-founder's ego allow for a position of diminished responsibility? Can our overhead continue to keep him or her on staff?

3. THE "EGO-CLASHING" PARTNER. Entrepreneurs, as leaders with strong values and integrity, also tend to have extra-large egos. These egos clash from time to time. Sometimes, the clash is short-lived and easy to overcome, and other times the continuing clashing of the egos creates a problem that cannot easily be resolved. The challenge is how to make everybody feel important without creating too many chefs in the kitchen.

4. THE "WE ALL HAVE DIFFERENT GOALS AND OBJECTIVES" PARTNER. Often, the co-founders are all slowly moving in different strategic directions, and each has different visions and plans for the company's future. This makes for strained communication. I've even seen a partner lose the "fire in the belly" once the company reached a particular stage of growth and when key goals and objectives were met. If this happens, it's best for that co-founder to step down, be reassigned or find new challenges to pursue. Just as the flame in an old marriage can be rekindled, so can the entrepreneurial spirit be resparked.

5. THE "SILENT MONEY" PARTNER. Few people I've met have gotten wealthy by being stupid or being silent, but entrepreneurs still want to believe there's such a thing as a "silent partner." My

CHAPTER SEVEN PARTING COMPANY

experience has been that silent partners are rarely silent, and most will go out of their way to interfere with the operations and management abilities of the operating partners.

6. THE "I WANT TO RETIRE EARLY" PARTNER. People tend to reach personal comfort levels or just plain "burn out" at different stages of a company's growth. One partner may want to pursue a life on the tennis court, another may want to take a trip around the world, while still others may simply feel that they have accumulated sufficient wealth and just want to take it easy. In addition, many growing companies are begun when all of the co-founders are either unmarried or in the early stages of their marriage. As the size of the company grows, so do the sizes of the co-founders' families. Co-founders with young children may feel the pressure to spend more time at home, but their absence will significantly reduce their ability to make a valuable contribution to the company's growth. Also, growing families may bring new income needs that the company may not be able to meet.

7. THE "HAND-CAUGHT-IN-THE-COOKIE-JAR" OR THE "CAUGHT-IN-THE-BACK-ROOM-WITH-A-SUBORDINATE" PARTNER. When a co-founder is caught doing something illegal or unacceptable on the company's premises, it can be very difficult to handle diplomatically. The issues—embezzlement, sexual harassment, employment discrimination, and other unacceptable or illegal acts—are sensitive, and the liability to the company is significant.

8. THE "I HAVE AN IMMEDIATE NEED TO CASH OUT" PARTNER. A demand for cash could result from ordinary circumstances, such as the need to buy a home, or it could be related to less-than-acceptable circumstances, like a gambling debt. This situation puts a strain on the relations among the co-founders. More important, it puts a strain on the company's ability to provide the cash to repurchase that co-founder's shares of the company. The company may not have readily available funds, and because nothing has happened by way of disability or death, insurance policies can rarely be drawn upon to fund this repurchase.

> **BOX 7-3** **Potential Solutions to Feuding Co-Founders**
>
> - **Sell** to each other
> - **Sell** to a third party
> - **Submit** to a mediator
> - **Contribute stock** into a voting trust
> - **Sell** to employees
> - **Sell stock** through a public offering
> - **Restructure** the ownership and operations
> - **Adopt** an advisory board
> - **Contribute stock** to a mediator
> - **Turn over control** to the next generation
> - **Initiate** formal litigation or seek a declaratory judgment

9. THE "WE ARE GETTING ACQUIRED AND THE BUYER WANTS ONLY ME" PARTNER OR "THE INVESTOR WANTS YOU OUT" PARTNER. In a rapidly growing business, the exit strategy is often either a sale of the company to a third party or the registration of the company's stock in a public offering. I've often seen that the buyer of the company wants only one or two of the co-founders due to lack of confidence or personality differences. Many times the investment bankers who are handling an initial public offering ("IPO") would prefer that one or more of the co-founders step down because of lack of experience or the disclosure of an incident in his or her past that might have an adverse effect on the public offering. I have even seen this scenario in venture-capital settings where two or three co-founders were asked to either leave or modify their positions as a condition to the venture capitalist's closing the transaction. Naturally, this situation creates divided loyalties among the co-founders. The post-closing status of each of the co-founders may dampen enthusiasm and add confusion to an already complex transaction, when it is necessary to either raise the needed capital or to consummate the sale of the company.

10. THE "I *THINK* I AM A PARTNER" NON-PARTNER. Often key employees get the idea that they are co-owners. This can occur in companies where there is open-book management, or where employees are issued phantom stock plans, or stock-appreciation rights, and become difficult on issues of governance. This is an issue to consider when planning a stock option or bonus plan. The "dark side" of empowerment is that the intent to "make

CHAPTER SEVEN PARTING COMPANY

> **BOX 7-4 Managing Co-Founder Disputes**
>
> **Be creative in seeking and structuring solutions.** It's shortsighted for co-founders to merely repurchase the shares when other types of strategic or creative solutions could be a better choice.
>
> **Be civil.** What goes around comes around. It *is* a small world.
>
> **Be reasonable and realistic regarding price and structure.** Whether you are a departing or remaining co-founder, it's important to be creative in the structure of the departure, such as how and when the payments will be made and whether they'll be made in cash or with other assets or key licensing agreements. There are several instances of post-closing lawsuits in which a former co-founder feels that information may have been wrongfully withheld from him concerning his buyout or the valuation used by his co-founders. These lawsuits are very difficult and complex and can go on for some time at a significant cost to both the co-founders (past and present) and the company. Consider an earn-out clause or some other participation right or post-sale adjustment to help avoid a future dispute.
>
> **Be sensitive to those around you when there are problems among the co-founders.** It is important to recognize that the media, key vendors, key customers, creditors, and especially employees must be treated with sensitivity when co-founders are having a problem.

them feel like an owner" may go too far. You may find yourself needing to justify that new home, car or raise to non-shareholders. Also, be certain to remember the legal impact of granting stock to a key employee when there are only two co-founders—guess who just got granted the swing vote? That's probably not what you intended!

Why Disputes Arise and How to Avoid Them

WE OFTEN DON'T GET TO KNOW OUR CO-FOUNDERS' PERSONALITY QUIRKS until well into the development of the business. Many of us rush into business relationships the same way we enter into

Dealing With Non-Family Co-Owners

Don't lose sight of the impact of these disputes on company morale and leadership. The rumor mill can be cruel and lead to the eventual demise of the company if certain kinds of problems are not treated properly.

Never litigate over matters of principle. Be sure that the potential rewards and remedies outweigh the many expenses and opportunity costs.

Be patient and disciplined in your breakup negotiations with your soon-to-be-former co-founder. Be sure to deal with the difficult issues, such as notice to creditors, the extent of assumption of liabilities by continuing co-founders, the valuation of the withdrawing co-founder's equity in the company, indemnification, and protection from post-breakup obligations and liabilities. Do not let emotion or impatience interfere with your otherwise strong negotiating skills.

Govern yourself accordingly. Remember that these problems and their solutions are as much psychological as they are legal and as much strategic as they are contractual.

Do not vacillate. If you see problems in your business marriage, don't avoid the need for confrontations on an unpleasant set of negotiations. The longer you wait the worse it typically seems. Few problems go away or cure themselves by being ignored.

---

personal relationships—with excitement, gumption and willingness to overlook character flaws.

NO ONE LIKES TO LOOK INTO A CRYSTAL BALL AND SEE BAD THINGS. It's very difficult to predict what problems may come up in the future. Many business relationships start out as friendships, and, as in a marriage, the thought of negotiating a business "prenuptial" agreement is not pleasant.

ENTREPRENEURS JUST STARTING OUT DON'T ALWAYS HAVE THE CAPITAL to hire lawyers who'll draft the shareholders' or partnership agreements necessary to protect against certain kinds of problems and provide pre-determined solutions to these problems if and when they occur. By the time the company *can* afford to have attorneys draft these agreements, it's often too late—the company is too far along in its development. These time bombs must be defused before the company blows up.

YOU CAN'T PREDICT EACH CO-FOUNDER'S COMMUNICATION- AND DECISION-MAKING STYLES, so there are often significant disparities between how decisions are *supposed* to be made and how they are *actually* made. Also, in rapidly growing, closely held companies, communication and plans aren't always properly documented or researched, so key strategic decisions are made on an ad hoc basis. Shareholders' and partnership agreements can spell out which kinds of decisions cannot be made on an ad hoc basis and can provide the rules under which those decisions will be made.

OWNERS OF SMALL COMPANIES, who wear many hats during the growth of a business, often find it hard to separate their roles as directors, officers, shareholders and key employees. As an example, it is important to know whether a meeting or decision has risen to the level of a board of directors (which requires detailed minutes) or whether it is more of a day-to-day strategic meeting, which would not require any formal notice or documentation.

SMALLER COMPANIES OFTEN FAIL TO PROVIDE for procedures in case of a deadlock (when there is an even number of founders). The founder must identify at an early stage how to break a deadlock.

THE ADAGE "FAILING TO PLAN IS PLANNING TO FAIL" often proves true in the context of disputes among co-founders. The lack of a clear and concise strategic-development plan (not the boilerplate type that gets used to raise capital) often leads to confusion and problems among co-founders.

ENTREPRENEURS TEND TO APPROACH PROBLEM-SOLVING on a reactive instead of proactive basis. By not taking the time to deal with these issues before they mature into problems, entrepreneurs fail to heed another adage, that "an ounce of prevention is worth a pound of cure."

ENTREPRENEURS ARE OFTEN BAD DELEGATORS, both among themselves and to key employees. This can lead to problems among co-founders and stifle the company's ability to truly departmentalize.

The best way to deal with problems like these is to prevent them from happening at all. Your willingness to communicate openly, prepare for the worst and detect problems before they mature is at the heart of the solution. Here are some of the key measures:

SCHEDULE PERIODIC VALUATIONS OF THE COMPANY. While expensive, valuations can provide you with a clear-cut and objective assessment of the company's worth. The valuations should be done annually depending on the company's growth patterns and the industry trends. Occasional financial and legal audits will help lend insight into the company's value and identify legal and financial problems before they arise.

PREPARE A SHAREHOLDERS' OR PARTNERSHIP AGREEMENT early in the development stages of the business in order to address decision-making procedures, restrictions on the transfer of stock, buyout provisions, and a shareholder's lack of participation in the business. Take comfort in knowing that these agreements are in place well in advance of a dispute. Here are some of the decisions that might require unanimous approval under a shareholders' agreement:

- **Changes to the company's** articles of incorporation or bylaws;
- **Increases or decreases in the company's** number of authorized shares of any class of stock;
- **The pledge of the company's assets** (real estate, computers, inventory or equipment), or the grant of a security interest or lien that affects these assets;
- **Creating, amending or funding** a pension, profit-sharing or retirement plan;

- **Signing any contract or agreement** deemed to be major; and
- **Making major changes** in the nature of the company.

Update these documents periodically to reflect changes in law or circumstances. Dust off your old shareholders' or partnership agreement and ask: Do these still work for us?

BUY KEY-PERSON INSURANCE POLICIES that provide a source of capital for the buyout of a co-founder's shares in the event of departure, death or disability.

CREATE EMPLOYMENT AGREEMENTS for each of the co-founders that will be separate and apart from the shareholders' or partnership agreements. The employment agreement will provide for conditions of termination, which are especially critical in sensitive problems such as alcohol and drug abuse, sexual harassment, or employment discrimination. These agreements should also clearly set forth each co-founder's duties and decision-making authority.

If you and your co-founders are in agreement on these topics, then you can probably avoid a future third-party investor from forcing the issue. Taking a dose of preventive medicine can go a long way in saving you legal fees, anxiety and feeling as if you've wasted a productive effort. It also helps to keep the relationship alive and avoid the types of break-up discussed below.

Managing the Inevitable Breakup

If you and your co-founders recognize that your working relationship is truly over and you've considered all reasonable alternatives, the following are possible options for administering a smooth breakup.

SCENARIO #1: Once you've decided that there are no solutions to the discord, the clearest and most obvious choice is for a repurchase of the co-founder's equity in the company either by the remaining shareholders or by the company (either on a lump-sum basis or over a period of time). The payment may be cash, assets, contractual rights, intangibles, or a combination thereof.

SCENARIO #2: Several companies have resolved disputes among co-founders by splitting up the business by function, essentially spinning off different operating divisions of the company based on each founder's interest. If technology is involved, there can be cross-licensing arrangements among the various companies (or joint-venture agreements between the now-separate companies). This allows each co-founder to pursue his or her own interests and strategic objectives without losing some of the efficiencies and economies of scale created when the company was all under one roof. Be as creative as possible. There may be ways to divide and subdivide the company—by function, product line, market, territory or target customers—that may not occur to you at first. Ask yourself, "How many different businesses are we *really* in?"

SCENARIO #3: Selling certain key assets (or even the company) to a third party may provide a means for a co-founder to transfer his or her interest to a separate company, providing a formal separation and an opportunity to pursue differing goals and objectives.

SCENARIO #4: Setting up a field office may create some operational and overhead inefficiencies, but in the event that one or more of the co-founders feels the need to relocate, the field office might be an effective way for the business relationship to continue.

SCENARIO #5: If there is a suspicion of fraud or embezzlement, consider a court-ordered accounting of the books and records of the company.

SCENARIO #6: Seeking a dissolution of the company through a judicial decree may also be an alternative. The court would have to be convinced that the company should be dissolved either because of a major event affecting the company, such as the mental illness of a co-founder, because the company may involuntarily go out of business, or because the company is operating at a financial loss.

SCENARIO #7: Consider arbitration, mediation, a mini-trial or other alternative dispute-resolution techniques that may be less expensive, less time-consuming and often less emotional than full-blown litigation. You may also try a less adversarial approach by appointing an advisory board to resolve disputes.

SCENARIO #8: If the co-founders cannot reach an amicable solution (as described in scenarios 1 through 7), then formal litigation is inevitable. The co-founders should be prepared for a lengthy and expensive battle, and cost-benefit analyses should be conducted at various stages of the litigation. It's possible to ask the court to appoint a receiver or independent trustee to manage the company while the disputes are still pending.

CHAPTER EIGHT | **PARTING COMPANY**

Selling to Your Employees

THERE ARE A NUMBER OF STRATEGIES FOR TRANSFERRING ownership to your employees. Many closely held companies sell all or a portion of their business either to key personnel or to almost all of their qualifying personnel through an employee stock ownership plan (ESOP). Others sell to selected executives through one or more stock-option programs.

If structured properly, the ESOP offers many tax advantages, and it may be a viable exit strategy where there's no family member available who has the acumen or the desire to take over the company.

This chapter will provide an overview of the various employee-driven transition strategies that are highlighted in the box on the following page. These exit strategies can be a very useful tool for increasing employee morale, productivity and loyalty, while at the same time providing you with a tax-advantaged succession plan. One thing to bear in mind: many of these strategies are implemented in stages and often do not provide for an immediate transition of management and control.

CHAPTER EIGHT PARTING COMPANY

BOX 8-1 Employee-Driven Exit Strategies

PLAN TYPE	FULL VERSUS PARTIAL TRANSFER	LUMP-SUM VERSUS GRADUAL TRANSFER OF OWNERSHIP	ALL ELIGIBLE EMPLOYEES VERSUS KEY EXECUTIVES
Employee Stock Ownership Plans (ESOPs)	Can be full or partial but must be at least 30% of total outstanding stock	Typically done on a lump-sum basis, but the ESOP could acquire greater than the 30% minimum over time	Typically all eligible employees participate in the ownership plan, not just a few executives
Non-Qualified Stock Options (NQSOs)	Typically used to grant ownership of the company to key employees (or directors, consultants, etc.) for up to a certain percentage of the company	Typically subject to a vesting schedule and other conditions	Can be much more selective and offered only to key employees or key consultants and advisers
Incentive Stock Options (ISOs)	Typically used to grant ownership to all eligible employees (and only employees) for up to a certain percentage of the company	Typically subject to a vesting schedule and other conditions	Must meet a wide variety of statutory requirements under Internal Revenue Code 401 in order for employee to enjoy tax benefits upon the exercise of the options
Restricted Stock Program	Typically used to transfer only a small portion (e.g., up to 10%) of the company to key employees	Subject to vesting schedule and risk of forfeiture if the key employee leaves or fails to meet performance targets	Typically only key executives are granted shares of the company subject to forfeiture if certain tenure requirements or management and financial goals are not attained

106

Selling to Your Staff: ESOPs As an Exit Strategy

Employee stock ownership plans (ESOPs) have been established by many companies to provide employees with shares of the company's stock through tax-deductible contributions made by the employer. ESOPs are also used to acquire a portion (or all) of a company's outstanding stock from its shareholders, resulting in employee-controlled ownership of the business through a tax-advantaged trust. Many small and midsize companies that can't find a suitable buyer (or that want to "sell" the company to their employees) can create an ESOP to serve as the eventual buyer of the company—or a large portion of it.

The Growing Role of ESOPs

The number of ESOPs increased steadily during the 1980s, particularly after tax-law changes made them more attractive financially to business owners. The increased activity stems from the economy's strength, the rapidly increasing number of closely held companies whose current owners are at or near retirement age, and the realization by closely held companies that an ESOP can provide a competitive edge by encouraging productivity.

Structuring the Deal

The company stock that ESOPs purchase and then allocate to individual employees' accounts can be acquired in various ways. Under some plans, the employer (that's you) would contribute securities or cash every year to the ESOP so it can buy company stock. Most ESOPs, however, obtain bank loans to buy the stock from you; you may use the proceeds of the stock purchase to expand the business or, if your company is small, to fund your personal retirement nest egg. ESOPs also provide you some important tax advantages—in addition to the ability to deduct the full payments (principal and interest) on loans obtained through the ESOP.

CHAPTER EIGHT PARTING COMPANY

If, after buying stock from you, the ESOP owns at least 30% of the company, you may defer capital-gains taxes if the proceeds are invested in other securities, such as stocks and bonds. No capital-gains tax is paid until those investments are sold.

Apart from tax advantages, the most impressive aspect of an ESOP is the potential for productivity gains. In a 1995 survey of 1,150 companies with ESOPs by the ESOP Association, 68% of the respondents said their financial figures improved after they instituted an ESOP, and 60% said productivity improved.

Risks of Creating an ESOP

ESOPs can be prohibitively expensive for small companies, for those with high employee turnover (such as fast-food outlets and gas stations), and for companies that rely heavily on contract workers (such as real estate agencies) who are barred from participating under applicable IRS guidelines. ESOPs may also pose too many problems for businesses with chronically uncertain cash flow. An ESOP is contractually obliged to repurchase stock from employees who leave the company or retire, and over time that obligation can cause big headaches if the money isn't there. In addition, an ESOP can be a catastrophe if the company creates one without a commitment to employee participation in the company's management. Employee owners come to expect that. If they are shunted aside, they become resentful and management finds that it has created a monster.

An ESOP poses risks for the employee, too: Most of his or her retirement nest egg is invested in the stock of one company. If the company goes bankrupt, the employee's holdings may be worthless. However, of the roughly 10,000 ESOPs created over the past 20 years, only 1% have had to file for bankruptcy.

The two general categories of ESOPs are:

LEVERAGED ESOP. A plan that borrows directly from the company or from a third-party lender based on the company's guaranty, with your securities as collateral, to acquire your securities. The ESOP will repay the loan with employer contributions, as well as any dividends that may be paid on the employer's securities.

NON-LEVERAGED ESOP. A stock bonus plan (or contribution stock bonus plan with a money-purchase pension plan) which purchases your securities with funds from you that would have been paid as some other form of compensation.

Legal Considerations in Structuring an ESOP

ESOPs must meet certain minimum requirements set by the IRS, as do all types of tax-qualified deferred compensation plans. Failure to do so will render your contributions not tax-deductible, thereby defeating many of the tax advantages of the ESOP as well as your strategic objectives. These requirements include:

ESTABLISHING A TRUST IN ORDER TO MAKE CONTRIBUTIONS AND ADMINISTER THE PLAN. The trust must be for the exclusive benefit of the participants and their beneficiaries.

STRUCTURING THE ESOP SO THAT IT IS NOT "TOP-HEAVY" in the allocation of assets and income distribution. The plan must not discriminate in favor of officers, major shareholders or highly compensated employees. For example, at least 70% of all non-highly-compensated employees must be covered by the plan (this is known as the coverage test).

INVESTING PRIMARILY IN THE SECURITIES OF THE SPONSORING EMPLOYER. Although there are no strict guidelines, it is assumed that the ESOP portfolio will include at least 50% to 60% of your securities at any given time. Remaining assets of the ESOP trust should be invested in prudent securities that offer liquidity and diversification of the portfolio.

VESTING IN COMPLIANCE WITH ONE OF THE MINIMUM VESTING SCHEDULES. The plan must adopt either: five-year "cliff" vesting (employee must be fully vested after five years of service but need not be vested at all before that time) or the seven-year "scheduled" vesting (20% fully vested after three years, increasing in 20% increments per year until 100% vesting is reached after seven years).

CHAPTER EIGHT PARTING COMPANY

ESTABLISHING VOTING REQUIREMENTS THAT CONFORM TO IRS RULES. Voting rights may be vested in the trust's fiduciary, except under certain circumstances where rights must be "passed through" to the plan's participants. Generally, passing through becomes an issue when the vote will involve mergers, consolidations, reorganizations, recapitalizations, liquidations, major asset sales and the like. You may, at your discretion, pass through voting rights "in toto" at the time you create the plan. Failure to fully pass through these rights may raise personnel and productivity problems; if the employees don't feel like true owners, they might become cynical about the ESOP, which defeats your main purpose in adopting such a plan.

COMPLYING WITH IRS RULES REGARDING THE DISTRIBUTION OF ESOP BENEFITS OR ASSETS. The plan must provide for a prompt (within one year) distribution of benefits to a beneficiary following the retirement, disability or death of an employee. The nature and specific timing of the distribution will depend in part on the cause for separation from service with the company as well as whether the company is closely held or publicly traded.

CONTRIBUTING BASED ON A SPECIFIC PERCENTAGE OF PAYROLL. This could take the form of a money-purchase pension plan (in which a contribution is required based on a percentage of pay) or use some other formula, such as a percentage of profits (as do some profit-sharing plans). This allows you maximum flexibility because contributions are at your discretion. Each year you simply make a determination of the appropriate contribution amount. However, the plan provides for a minimum contribution that is sufficient to pay any principal and interest due on a loan used to acquire your securities. Your contribution may be made in cash, securities or other property. In the event that you contribute your own securities, you may obtain a "cashless deduction"; you're entitled to deduct the fair market value of the securities, and the contribution involves no cash outlay on your part.

PROVIDING "ADEQUATE CONSIDERATION" IN CONNECTION WITH THE PURCHASE OF EMPLOYER STOCK IN AN ESOP. This requires that some

Selling to Your Employees

| CASE STUDY | **Selling to an ESOP** |

The Situation

BILL FREED, the founder of GrowCo Enterprises, wanted to create a succession plan that would benefit him, his family, his 250 employees and his long-standing customers. He also needed liquidity because most of his net worth was tied up in the company, the product technology was changing rapidly, and he didn't want the company to lose its momentum. He also wanted to minimize income and estate taxes.

Bill's two sons were in management at the company. While he liked having his children in the business, he'd never promised them they would take over. He had always left that question open. When he was ready to retire as CEO, Bill considered phasing them in gradually as his successors. However, he felt they would need time to learn the job, and he didn't think the business could afford that luxury. He could have sold the company, but that would have jeopardized jobs—and he wanted to remain active and involved with the company.

Bill's last option was an ESOP. The more he considered it, the more sense an ESOP made. He could have said, "I just want to take care of my family." But he felt GrowCo wouldn't be where it was today without the employees, so they represented a much larger family, whose welfare he also had to consider.

The Solution

Bill decided to establish a leveraged ESOP. He made arrangements with a local commercial lender for the ESOP to borrow the funds necessary to purchase 51% of the company. Herb Klein, Bill's long-time COO and a very skilled leader with broad experience, became CEO. Bill and his family retained 49% of the company; Bill will gradually give more of his voting shares to his sons, who expect to remain with the company, and other, non-voting shares to non-participating family members.

The Result

GrowCo is current on its ESOP loan payments; its revenues and profits are up; the ESOP defers taxes; and Bill has invested the proceeds from the initial sale in stock and bond mutual funds, setting up a solid retirement nest egg.

---

method for valuation of the shares must be available. For publicly traded companies, this is generally not a problem because the prevailing market price is a sufficient indication of value. For privately held companies, however, value must be determined by the fiduciaries of the plan acting in good faith. This will generally require an independent appraisal, initially upon the establishment of the ESOP and at least annually thereafter.

Legal Documents You Need to Establish an ESOP

There are many legal documents that must be prepared to organize and implement an ESOP. Your counsel will prepare these documents only after getting input and analysis from all key members of the company's ESOP team (which includes financial and human-resources staff, accountants, investment bankers, commercial lenders, the designated trustee and the designated appraisal firm). This preliminary analysis should include:

- **impact on ownership,** control and earnings of the company;
- **type of securities to be issued** (common versus preferred);
- **tax deductibility of contributions,** and related tax issues;
- **the extent to which the sale of shares to an ESOP** will dilute the ownership of the remaining owners;
- **registration of the securities,** where required, under federal and state securities laws;
- **employee-motivation** and productivity-improvement analyses;
- **the company's current and future capital** requirements and growth plans;
- **interplay of the ESOP** with other current or planned employee benefit plans; and
- **timetable for planning,** organization and implementation of the ESOP.

Once you've considered these factors and made strategic decisions, you may instruct your counsel to prepare the necessary documentation. In a leveraged ESOP, the documents may include: the ESOP plan; the ESOP trust agreement (which may be combined with the plan); the ESOP loan documentation (the loan agreement and note guaranty, for example; [you might get more than one set—one for you from the lender, and one for you to give to the ESOP when you make a "mirror-image" loan to the plan]); the ESOP stock-purchase agreement (for stock that is to be purchased

> **BOX 8-2** | **The ESOP Plan and ESOP Stock Purchase Agreement**
>
> The primary issues to be addressed by each of these documents are:
>
> **THE ESOP PLAN (WHERE TRUST AGREEMENT IS SELF-CONTAINED)**
> 1. **Designation of a name** for the ESOP
> 2. **Definition of key terms** (e.g., "participant," "year of service," "trustee")
> 3. **Eligibility to participate** (standards and requirements)
> 4. **Contributions by employer** (designated amount or formula; discretionary)
> 5. **Investment of trust assets** (primarily in employer securities; plans for diversification of the portfolio; purchase price for the stock; rules for borrowing by the ESOP, and so on)
> 6. **Procedures for release of the shares from encumbrances** (formula as ESOP obligations are paid down)
> 7. **Voting rights** (rights vested in trustee; special matters that trigger employee voting rights)
> 8. **Duties of the trustee(s)** (accounting, administrative, appraisal, asset management, record keeping, voting obligations, preparation of annual reports, allocation and distribution of dividends)
> 9. **Removal** of trustee(s)
> 10. **Effect of retirement,** disability, death and severance of employment
> 11. **Terms of the put option** (for closely held companies)
> 12. **Rights of first refusal** upon transfer
> 13. **Vesting** schedules
>
> **ESOP STOCK-PURCHASE AGREEMENT**
> 1. **Background information** in the form of Recitals (the "Whereas..." clauses)
> 2. **Purchase** terms for the securities
> 3. **Conditions** to closing
> 4. **Representations** and warranties of the seller
> 5. **Representations** and warranties of the buyer
> 6. **Obligations** prior to and following the closing
> 7. **Termination**
> 8. **Opinion** of counsel
> 9. **Exhibits,** attachments and schedules

from you or your principal shareholders); the corporate charter amendments and related board resolutions; and the legal-opinion and valuation reports.

Raising Equity Capital for an ESOP Transaction

While many business owners borrow money from a commercial lender to establish an ESOP, you might want to look into another option. Instead of borrowing the money yourself, you could work with a private-equity or venture-capital firm that specializes in providing the capital needed both to structure the ESOP and to finance the partial sale of the company to the ESOP. The investment firm then becomes part owner of the company along with the employees through the ESOP, and the proceeds of that sale are paid to you as a component of the full or partial exit strategy.

As with all sources of equity capital, the fund managers will require that you and your employee group prepare and present a business plan.

For example, American Capital Strategies Inc. based in Bethesda, Md., provides equity financing for ESOPs and management buyout (MBO) transactions. ACS has provided capital for or participated in more than 30 ESOP transactions. In a typical transaction, the employee group will have majority ownership of the company, but ACS will protect its investment and minority stake with control of the board of directors, and a series of covenants affecting operations and performance. It may also require wage-and-benefit concessions, particularly if unions are involved in the negotiations and restructuring.

Alternatives to an ESOP

There are other ways to transfer or award ownership rights to key (but not all) employees. These methods are more commonly used as incentives to retain top employees or as bonuses for outstanding work. When employed as an exit strategy, they typically result in a more gradual transfer of the business.

Selling to Your Employees

| CASE STUDY | **Gradual Sale to Key Employees** |

The Situation
SMITH AND JONES have a partnership that employs 15 workers full-time and about ten more seasonally. They expect to earn revenues of about $5 million this year. The two owners have four children between them, but none wants to take over the business. They have key-person insurance to protect the business in case one of them suddenly dies, but they also want to set up a succession plan to anticipate their retirement.

The Solution
Smith and Jones have two highly valued employees, and would like those employees to eventually run the business. After conferring with their lawyer, they set up a buy-sell agreement with the pair under which the two employees will begin to buy the company over two consecutive five-year periods. Each employee will purchase 12% of the company's stock during the first five years and another 12% during the second, at a fixed price of two times book value (with book value recalculated annually). Payments will be made on an installment plan charging interest at the prime rate plus 1.5 percentage points. Proceeds from the sale of stock will be used to purchase annuities.

After the ten years, all four principals will decide how to proceed regarding Smith and Jones's remaining shares. Jones, now 55, may retire then, but Smith, 42, isn't certain what he'll do. Options include having the two employees purchase the remaining 52% of the company or allowing a small number of other key employees to purchase some of that stock.

The Result
Either way, Smith and Jones are glad that the two employees are now positioned to take over the business when necessary. The company now has key-person insurance policies held on each of the four shareholding partners; the insurance is sufficient to ensure that if any of the partners dies before the buy-sell agreement is completed, the other partners will be able to meet their obligations under the agreement.

These stock-ownership plans include: *stock bonus award plans,* which pay key employees bonuses in company stock—and often include cash to cover the recipient's tax liability because the stock is considered compensation; and *stock options,* both "qualified" and "non-qualified," under which executives are granted options to purchase shares in the future at a per-share price as of the day of the issuance of the option. These plans can be complicated, have stringent requirements and should be discussed with and implemented by your counsel, accountant and financial advisors. (See a sample stock option plan on page 224 in the Appendix.) If you give shares in lieu of cash bonuses as a means of transferring ownership, there won't be cash proceeds to feather your retirement nest.

Stock Award and Option Plans

STOCK BONUS AWARD PLANS

Generally, executive-bonus plans pay awards in the form of cash. A company may, however, pay the award in the form of company stock. In some circumstances, an award of company stock can have a greater motivational impact and build long-term loyalty toward the company. If the award is paid in the form of company stock, cash is sometimes included along with the stock award to cover the income-tax liability that will accrue to the executive from the receipt of stock. The value of the stock award will be subject to income tax withholding and employment taxes. Because the stock award is a form of compensation, the company will be entitled to a tax deduction equal to the value of the stock award.

STOCK OPTIONS

Incentive Stock Options. An incentive stock option (ISO), is a right granted by an employer to an executive, allowing him or her to purchase shares of the company's capital stock. ISOs qualify for special tax treatment. Basically, an ISO is a right to purchase a set number of shares during a specific period at a fixed price. The fixed price is the market price of the stock (or the value of the stock, if the stock is not regularly traded) at the date the ISO is granted. The executive can delay the purchase of the stock (that is, she can delay the "exercise" of the ISO) for a period of up to ten years, during which time the stock will presumably increase in value. She can then purchase the stock at what is, at the time of purchase, a bargain price. She won't recognize any taxable income when the ISO is granted nor when she exercises the ISO, as long she meets the following holding-period requirements: She must hold the stock that she receives upon exercising the

ISO for a period of two years after the grant date *and* one year after the exercise date. When she finally sells the stock, the income from the sale is subject to capital-gains tax. The company receives no deduction in an ISO program, except in the case of a disqualifying disposition, as explained below.

If an executive sells the stock *within* two years of the ISO's grant date or *within* one year of the exercise date, it is called a "disqualifying disposition." She will have to recognize ordinary income as a result of the sale of the shares. The amount will equal the difference between the strike price (the amount paid for the shares) and the amount received on the sale of those shares. The difference between the strike price and the fair market value at exercise is ordinary income, and the increase in value from exercise to disposition is a capital gain. When a disqualifying disposition occurs, the company will be entitled to a deduction equal to the amount the executive is required to recognize as ordinary income.

Non-qualified stock options. Non-qualified stock options (NQSOs) are stock options that don't ordinarily result in taxable income at the time of grant unless the options are immediately transferable, immediately exercisable in full, subject to no restrictions that would offset the fair market value of the option, and have a readily ascertainable fair market value.

If NQSOs don't satisfy all of these conditions (which is the usual case), federal income tax is not applicable at the time of grant. Upon the *exercise* of an NQSO, however, the executive will recognize ordinary taxable income, equal to the difference between the strike price (amount paid for the shares) and the fair market value at the date of exercise. The amount of taxable income is subject to income-tax withholding and employment taxes.

A subsequent sale of the shares will result in capital gains to the executive; his basis for purposes of reporting gain or loss will be the fair market value of the shares on the exercise date.

From your perspective, there are certain advantages to NQSOs. The company incurs no cash expense (other than administrative costs) in granting NQSOs, but receives a tax deduction equal to the amount the executive is required to recognize as ordinary income; the company receives this deduction at the same time the executive recognizes the taxable income.

Some Final Thoughts

Although these employee-driven exit strategies offer a strategic and tax-advantaged way of transferring ownership to one or more employees, they must be implemented with careful planning and a genuine understanding of the needs and wants of your employees. In addition to seeking sound legal and accounting advice, take the time to survey current employees and consider the following:

CURRENT EMPLOYEES MAY NOT BE MENTALLY AND FINANCIALLY prepared to act like owners. Are they too young or inexperienced? Is there high employee turnover? Will they be motivated by ownership of the company, or would they actually prefer cash-driven rewards?

THE TRANSITION MUST BE GRADUAL. Current employees may not have the management or leadership skills to assume control overnight. A hasty turnover can have a significant negative impact on the value of your residual stock in the company.

YOU MUST PLACE A PREMIUM on *how* and *when* the employee-ownership plans will be communicated to the affected employees. The details of the plan should be communicated in a clear and easily understood fashion, without legalese, and *not* via the rumor mill. Confusion over the details of the plan's benefits will result in a lack of enthusiasm and a failure to meet the key objectives of the transition plan.

BEAR IN MIND THAT STOCK-OPTION and ownership plans create new owners of the business. This is a new experience for family and closely held businesses that may not be used to having non-family owners. If you're not prepared to deal with the new legal rights that these employees will have in addition to those that they already have as employees under federal and state laws—including voting rights, rights to receive reports, rights to inspect books and records—then consider alternatives to employee ownership. If you're not ready for them to look over your shoulder, then you're *not* ready for employee ownership.

LINK REWARDS TO TENURE. Give careful thought to vesting schedules so that the plan strongly encourages employees to remain on the job as a condition of enjoying ownership benefits.

BE SURE YOU HAVE A WAY TO GET IT BACK. The plan should include a shareholders' agreement that provides for buy-back rights and allows you to get the stock back at a predetermined value or formula after the employee leaves. You certainly don't want to wind up with a bunch of disgruntled ex-employees as stockholders.

Remember to carefully assess the impact that employee-driven exit strategies will have on all affected parties—including family members, vendors, customers, licensees or franchisees, competitors and, of course, the employees themselves. Talk to the employees about their concerns—which may include a clarification of their roles in the company, long-term job security, the financial health of the business, and how the transition plan will affect their own estate and retirement planning. Your failure to listen carefully to these concerns could result in massive confusion or even an attempt by key employees to sabotage or obstruct the implementation of the transition plan. You should also clarify whether employee ownership is part of the company's long-term strategy or whether it's an interim step until the next generation of the family has been sufficiently groomed to assume control of the business, which naturally will influence the type of plan selected and its terms.

CHAPTER NINE | PARTING COMPANY

Selling to a Third Party

THERE WILL BE TIMES WHEN THE OWNERS OF SMALL and growing businesses determine that the most effective transition plan would be to sell the company. That might occur when family members are unable, unwilling or incapable of succeeding the current ownership. Or the owners might keep the business in the family but need to sell it as a means of funding their retirement. Or if selling or transferring ownership to employees is not a viable option (as discussed in Chapter 8), then owners may want to consider selling the business to a third party. The decision to sell a closely held or family business can be very difficult and emotional. It should not be made without a fair degree of analysis and planning.

The factors leading to the decision to sell the business to a third party will vary from case to case, but often involve challenging issues such as a decline in the health of the founder or co-owners, an inability to resolve disputes among the co-owners or within the family, or competitive market pressures that are slicing into the profitability of the business and causing a devaluation of the family's key asset. The traditional thinking in family-business circles has been that selling out is a type of failure—an admission by the current generation of owners that

CHAPTER NINE PARTING COMPANY

they couldn't make things work or had failed to adequately plan for the future. The more modern view is that in some situations the sale of the business can be in the best long-term interests of the family's current and future generations, provided that the impact on and expectations of the next generation are carefully considered, and that the proceeds from the sale are properly invested and protected through estate-planning and wealth-preservation strategies. It may also be the only way that the legacy of the business—in some form or another—can be preserved as a surviving and competitive organization, even if the original owners are no longer responsible for management and control. It is also critical to consider dividing the business into distinct parts, with an emphasis on the sale of one division. This can be done to more fully devote the family's or founder's time, energy and resources to the remaining divisions, or where less than 100% of the assets or stock of the business will be sold to a third party, essentially bringing on board a financial or operating partner or venture investor.

The emotional side of selling the family business should not be taken lightly. The founder may have spent decades serving as the patriarch or matriarch and provider to the family, and can't imagine any other role. This "identity crisis" may lead the founder to be skeptical or distrustful of the possibility or even the viability of turning the business over to some third party who he or she is convinced will only ruin the business. The family may be very used to enjoying certain perquisites and benefits that will need to be sacrificed or substituted if the business is sold. These psychological and emotional factors often serve as barriers to the type of advance planning that must be done to sell a business properly and to obtain the best valuation. And even if the founder is focused on the process, hires the proper advisers, prepares audited financials and begins the kind of corporate and legal housekeeping that's necessary before meeting with a prospective buyer, many family or closely held business owners are overcome with "seller's remorse" as the actual date of sale approaches. This chapter will focus on helping you get ready for the process once the decision has been made and discussed with all affected parties.

Will I Be Able to Find a Buyer? When Is the Right Time to Sell?

During the turbulent 1980s, nearly half of all companies in the United States were restructured, more than 80,000 were acquired or merged, and more than 700,000 sought bankruptcy protection in order to reorganize to continue operations. The general public's perception of the go-go '80s, however, was depicted by Michael Douglas's portrayal of Gordon Gekko, the corporate raider in the movie *Wall Street*, who declared, "Greed is good." The era featured swashbucklers who used Rambo tactics to gain control over targets.

The 1990s have proved to be even *more* dynamic in terms of companies evolving through strategic acquisitions, downsizing, rightsizing, spinoffs, roll-ups, and industry consolidations and divestitures. There is, however, a different focus on post-closing synergies, operating efficiencies, increases in customer bases, strategic alliances, market share and access to new technologies.

A variety of factors may lead you, as the owner of the small or closely held, business to consider sale as an exit strategy. These could include the inability to compete as an independent, the desire to obtain cost savings, and access to the greater resource of the acquiring company. These may compete with the motivations of the buyer (see the box on page 124).

Getting Your House in Order: Preparing to Sell Your Business

Two houses in my neighborhood recently went up for sale. Each seller took a very different approach to preparing for the transaction. One couple, nearing retirement, began the process almost two years ago. Every weekend they would work on a different part of the house or garden, taking steps to increase the value and hence the ultimate selling price of the home. The proceeds represented the bulk of their retire-

CHAPTER NINE PARTING COMPANY

> **BOX 9-1 Understanding Each Party's Motivations**
>
> AT THE HEART of gaining an understanding into why the buyer and seller have competing objectives is the realization that each party has an entirely different set of motivations for entering into the transaction.
>
> **COMMON SELLER MOTIVATIONS**
> 1. **Desire** to retire
> 2. **Lack** of successors
> 3. **Business** adversities
> 4. **Inability** to compete
> 5. **Lack of capital** to grow or modernize the business
> 6. **Inadequate** distribution system
> 7. **Desire to eliminate** personal obligations
> 8. **Inability** to diversify
> 9. **Age** and health concerns
> 10. **Need for particular** amount of money for estate planning
> 11. **Irreconcilable conflict** among owners or resources
> 12. **Loss of key people** or key customers
>
> **COMMON BUYER MOTIVATIONS**
> 1. **Desire** to grow
> 2. **Opportunity** to increase profits
> 3. **Desire** to diversify
> 4. **Value-driven** acquisition strategy
> 5. **Acquisition** of competitors
> 6. **Use** of excess capital
> 7. **New** distribution channels or efficiencies
> 8. **Diversification** into new products or geographic markets
> 9. **Need for particular** people, existing business or assets
> 10. **Access to new** or emerging technologies
> 11. **Need to efficiently deploy** key people
> 12. **Strategic fit** between buyer's and seller's current operations

ment nest egg, and every dollar of value was critical. Naturally, certain items, such as wallpaper and paint, were hard to upgrade because they didn't know the potential buyer's wants and needs. Therefore, they made the walls and rooms "generic," to appeal to the varying tastes of prospective buyers.

The other couple, in their mid thirties with three young children, seemed as if they started preparing about one week before the first prospective buyer arrived. They had already purchased their next home, and although the selling price mattered, it really affected only the size of their next mortgage. In fact, with three wild and destructive children, it seemed that they were taking steps to decrease the value of the house on a weekly basis! Clearly, their approach to the buyer was "take it as is and hopefully it will meet your needs." Prospective buyers came into the transaction knowing that a lot of time, care and attention would need to go into the house after closing.

In many ways, these two approaches mirror the attitudes of sellers of businesses. Some companies become available for sale after years of planning and preparation by the seller, who has laid the groundwork for maximizing value and takes to heart the phrase "getting your house in order." This seller takes the time to anticipate the needs and wants of the different types of buyers, yet realizes that some items must be kept "plain vanilla" because each buyer will have different objectives and motivations.

Other companies become available for sale because the founder has become bored, or because of competitive or financial factors that may have only recently occurred. Although each set of circumstances will be different, this second type of seller will not invest much time, energy or resources in preparing for the sale of his business. It may be that he simply does not want to make the significant capital investments that may be necessary to continue operations, or the industry may have become less profitable, or there may be irreconcilable shareholder or management disputes that are driving the transaction. In each of these cases, the buyer is likely to be purchasing a "fixer-upper" and the price and valuation will be negotiated accordingly. In rare cases the hasty decision to sell may be for positive reasons—for instance, a particular industry may be perceived as "hot" by the financial markets, thereby creating an ability to sell at an inflated price for a limited time, or a competing business opportunity has been presented and the seller needs to diversify his or her assets in order to pursue it.

If you're considering the sale of your small or closely held business as an exit strategy, you have many important tasks to perform. The first and most important is the selection of a team of advisers (see the box on page 127). This team will not only help prepare the company for the sale itself, but also assist you in developing an "offering memorandum" that will summarize the key aspects of the company's operations, products and services, personnel and financial performance. In many ways, this offering memorandum is akin to a traditional business plan and will serve both as a road map for you and an informational tool for the buyer. When selecting team members, look for the following qualities:

- **Knowledge of the company,** its history and its founders;
- **An understanding of your motivation,** goals and post-closing objectives;
- **Familiarity with trends in your industry;**
- **Access to a network of potential buyers;**
- **Track record and experience in mergers** and acquisitions with emerging-growth and middle-market companies;
- **Expertise with the financing issues** that will face prospective buyers; and
- **Knowledge of tax and estate-planning issues** that may affect you both at closing and beyond.

Once your team is assembled, schedule a meeting to:

- **Identify your financial and structural objectives;**
- **Develop an action plan and timetable;**
- **Begin preparing the offering memorandum;**
- **Identify potential legal and financial hurdles to a successful transaction** (for example, think about what "clouds to title" may exist that could be a turn-off to a prospective buyer);
- **Develop a definitive "to do" list** of corporate housekeeping matters; and
- **Identify how and when to recruit prospective buyers,** evaluate offers and select final candidates

Before preparing the offering memorandum, as explained below, you must get the company ready for the buyer's analysis and due-diligence investigation. A mini legal audit should be conducted in order to assess the "state of the union." The legal audit should address numerous issues, including corporate housekeeping, necessary consents from third parties, the status of your intellectual property and key contracts (including their assignability), regulatory issues, and litigation.

The goal here is to find as many "bugs" as possible and

Selling to a Third Party

> **BOX 9-2 | Assembling Your Team**
>
> **Financial Adviser/Investment Banker.** In tandem with the certified public accountant, a financial adviser (or investment banker) will counsel you on issues affecting valuation, pricing and structure, and assist you in the identification and evaluation of prospective buyers. In some cases, multiple offers may have both different structures and different consequences for you, and a financial adviser will counsel you on how to evaluate each proposed transaction.
>
> **Certified Public Accountant.** A certified public accountant (CPA) will assist you in preparing the financial statements and related reports that the buyer (or buyers) will inevitably request, and advise you on the tax implications of the proposed transaction. The CPA will also assist in estate planning and structuring a compensation package for you that will maximize the benefits of the proposed transaction.
>
> **Legal Counsel.** The transactional attorney is responsible for a wide variety of duties, including: (a) assisting you in pre-sale corporate "housekeeping," which involves cleaning up corporate records, developing strategies for dealing with dissident shareholders and shoring up third-party contracts; (b) working with the financial adviser to guide you on how to evaluate competing offers; (c) assisting in the negotiation and preparation of the letter of intent and confidentiality agreements; (d) negotiating definitive purchase agreements with the buyer's counsel; and (e) working with you and the CPA on certain post-closing and estate- and tax-planning matters.

exterminate them before the first potential buyer is entertained. If the buyer's counsel discovers the bugs *for* you, it will be embarrassing and costly from a negotiating perspective. Now is the time to resolve any disputes with minority shareholders, complete the registration of copyrights and trademarks, deal with open issues in your stock-option plan, or renew or extend your favorable commercial leases. It may also be a good time to set the stage for the prompt response of those third parties whose consent may be necessary to close the transaction, such as landlords, bankers, key customers, suppliers, (if they have a restriction on change in control) or venture capitalists. If any bugs can't be killed, don't try to hide them under the carpet—explain the status of any remaining problems to

CHAPTER NINE PARTING COMPANY

the prospective buyer, and negotiate and structure the deal accordingly.

Although the audit will help to resolve certain legal problems, it may also be necessary to change certain business practices before you sell your company. This "strategic re-engineering" will help build value and remove unnecessary clutter from your financial statements and operations. The process involves an examination of certain key financial ratios such as debt-to-equity, turnover and profitability. It also involves looking carefully at the company's cost controls, overhead management and profit centers to ensure the most productive performance. Even if you don't have the time, inclination or resources to make improvements, it will still be helpful to identify these areas and address how the company could be made more profitable to the buyer in the offering memorandum.

Once your objectives have been identified, you should develop a game plan for attracting buyers and begin preparing the offering memorandum. This document must present the data truthfully and attractively, and include the following:

- **Overview of the company;**
- **Description of products and services;**
- **Description of management team** and organizational structure;
- **Summary of company's financial performance to date;**
- **Description of key customer relationships** and intangible assets;
- **Hurdles (if any) to accomplishing the sale;** and
- **Supplemental materials.**

Once a letter of intent (or preliminary agreement) has been executed, you should anticipate that a buyer and its acquisition team will want to embark immediately on the complex and extensive legal and business due diligence, which must occur before closing the transaction. As a result, you and your advisers should be prepared to accommodate all reasonable requests made by the buyer. *Legal* due diligence will focus on the potential legal issues and problems that may serve as impediments to the transaction, and will shed light on how the documents should be structured. *Business* due diligence will focus on the strategic issues surrounding the transaction, such as: integration

> **BOX 9-3 Common Reasons Why Deals Die at an Early Stage**
>
> **1. Seller has not prepared adequate financial statements** (for example, going back at least two years and reflecting the company's current condition).
>
> **2. Seller and its team are uncooperative** during the due-diligence process.
>
> **3. Buyer and its team discover a "deal breaker"** in the due diligence (e.g., large unknown or hidden actual or contingent liabilities, such as a potential liability for violation of federal environmental laws.
>
> **4. Seller has seller's remorse,** cold feet or second thoughts about its after-tax consideration or compensation.
>
> **5. Seller suffers from "don't call my baby ugly" syndrome.** Seller gets defensive when the buyer and its team find flaws in anything—the operation of the business, the valuation, customer loyalty, the quality of the accounts receivable or personnel skills, for instance—and focus on these flaws during negotiation.
>
> **6. A strategic shift** (or set of extenuating circumstances) affecting the acquisition strategy or criteria of the buyer (for example, a change in the buyer's management team during the due-diligence process).
>
> **7. Seller is inflexible on price** and valuation when the buyer and its team discover problems during due diligence.

of the human and financial resources of the two companies; confirmation of the operating, production and distribution synergies and economies of scale to be achieved by the acquisition; and the gathering of information necessary for financing the transaction.

The due-diligence process can be tedious, frustrating, time-consuming and expensive. Yet it is a necessary prerequisite to a well-planned acquisition, and may assist you as well as the buyer in analyzing the benefits of the transaction and measuring its costs and risks. Ultimately, you and your counsel should ensure that buyers are prevented from "due diligence overkill," keeping in mind that due diligence is *not* a perfect process and that information may slip through the cracks. Therefore, prior to business due diligence, you should make every effort to prevent or correct any undervaluation of inventories, overdue tax liabilities, incomplete financial documentation or customer information, aging accounts receivable or unrecorded liabilities (such as warranty claims, vacation pay, claims, sales returns and allowances).

Common Preparation Mistakes Sellers Make

Once you and your team conduct an internal pre-sale legal audit and pull together "the good, the bad and the ugly" into a detailed offering memorandum, you're ready to start meeting with buyers. The following are a few preliminary steps as well as some of the more common preparation mistakes sellers make in getting ready to sell their company.

GUARD AGAINST IMPATIENCE OR INDECISION. Timing is everything. If you seem too anxious to sell, buyers will take advantage of your impatience! But if you sit on the sidelines too long, the window or market cycle for obtaining a top selling price may pass you by.

TELL OTHERS IN A TIMELY FASHION. Again, timing is critical. If you tell key employees, vendors or customers too early in the process that you are considering a sale, they may abandon your relationship out of fear of the unknown or in anticipation of losing their jobs. Key employees may not want to take the chance of relying on the unknown buyer to honor their salary or benefits. Yet these key employees and strategic relationships may be items of value that the buyer is counting on after closing. On the other hand, if you wait too long and disclose at the last minute, employees may resent having been kept out of the loop, and customers or vendors may not have the time to react and evaluate the impact of the transaction on their businesses (or, where applicable, provide their approvals).

ELIMINATE THIRD-PARTY TRANSACTIONS WITH FAMILY MEMBERS when those relationships would not carry over to the new owner. For example, a family member who's not really working at the company should be let go as soon as possible.

PURCHASE MINORITY SHAREHOLDER INTERESTS so the new owner won't have to contend with their demands after the sale.

BE READY TO RECAST YOUR FINANCIAL STATEMENTS. Privately owned companies tend to keep reported profits and thus taxes as low as possible; financial recasting is a crucial element in understanding the real earnings history and future profit potential of your business. Buyers are interested in real earnings, and recasting shows how your business would look if its philosophy matched that of a public corporation in which earnings and profits are maximized. In presenting the complete earnings history of your company, your financial statements should be recast for the preceding three years. For example, adjust salaries and benefits to prevailing market levels (and don't overinflate), and eliminate expenses that are avoidable, unusual or non-recurring, such as personal expenses, country-club dues or expensive car leases. Recasting presents the financial history of your business in a way that buyers understand. This is key to translating your company's past into a valuable, saleable future, and allows sophisticated buyers the means and opportunity for meaningful comparisons with other investment considerations.

CONVINCE THE BUYER YOUR FINANCIAL PROJECTIONS ARE CREDIBLE. The price that a buyer may be willing to pay depends on the quality and reasonableness of profit projections that you are able to provide. The profit-and-loss statement, balance sheet, cash flow and working-capital requirements are developed and projected for each year over a five-year planning period. Using these documents, plus the enhanced value of your business at the end of five years, the discounted value of future cash flow is calculated. This establishes the primary economic return to the buyer for his acquisition investment.

PRE-QUALIFY YOUR BUYER. It's critical to pre-qualify your buyers, especially if the transaction creates a continuing business relationship after closing. The buyer must demonstrate its ability

CHAPTER NINE PARTING COMPANY

to meet one or more of a series of pre-closing conditions, such as availability of financing. You should take the time to understand the buyer's post-closing business plan, especially in a roll-up or consolidation, where the buyer is purchasing several different companies in your industry hoping to achieve certain economies of scale, and where your upside will depend on the ability of the buyer to meet its business and growth plans.

The Letter of Intent

At this stage of the transaction, both you and the buyer (and your respective advisers) have developed a strategic plan and hopefully have taken the time to understand each other's perspective and competing objectives. The field of available candidates has been narrowed, the preliminary get-acquainted meetings are over, and a tentative selection has been made. After the completion of the pre-sale review, the next step involves the preparation and negotiation of an interim agreement, which will govern the conduct of the parties up until closing.

There are valid legal arguments against the execution of any type of interim document. Some courts have interpreted them to be binding legal documents (even if one or more of the parties did not initially intend to be bound). But it has been my experience that a letter of intent, which includes a set of binding terms and non-binding terms as a road map for the transaction, is a necessary step in virtually all mergers and acquisition transactions. I've found that most parties prefer the organizational framework and psychological comfort of knowing that there is some type of written document in place before proceeding further and before incurring significant expenses.

There are many different styles of letters of intent, which vary from law firm to law firm and business lawyer to business lawyer. These styles usually fall into one of three categories: binding, non-binding and hybrids, like the sample on page 240 of the Appendix. In general, the type selected will

BOX 9-4 — The Selling Process and Seller's Decision-Making Path

1. Reaching the Decision to Sell
- Understanding your motivations and objectives
- Building the foundation for value
- Timing and market factors

2. Getting the House in Order
- Assembling your advisory team.
- Legal audit and housekeeping
- Establishing preliminary valuation
- Preparing the offering memorandum
- Estate and exit planning

3. Marketing Strategy
- Targeting qualified buyers
- Use of third-party intermediaries
- Narrowing the field of candidates

4. Choosing a Dance Partner
- Selecting the most qualified and synergistic candidate (or strongest financial candidate, depending on your objectives)
- Preliminary negotiations
- Execution of confidentiality agreement
- Preliminary due diligence

5. Fighting It Out
- Execution of more detailed letter of intent or memorandum of understanding
- Extensive negotiations and strategic adjustments
- Structuring the deal
- Accommodating the buyer's team for legal and strategic due diligence

6. Preparing for the Closing
- Preparation and negotiation of the definitive legal documents
- Meeting conditions to closing
- Obtaining necessary third-party consents

7. The Closing

8. Post-Closing Issues
- Monitoring post-closing compensation/earn-outs
- Facilitating the post-closing integration plan
- Post-closing challenges

---

depend on (a) the information to be released publicly concerning the transaction, (b) the degree to which negotiations have been definitive and necessary information was gathered, (c) the cost to the buyer and you of proceeding with the transaction before making binding commitments, (d) the speed with which the parties estimate a final agreement could be signed, and (e) the degree of confidence in the good faith

CHAPTER NINE PARTING COMPANY

> **BOX 9-5 Pros and Cons of Executing a Letter of Intent**
>
> **ADVANTAGES**
> - **Tests parties' seriousness**
> - **Morally commits parties to sale**
> - **Sets out in writing areas of agreement** (important because there may be a long delay before a sales agreement is executed)
> - **Highlights differences** and matters needing further negotiation
> - **Discourages seller** from shopping around for a better deal
>
> **DISADVANTAGES**
> - **May be considered a binding agreement** (important to state whether or not letter of intent is meant to constitute an enforceable agreement)
> - **Public announcement of prospective sale** may have to be made due to federal securities law if either company is publicly held

of each party, and the absence (or presence) of other parties competing for the transaction. In most cases, the hybrid is the most effective format to protect the interests of both parties and to level the playing field from a negotiations perspective.

Although formally executed by the buyer and the seller, a letter of intent is often considered an agreement in principle. As a result, the parties should be very clear as to whether the letter of intent is a binding preliminary contract or merely a memorandum from which a more definitive legal document may be drafted upon completion of due diligence. Regardless of the legal implications, however, by executing a letter of intent, the parties make a psychological commitment to the transaction and provide a road map for expediting more formal negotiations.

A well-drafted letter of intent will also provide an overview of matters that require further discussion and consideration, such as the exact purchase price. Although a purchase price cannot realistically be established until due diligence has been completed, you may hesitate to proceed without a price commitment. Instead of creating a fixed price, however, the letter of intent should incorporate a price range that is qualified by a clause or provision that sets forth all of the factors that will influence and affect the calculation of a final fixed price.

Proposed Terms

As you can see from the sample letter of intent on page 240 of the Appendix, the first section addresses certain key terms of the deal, such as price and method of payment, but these terms are usually non-binding so that the parties have an opportunity to conduct thorough due diligence and have room for further negotiation, depending on the specific problems uncovered during the investigative process.

Binding Terms

The sample letter of intent on page 240 also includes certain binding terms which will not be subject to further negotiation. These are certain issues that at least one side (and usually both sides) will want to ensure are binding, regardless of whether the deal is actually consummated. These include:

LEGAL ABILITY OF SELLER TO CONSUMMATE THE TRANSACTION. Before wasting too much time or money, the buyer will want to know that you have the resources and authority to close the deal.

PROTECTION OF CONFIDENTIAL INFORMATION. You in particular (and in general both parties) will want to ensure that all information provided in the initial presentation as well as during due diligence remains confidential.

ACCESS TO BOOKS AND RECORDS. The buyer will want to ensure that you and your advisers will fully cooperate in the due-diligence process.

BREAKUP OR WALK-AWAY FEES. The buyer may want to include a clause in the letter of intent to attempt to recoup some of its expenses if you try to walk away from the deal. (A seller might do this either because of a change in circumstances or to accept a more attractive offer from a different potential buyer.) You may want a reciprocal clause to protect against your own expenses if the buyer walks away or defaults on a preliminary obligation or condition to closing, such as an inability to raise acquisition capital.

NO-SHOP/STANDSTILL PROVISIONS. The buyer may want a period of exclusivity during which it can be confident that you will not be entertaining any other offers. You will want to place a limit or outside date on this provision so that you can begin entertaining alternate offers if the buyer is unduly dragging its feet.

GOOD-FAITH DEPOSIT: REFUNDABLE VERSUS NON-REFUNDABLE. In some cases you will request a deposit or option fee; the parties must then determine to what extent, if at all, this deposit will be refundable and under what conditions. There are often timing problems with this provision that can be difficult to resolve. For example, the buyer will want the deposit to remain 100% refundable if you are being uncooperative, or at least until the buyer and its team complete the initial round of due diligence to ensure that there are no major problems discovered that might cause them to walk away from the deal. You will want to set a limit on the due-diligence and review period at which point the buyer forfeits all or a part of its deposit. If the buyer forfeits some or all of the deposit, and the deal never closes, the buyer may want to negotiate an eventual full or partial refund if you find an alternative buyer within a certain period of time, say, 180 days.

IMPACT ON EMPLOYEES. If an announcement isn't made directly to your employees, they may get the unmistakable message that their jobs are unimportant or in jeopardy, or both. Brief supervisory personnel first, and answer all of their questions so that they can inform their subordinates. After the closing, it's imperative that the top management of the acquiring company assure your employees of the continuation of beneficial policies and welcome them into a larger and better organization if that is their intent. Employees who don't feel they are part of a team will have poor morale and poorer productivity. It is essential that lines of communication be kept open at the time of the acquisition.

KEY TERMS FOR THE DEFINITIVE DOCUMENTS. The letter of intent is often subject to "definitive documents," such as the purchase agreement; those definitive documents will address key matters or include certain key sections, such as covenants, indemnification, representations and warranties, and key conditions for closing.

CONDITIONS FOR CLOSING. Both parties will want to specify a set of conditions or circumstances under which they will not be bound to proceed with the transaction. These could include certain contingencies that might not be met or events that might occur after the execution of the letter of intent. Be sure to articulate these conditions clearly so that there are no surprises down the road.

CONDUCT OF THE BUSINESS PRIOR TO CLOSING. The buyer usually wants some protection that what he or she sees today will be there tomorrow. Thus, you will be obligated to operate your business in the ordinary fashion: Assets can't start disappearing from the premises, equipment can't fall into disrepair, new-customer leads must be pursued, bonuses can't suddenly be declared, and personal expenses can't be paid "the night before." These are just a few examples of steps that could deplete the value of the company prior to closing. These "negative covenants" help protect the buyer against unpleasant surprises at, or after, closing.

LIMITATIONS ON PUBLICITY AND PRESS RELEASES. The parties may want to place certain restrictions on the content and timing of any press releases or public announcements of the transaction. In some cases it may be necessary to follow Securities and Exchange Commission (SEC) guidelines.

If either or both of the parties to the transaction are publicly traded, the general rule is that once the essential terms of the transaction are agreed to in principle (such as through the execution of a letter of intent), there must be a public announcement. The timing and content of this announcement must be weighed carefully by the parties, including an analysis as to how the announcement will affect the price of the stock. The announcement should not be too early or it may be viewed by the SEC as an attempt to influence the price of the stock.

CHAPTER NINE PARTING COMPANY

EXPENSES AND BROKERS. The parties should decide, where applicable, who will bear responsibility for investment-bankers' fees, finder's fees, legal expenses, and other costs pertaining to the transaction.

Preparing the Work Schedule

Following the execution of the letter of intent, one of the first responsibilities of legal counsel for both parties is to work together to prepare a comprehensive schedule of activities ("work schedule") that serves as a task checklist and assignment of responsibilities. The primary purpose of the schedule is to outline all of the events that must occur and documents that must be prepared prior to the closing date and beyond.

In this regard, the buyer's legal counsel acts as an orchestra leader assigning primary areas of responsibility to the various members of the acquisition team as well as to you and your counsel. The buyer's counsel must also act as a taskmaster, to ensure that the timetable for closing is met. Once all tasks have been identified and assigned, and a realistic timetable established for completion, then a firm closing time and date can be determined.

Naturally, the exact list of legal documents that must be prepared and the specific tasks to be outlined in the work schedule will vary from transaction to transaction, usually depending on the specific facts and circumstances of each deal, such as:

- whether the transaction is a stock or asset purchase,
- the form and terms of the purchase price,
- the nature of the business being acquired,
- the nature and extent of the assets being purchased or liabilities being assumed, and
- the sophistication of the parties and their respective legal counsel.

A sample work schedule for an asset purchase transaction, which is not intended to be overly complex or comprehensive, is found on page 140.

Structuring the Deal

There are countless ways to structure a corporate merger or acquisition. There are probably as many potential deal structures as there are qualified and creative attorneys and bankers. The goal is not to create the most complex deal, but rather to create a structure that fairly reflects the goals and objectives of the buyer and seller. Naturally, not all of the objectives of each party will be met each time—there will almost always be a degree of negotiation and compromise. Virtually all structures, even the most complex, boil down to either mergers or acquisitions, including the purchase or consolidation of either stock or assets. The creativity often comes in structuring the deal to achieve a particular tax or strategic result or to accommodate a multi-step or multi-party transaction. At the heart of each transaction are the following key issues which will affect the deal's structure:

- **How will tangible and intangible assets** be transferred to the purchaser from you? At what price and according to what terms?
- **What issues discovered during due diligence** may affect the structure of the deal?
- **What liabilities will be assumed by the buyer?** How will risks be allocated among the parties?
- **What are the tax implications to each party?**
- **What are the buyer's long-term objectives?**
- **What role will you have in the management** and growth of the business after closing?
- **To what extent will third-party consents** or governmental filings and approvals be necessary?
- **What arrangements will be made for your key management team** (who may not necessarily be among the selling owners of the company)?
- **Does the buyer currently have access to all of the cash to be paid** to you, or will some of these funds need to be raised from debt or equity markets?

There are a wide variety of corporate-, tax- and securities-law issues that affect the final decision as to the structure of any given transaction. Each issue must be carefully consid-

CHAPTER NINE PARTING COMPANY

BOX 9-6 — A Sample Work Schedule

TIMETABLE	TASK	RESPONSIBLE PARTIES
6 weeks before closing	Sign letter of intent; obtain board resolutions to authorize negotiations	Seller, buyer and counsel
	Deliver due-diligence report to seller	Buyer's counsel
5 weeks before closing	Organize and deliver due-diligence materials	Seller's counsel
	Review due-diligence materials	Buyer's counsel
	Draft the asset purchase agreement, information schedules, and exhibits to purchase agreement and consulting agreements	Buyer's counsel
	Order lien searches on assets to review encumbrances	Buyer's counsel
	Review seller's financial statements	Buyer's accountants
3 to 4 weeks before closing	Review, negotiate and redraft asset purchase agreement (may continue until the night before closing)	Buyer's and seller's counsel
	Prepare and negotiate opinion(s) of counsel	Buyer's and seller's counsel
	Complete review of all initial due-diligence materials and make follow-up requests	Buyer's counsel
	Ensure that all board and shareholder approvals have been obtained (as required by state law)	Buyer's and seller's counsel

TIMETABLE	TASK	RESPONSIBLE PARTIES
3 to 4 weeks before closing (continued)	Prepare checklist and commence process for all third-party regulatory and contractual approvals (banks, landlords, insurance companies, key customers)	Buyer's and seller's counsel
2 weeks before closing	Mutual review of press releases or other third-party communications regarding the deal (or sooner, as required by the SEC)	Buyer's and seller's counsel
	Prepare schedule of closing documents (including opinions, results of lien searches, compliance certificates)	Buyer's counsel
1 week before and up to closing	Finalize any last-minute negotiations to the asset purchase agreement	Buyer's and seller's counsel
	Obtain closing certificates from state authorities (good-standing certificates, taxes paid, and current charter and amendments)	Seller's counsel
	Check to ensure that all conditions to closing have been met or waived	Buyer's and seller's counsel
	Conduct dry-run closing to identify open issues (recommended two to three days before closing)	Buyer and seller
	Close	All parties
	Resolve post-closing matters and conditions	All parties

CHAPTER NINE PARTING COMPANY

ered from a legal and accounting perspective. However, the following basic questions are at the heart of each structural alternative:

- **Will the buyer be acquiring stock** or assets of the target company?
- **In what form will the consideration from the buyer to you be made** (e.g., cash, notes or securities)?
- **Will the purchase price be fixed,** contingent or payable over time on an installment basis?
- **What are the tax consequences of the proposed structure** for the acquisition?

142

CHAPTER TEN | PARTING COMPANY

Going Public

DEPENDING ON YOUR COMPANY'S SIZE AND TRACK record, the sale to the public of a significant portion of your company's securities may be a viable exit strategy. From a succession-planning and exit-strategy perspective, a public offering will achieve the liquidity and cash that you desire, and the remaining issues regarding the transfer of wealth can be dealt with in the estate plan. To a family-owned business, the rewards of going public can be bittersweet and present new types of challenges within the family. As Bob Davidson, the founder of family-owned software publisher Davidson & Associates, observed shortly after going public: "When we started, we worried about wiping out the kids' savings. Now we've made them rich. I don't know which is worse."

There are numerous examples of medium-to-large family businesses that went public for many reasons, including to provide liquidity for the original founders and family members. Well-known companies such as William Wrigley Co. (the Wrigley family), The Washington Post Co. (the Graham family), Manor Care (the Bainum family), Berkshire Hathaway (the Buffett family), Tyson Foods (the Tyson family), Corning Glass Works (the Houghton family), Danaher Corp. (the

CHAPTER TEN PARTING COMPANY

Rales family) and General Dynamics (the Crown family), have all struck a delicate balance between maintaining family control and enjoying the liquidity that comes with being a public company. In fact, a new Family Business Stock Index (FBSI) tracks the current and past performance of 210 of the nation's largest family-owned but publicly traded businesses. FBSI companies provided an average annual return of 16.6% from 1976 to 1996, nearly three points ahead of the companies in the Standard & Poors 500 stock index.

The market for initial public offerings (IPOs) is like a well-designed roller coaster—it will always have steep peaks and deep valleys. The mid to late 1990s presented one of the wildest rides in history for the IPO market as hundreds of new companies, at stages much earlier than ever before, brought their shares for sale to the public and then watched their prices and valuations soar to new heights.

An IPO is a legal process through which a company initially registers its securities with the Securities and Exchange Commission (SEC) for sale to the general investing public. Many entrepreneurs view the process of "going public" as the epitome of financial success and reward; however, the decision to go public requires considerable strategic planning and analysis from both legal and business perspectives. The planning and analysis process involves: (a) weighing the costs and benefits, (b) understanding the process and expense of the offering and (c) understanding the obligations of the company, its advisers and shareholders once the company has successfully completed its public offering.

For you, as the current owner of a closely held or family business, the process of going public represents a number of benefits, including:

- **significantly greater access to capital;**
- **increased liquidity for the company's shares;**
- **market prestige;**
- **enhancement of public image;**
- **flexibility for employee ownership** and participation;
- **improved opportunities for mergers,** acquisitions and further rounds of financing;

- **increased ability to recruit senior executives;**
- **an immediate increase in your wealth** and that of future generations; and
- **cash available to cover estate taxes** as the remaining ownership passes from one generation to the next.

The many benefits of going public are not without their corresponding costs, however, and the downside of being a public company must be strongly considered in the exit-strategy planning process. Among these costs are:

- **dilution of your control of the entity,** the management and control of which had traditionally been vested only in the family or among the co-founders;
- **pressure to meet market and shareholder expectations** regarding growth and dividends (the "living from quarter to quarter" syndrome);
- **changes in management styles** and employee expectations;
- **compliance with complex reporting** and disclosure regulations imposed by federal and state securities laws;
- **loss of the privacy enjoyed in a closely held or family business**—corporate life is often lived in a fishbowl;
- **stock resale restrictions for company insiders;**
- **vulnerability to shifts in the stock market;** and
- **sharing the company's financial success with hundreds,** even thousands of other shareholders.

The Hidden Legal Costs

In addition to some of the more obvious business costs, the most expensive aspect of registering the securities is often the hidden costs that are imposed by federal and state securities laws. The rules and regulations imposed by the SEC make going public a time-consuming and expensive process that in reality begins several years before the public offering and continues (through the SEC periodic-reporting process) for as long as the company remains public. From a legal perspective, the following factors should be strongly considered:

CHAPTER TEN PARTING COMPANY

PLANNING AND PREPARING THE BUSINESS FOR THE IPO. From the day that the company is formed there are a host of legal and structural pitfalls that must be avoided if an initial public offering is in your company's future. Some of these pitfalls, if not avoided early on, will serve as significant impediments to a successful IPO and will be expensive to remedy once the damage has been done. In addition, being a public company requires a more formal management style (from a legal perspective), which normally entails more regular meetings of the board of directors and the observance of formalities imposed by state corporate laws.

DUE DILIGENCE AND HOUSECLEANING. Many owners (and their managers) who take their companies public complain that they feel as though their company and personal lives are conducted in a fish bowl. Federal and state securities laws dictate that a prospective investor must have access to all material information about the company offering its securities to the public. As a result, you must go through the due-diligence process well before you're ready to file a registration statement with the Securities and Exchange Commission. The corporate charters, bylaws, shareholders' agreements, employment agreements, leases, licenses, accounting methods, and related documents and procedures may need to be formalized, amended or even terminated before you're ready to operate in the public eye.

THE REGISTRATION PROCESS. The time, effort and expense required to prepare the registration statement should not be underestimated. In fact, the six- to 12-month time frame and the out-of-pocket expenses alone can make the cost prohibitive for many growing businesses that are going public to raise capital. While costs will vary depending on a number of factors, a company planning to offer its securities to the public should be prepared to spend anywhere from $200,000 to $500,000 in legal and accounting fees, appraisal costs, printing expenses, and consulting and filing fees. This amount does not include the underwriters' and brokers' commissions, which may run 10% or more of the total offering. However, as discussed further in this chapter, the SEC has implemented new regulations for small-business owners that have decreased legal and accounting fees. You must remember that few, if any, of these costs will be contingent on the success of the offering and, therefore, must be paid regardless of how many shares are actually sold.

In addition to the registration statement, exhibits and attachments that document major business transactions (such as plans for acquisition, reorganization or liquidation), customer and vendor arrangements and financial statements must be filed prior to the offering. These required disclosures will result in a loss of confidentiality that may be costly, because competitors, creditors, labor unions, suppliers and others will have access to these documents once they become available to the public.

PERIODIC REPORTING AND ONGOING COMPLIANCE. Most public companies are subject to the ongoing periodic-reporting requirements imposed by the Securities and Exchange Commission, such as quarterly financial reporting (Forms 10-Q and 10-QSB), annual financial reporting (Forms 10-K and 10-KSB), reporting of any major developments or substantial events that might affect the company or its stock price (Form 8-K), and related reporting requirements, such as those for the sale of control stock and tender offers. The ongoing costs of being a public company also include an increased use of attorneys, accountants and other advisers; a dedication of staff time to meet with securities analysts and financial press; the implementation of shareholder- and media-relations programs; and the significantly greater cost of annual reports, shareholder meetings, and solicitations of proxies when shareholder approval is needed for major corporate transactions.

In preparing for a public offering, you should immediately implement a more formalized management structure, which will include the recruitment of an experienced and independent board of directors who will be acceptable and attractive to the investing public, meet formally on a monthly or quarterly basis, and maintain complete and accurate corporate minutes and resolutions. Of greatest interest to any prospective underwriter or investor analyzing a company will be the three Ps of due diligence: people, products and profits. From a legal perspective, the intangible assets that will be critical to a successful offering should be protected as early as possible in the company's history.

Selecting an Underwriter

At the heart of the network established for the distribution and sale of securities is the managing, or "lead," underwriter, whose selection is a key ingredient for the success of the IPO. A significant amount of time should be devoted to the selection of the lead underwriter. Consider a wide variety of underwriters. They range from smaller but well-established regional firms such as Ferris Baker Watts and Legg Mason in the mid-Atlantic region (who may devote a considerable amount of time and attention to the transaction) to large firms, such as Goldman Sachs, Salomon Smith Barney and Morgan Stanley Dean Witter, with a genuine "Wall Street" presence (but whose size heightens the risk that the offering will be lost among bigger transactions or delegated to junior staff).

There are many factors that should be considered in selecting the lead underwriter. The size and reputation of the underwriter that the company is able to attract will typically depend on (1) the strength of the company, (2) the amount of stock being offered, and (3) the company's future business plans. Underwriters typically offer a wide range of support services, such as management consulting services, business valuations, development of media- and shareholders- relations programs, assistance in developing an optimum capital structure or location, and analysis of merger and acquisition candidates (which may or may not be needed when considering a public offering). Any company, regardless of size or industry type, should closely examine the reputation, experience, distribution capability, market-making ability, research capabilities and specific industry expertise of the potential underwriter.

Going Public

> **BOX 10-1 Deterrents to the IPO**
>
> HERE ARE A few items that will have a negative effect on the company's valuation and the underwriter's willingness to take the company public.
>
> - **Inefficient** management structure
> - **Overly restrictive shareholders'** agreements (which affect the company's control)
> - **Self-dealing** among the board of directors and key stockholders
> - **Inadequate** corporate records
> - **Capital structure** with excessive debt
> - **Series of unaudited** and uncertain financial statements
> - **Poor** earnings history
> - **Family members** or others on the payroll who are not really working at the business

Once selected, the lead underwriter will usually execute a letter of intent. That states the terms and conditions of the proposed distribution of the securities, and usually also sets a range for the price of the securities and hence the valuation of the company. However, the final decision on these issues will be determined by the post-effective price amendment (which may adjust the price based on recent events affecting the company or any changes in market conditions). The letter of intent will also govern the relationship throughout the preparation and registration process because the final underwriting agreement is usually not signed until the day that the registration statement becomes effective following SEC approval.

The first step is setting up a meeting of all key members of the registration team (attorneys, accountants, lead underwriter, chief executive officer and chief financial officer, among others), during which responsibility for the preparation of each aspect of the registration statement is delegated, and a timetable for completion of each task is developed and agreed upon.

The registration statement consists of two parts. The first is the offering prospectus (which is used to assist the underwriters and investors in analyzing the company and the securities being offered). The second is the exhibits and additional information (which are provided directly to the SEC as part of the disclosure and registration regulations). The registration statement is part of the public record and is available for public inspection.

The SEC's "Small Business Initiatives"

In 1992, the SEC implemented its Small Business Initiatives (SBIs), significantly modifying its special provisions for offerings by small businesses that are not already subject to the reporting requirements of the Exchange Act. The SBIs were designed to streamline the federal registration process in connection with IPOs to encourage investment in small businesses. A "small business issuer" is defined as a company meeting all of the following criteria:

- **has revenue of less than $25 million;**
- **is a U.S. or Canadian issuer;**
- **is not an investment company; and**
- **if a majority-owned subsidiary,** the parent corporation is also a small-business issuer.

Small-business issuers can use Forms SB-1 or SB-2 to register securities to be sold for cash with the SEC.

The SB-1 can be used *only* to register up to $10 million of securities. Also, if the company is a secondary one, it must not have registered more than $10 million in any continuous 12-month period (including the transaction being registered). In addition, it allows for financial statements (which must be audited by an independent party) to be given in accordance with generally accepted accounting principles (commonly referred to as "GAAP"), and not the detailed requirements of the SEC.

The SB-2 lets small-business issuers to offer an unlimited dollar amount of securities, thereby allowing companies that meet the SEC's definition of a small business to sell more securities without having to undergo the same extensive disclosure process as larger companies. The advantages to using the SB-2 include: (a) repeated use, (b) a database of these filings and (c) the option of filing with either the SEC's regional office (which should be nearer to your company's principal location) or headquarters office in Washington, D.C. (They also encompass the benefits of using the SB-1.) These advantages have translated into economic benefits. For example, the average cost of the legal and accounting fees for small businesses registering to make an IPO dropped from a range of between $200,000 and $500,000 to between $75,000 and $150,000.

An Overview of the Registration Process

When the initial draft of the registration statement is ready for filing with the SEC, you have two choices: Either file the document with the transmittal letter and required fees, or schedule a pre-filing conference with an SEC staff member to discuss any anticipated questions or problems regarding the disclosure document or the accompanying financial statements. The initial registration process is generally governed by the Securities Act, which is designed to ensure full and fair disclosure of material facts to prospective investors in connection with the offer and sale of securities. The Securities Act requires the company to file a registration statement with the SEC as well as provide a prospectus to each prospective investor.

Once the registration statement is officially received by the SEC, it is assigned to an examining group (composed usually of attorneys, accountants and financial analysts, within a specific-industry department of the Division of Corporate Finance). The length of time and depth of the review by the examining group will depend on the history of the company and the nature of the securities offered.

A closely held or family-owned business that files its registration statement with the SEC should also bear in mind that the filing may trigger purchase offers from outside parties. There are a wide variety of private equity funds, buyout funds and acquirers that regularly monitor the filing of registration statements as a form of shopping for acquisition candidates.

Following the initial review, a comment letter will be sent, suggesting changes to the registration statement. The modifications to the statement will focus on the quality of the dis-

CHAPTER TEN PARTING COMPANY

closure (such as an adequate discussion of risk factors or the verbiage in management's discussion of the financial performance), not on the quality of the company or the securities being offered. In most cases, the company will be required to file a material amendment in order to address the staff's concerns. This process continues until all concerns raised by the examining group have been addressed. The final pricing amendment is filed after the pricing meeting of the underwriters and the execution of the final underwriting agreement.

The SEC has detailed regulations and restrictions on what information may be released to the public or the media during this period (the "quiet period"), especially those communications that appear to be designed to influence the price of the shares. The registration statement then is declared effective and the securities can be offered to the public. The registration's "effective date" is 20 days after the final amendment is filed, unless the SEC accelerates it at the issuer's request. Most companies seek an accelerated effective date, and it's usually made available if the company has complied with the examining group's suggested modifications.

In addition to SEC regulations, a company offering its securities to the public must also meet the requirements of the National Association of Securities Dealers (NASD) and state securities laws. The NASD will analyze all elements of the proposed corporate package for the underwriter in order to determine its fairness and reasonableness. The SEC will not deem a registration statement effective for public offering unless and until the NASD has approved the underwriting arrangements as being fair and reasonable.

The Securities Act states that federal securities laws do not supersede compliance with any state securities laws. Therefore, the requirements of each state's applicable securities laws must also be satisfied. Although various exemptions from formal registration are often available, the state securities laws must be checked very carefully as to the filing fees, registered-agent requirements, disclosure obligations, and underwriter or broker/dealer regulations for each state in which the securities will be offered.

Ongoing Reporting and Disclosure Requirements

The Exchange Act generally governs the ongoing disclosure and periodic-reporting requirements of publicly traded companies. The act grants broad powers to the SEC to develop documents and reports which must be filed. The three primary reports required are:

FORM 10-K OR 10-KSB (for small-business issuers) is the annual report which must be filed within 90 days after the close of the company's fiscal year covered by the report. It must also include a report of all significant activities of the company during its fourth quarter, an analysis and discussion of the financial condition, a description of the current officers and directors, and a schedule of certain exhibits. The 10-K requires the issuer's income statements for the prior three years and the balance sheets for the prior two years. The 10-KSB requires the income statement for the prior two years and the balance sheet for the prior year (which can be prepared in accordance with GAAP).

FORM 10-Q OR 10-QSB (for small-business issuers) is the quarterly report which must be filed no later than 45 days after the end of each of the first three fiscal quarters of each fiscal year. This filing includes copies of quarterly financial statements (accompanied by a discussion and analysis of the company's financial condition by its management) and a report on any litigation as well as any steps taken by the company that affect shareholder rights or that may require shareholder approval. The difference between the 10-Q and the 10-QSB is the same as that between the 10-K and 10-KSB. The 10-Q requires an issuer's balance sheet from the previous year and a report of the most recent fiscal quarter; however, the 10-QSB requires a report on the most recent calendar quarter.

FORM 8-K is a periodic report that's designed to ensure that all information pertaining to significant events affecting the company is disclosed to the investing public as soon as it is available, (but not later than 15 days after the occurrence of the particular event that triggers the need to file the form; such events include mergers, acquisitions and significant changes in management).

As you can see, the pre-IPO planning process, the offering itself and the post-IPO reporting obligations can be burdensome, expensive and complicated. But IPOs remain a viable and increasingly popular exit strategy among midsize and large family-owned and closely held companies. It is critical, however, to start the planning process early and work with your financial and legal advisers to eliminate the more common deterrents mentioned in this chapter and any other management or accounting practices which that close off this exit strategy down the road.

CHAPTER ELEVEN | PARTING COMPANY

Creative Exit Strategies

FOR SOME CLOSELY HELD OR FAMILY-OWNED BUSINESSES, the options of keeping the business in the family, selling to employees, selling to competitors or financial buyers, and even selling to the general public through an initial public offering are simply not viable choices. Does that mean that you should just liquidate the business and just close the door? *Absolutely not.* Whether your goal is to provide liquidity for your retirement needs, to fund estate-planning objectives, to preserve the legacy of the business or to grow the business (but without investing any more capital or resources), you still have several options. Franchising, licensing or joint ventures may provide you a full or partial exit while leaving behind a business that the next generation will control in the coming years.

Consider the following scenarios:

A MIDWESTERN 50-store retailer torn between keeping the business within the family and selling to his employees selects "retro-franchising" as a solution, whereby he will sell 30 of his stores to his store managers and convert each separately owned unit into a franchise. The family enjoys the proceeds of the various sales for estate-planning purposes and continues to run the business

CHAPTER ELEVEN PARTING COMPANY

as a licensor of the company's brand and systems.

A NEW ENGLAND-BASED family-owned research laboratory, which is having trouble competing with larger firms, recruiting employees and breaking through complex distribution channels, cuts back on overhead and converts to an intellectual-property holding company. It now grants licenses to former direct competitors to use its patented discoveries. By doing so, it creates a valuable royalty income stream for the family and averts disaster.

A SOUTHWESTERN closely held real estate developer turns to joint ventures as a method for future expansion. It builds hotels in joint ownership with local investors; with management and operational skills are its primary capital contribution. This averts the damaging dilution of equity that would be suffered if the developer owned and operated the hotels on its own. Future generations enjoy the income from these joint-venture operations without the burdens of management.

A GEORGIA-BASED chain of printing shops that's been owned by the same family for three generations chooses to leverage its reputation and operational systems by entering new markets through business-format franchising in lieu of selling the business. The expansion plans allow the family business to remain competitive and continue to grow without bringing in outside ownership. An internal family dispute is resolved by granting master franchise rights in Florida and North Carolina to two cousins who had been complaining that they had insufficient equity and limited senior-management opportunities.

AN OHIO-BASED conglomerate of successful hardware stores licenses its recognized brand name to a manufacturer of lawn-care products. The lawn-care product line and brand continue to grow in popularity and use even though the stores themselves are suffering. Over time, the stores close, but the family and the estate continue to enjoy the income stream from the royalties produced by the license of the brand name. The founder's son (who was designated to take over the operation of the stores) winds up taking a job in the marketing department of the lawn-care products manufacturer.

These examples demonstrate that creative growth strategies such as franchising, joint ventures and licensing can be used to resolve family-business disputes, open up non-traditional succession-planning alternatives and provide partial-exit strategies to current owners of closely held and family businesses. Let's take a look at a few of these strategies in greater detail.

Business Format Franchising

Franchising can be viewed as an exit strategy in that you are no longer directly responsible for the financial investment needed to fuel growth and expansion. This financial responsibility is shifted to franchisees who pay you for the right to use your trademarks and systems. Over time, this income stream—both initial franchise fees and royalties—can be a very lucrative asset around which to build an estate plan.

Over the past three decades, franchising has emerged as a popular expansion strategy for a variety of product and service companies, especially for small businesses that cannot afford to finance internal growth. Recent Department of Commerce statistics demonstrate that retail sales from franchised outlets totaled $850 billion in 1997, nearly half of all retail sales in the U.S. Franchised outlets employed some nine million people in 1997. Despite these impressive figures—and favorable media attention—franchising as a method of marketing and distributing products and services is really appropriate only for certain kinds of companies. This is because there are a host of legal and business prerequisites that must be satisfied before any company can seriously consider franchising as a method for rapid expansion.

Many companies prematurely select franchising as a growth alternative or exit strategy and then haphazardly assemble and launch the franchising program. Other companies are urged to franchise by unqualified consultants or advisers who may be more interested in professional fees than in the long-term success of the franchising program. This has caused financial distress and failure on both the franchisor and franchisee sides, usually resulting in litigation. Current and future members of the franchising community must be urged to take a responsible view toward the creation and development of their franchising programs.

Responsible franchising starts with an understanding of the key components of the business structure. There are three critical components of the franchise system—the brand, the operating system, and the ongoing support provided by you, as the franchisor, to the franchisee. The brand creates the demand, allowing the franchisee to initially *obtain* customers. The brand includes your trademarks and service marks, your trade dress and decor, and all of the intangible factors that create customer loyalty and build brand equity. The operating system essentially "delivers the promise," thereby allowing the franchisee to *maintain* customer relationships and build loyalty. The ongoing support and training provide the impetus for growth, providing the franchisee with the tools and tips to expand its customer base and build its market share. The responsibly built franchise system is one that provides value to its franchisees by teaching them how to get and keep as many customers as possible, who consume as many products and services as possible, as often as possible. In fact, most litigation in franchising revolves around the gap between the actual needs of the franchisees to remain competitive in the marketplace and the reality of the support the franchisor is capable of providing. Unless the franchisor delivers on its promises and is committed to providing excellent initial and ongoing training and support, the disappointment begins during the recruitment phase of the relationship and continues beyond the start-up as the franchisee struggles to remain competitive.

Reasons for Franchising

Successful growing companies cite many reasons why they

selected franchising as a method of growth and distribution. These reasons include:

- **Obtaining operating efficiencies** and economies of scale;
- **Achieving more rapid market penetration** at a lower capital cost;
- **Reaching the targeted consumer more effectively** through cooperative advertising and promotion;
- **Selling products and services to a dedicated network** of franchisees;
- **Replacing the need for internal personnel** with motivated owner-operators; and
- **Shifting the primary responsibility for site selection,** employee training and personnel management, local advertising, and other administrative concerns to the franchisee, licensee or joint-venture partner (with your guidance).

In the typical franchising relationship, the franchisee shares the risk of expanding the market share of the growing company by committing its capital and resources to the development of satellite locations modeled after the proprietary business format of the growing company. The risk of business failure of the growing company is further reduced by the improvement in competitive position, reduced vulnerability to cyclical fluctuations, the existence of a captive market for the growing company's proprietary products and services (due to the network of franchisees), and the reduced administrative and overhead costs enjoyed by a growing company.

The Foundation for Franchising

Responsible franchising is the only way that growing companies and franchisees will be able to harmoniously co-exist in the 21st century. Responsible franchising means that there must be a secure foundation from which the franchising program is launched. Closely held and family-owned businesses that are considering franchising as a method of growth and distribution, or as a transition strategy, must understand the components of this foundation. The key components are as follows:

A PROVEN PROTOTYPE (either a single store or chain of stores) that will serve as a basis for the franchising program. The store or stores (or service-based operations) must have been tested, refined and operated successfully and must be consistently profitable. The success of the prototype should not be overly dependent on your physical presence or specific expertise.

A STRONG MANAGEMENT TEAM made up of internal officers and directors (as well as qualified consultants) who understand both your particular industry and the legal and business aspects of franchising as a method of expansion.

SUFFICIENT CAPITALIZATION TO LAUNCH and sustain the franchising program. There should be capital available for you to provide both initial and ongoing support and assistance to franchisees. The lack of a well-prepared business plan and adequate capital is the principal cause of the demise of many early-stage franchisors.

A DISTINCTIVE AND PROTECTED TRADE IDENTITY that includes federal and state registered trademarks as well as a uniform trade appearance, signage, slogans, trade dress and overall image.

PROPRIETARY AND PROVEN METHODS OF OPERATION and management that can be conveyed in writing in a comprehensive operations manual, not be too easily duplicated by competitors, maintain its value to the franchisees over an extended period of time, and be enforced through clearly drafted and objective quality-control standards.

A COMPREHENSIVE TRAINING PROGRAM FOR FRANCHISEES that integrates all of the latest education and training technologies. Training should take place both at your headquarters and on site at the franchisee's proposed location, both at the outset of the relationship and on an ongoing basis.

FIELD SUPPORT STAFF WHO ARE SKILLED TRAINERS and communicators, and who are available to visit, inspect, and periodically assist franchisees and monitor quality-control standards.

A SET OF COMPREHENSIVE LEGAL DOCUMENTS that reflect the company's business strategies and operating policies. Offering documents must be prepared in accordance with applicable federal and state disclosure laws. Franchise agreements should strike a delicate balance between the rights and obligations of the growing company and the franchisee.

A DEMONSTRATED MARKET DEMAND FOR THE PRODUCTS and services you developed that will be distributed through the franchisees. Your products and services should meet certain minimum quality standards, be proprietary in nature, and not be faddish or subject to rapid shifts in consumer preferences. Market research and analysis should be sensitive to trends in the economy and specific industry, the plans of direct and indirect competitors, and shifts in consumer preferences.

A CAREFULLY DEVELOPED SET OF UNIFORM SITE-SELECTION CRITERIA and architectural standards that can be readily and affordably secured in today's competitive real estate market.

A GENUINE UNDERSTANDING OF THE COMPETITION (both direct and indirect) that you'll face in marketing and selling franchises to prospective franchisees, as well as the competition the franchisee will face when marketing products and services.

RELATIONSHIPS WITH SUPPLIERS, LENDERS, REAL ESTATE DEVELOPERS and others, which are described in the operations manual and provide cost savings, volume discounts and preferred-customer services to your network of franchisees.

A FRANCHISEE PROFILE AND SCREENING SYSTEM that will identify the minimum financial qualifications, business acumen and understanding of the industry required of a successful franchisee.

AN EFFECTIVE SYSTEM OF REPORTING AND RECORD KEEPING to monitor the performance of the franchisees and ensure that royalties are reported accurately and paid promptly.

RESEARCH AND DEVELOPMENT CAPABILITIES for introducing new products and services to consumers through the franchised network on an ongoing basis.

A COMMUNICATION SYSTEM that promotes a continuing and open dialogue with the franchisees, and as a result reduces the chances for conflict and litigation.

NATIONAL, REGIONAL AND LOCAL ADVERTISING, marketing and public relations programs designed to recruit prospective franchisees as well as consumers to the sites operated by franchisees.

Regulatory Issues

The offer and sale of a franchise is regulated at both the federal and state levels. At the federal level, the Federal Trade Commission's Rule 436 specifies the minimum amount of disclosure that must be made to a prospective franchisee in any of the 50 states. In addition to the Federal Trade Commission rule, more than a dozen states have adopted their own regulations for the offer and sale of franchises within their borders. Known as the registration states, these states generally require a more detailed disclosure format, known as the Uniform Franchise Offering Circular (UFOC). The registration states are: California, Hawaii, Illinois, Indiana, Maryland, Michigan, Minnesota, New York, North Dakota, Rhode Island, South Dakota, Virginia, Washington and Wisconsin.

Each of the registration states has slightly different procedures and requirements for the approval of a growing company prior to authorizing its offers and sales. In all cases, however, a package of disclosure documents is assembled; it consists of a UFOC, franchise agreement, supplemental agreements, financial statements, franchise roster, an acknowledgment-of-receipt form and the special disclosures required by each state. These could include corporation verification statements, salesperson disclosure forms and consent-to-service-or-process documents. The specific requirements of each state should be checked carefully by the principals of the business and its counsel.

Joint Ventures

Another exit strategy available to closely held and family-owned businesses is a legal structure known as a "joint venture," which is most often used to leverage a company's growth and expansion, rather than having the founder invest additional capital on his or her own. A joint venture is structured as a partnership or as a newly-formed co-owned corporation where two or more parties are brought together to achieve a series of strategic and financial objectives on a short-term or a long-term basis. But the structure can also provide for a full or partial exit strategy. Small-business owners who wish to explore this strategy should give careful thought to the type of partner they're looking for and what resources the partner will contribute to the newly formed entity. Much like parents raising a child, each partner will make its respective contribution of skills and resources.

Regardless of the specific structure, the industry or even the purpose of the strategic relationship, all successful joint-venture and strategic-alliance relationships share a common set of factors essential to success. These factors include:

- **a complementary unified force** or purpose that bonds the companies together;
- **a management team committed at all levels to the success** of the venture, free from politics or personal agendas;
- **a genuine synergy,** where the sum of the whole exceeds its individual parts
- **a cooperative culture and spirit** among the strategic partners that creates trust, resource sharing and a friendly chemistry among the parties;
- **a degree of flexibility in the joint venture's objectives** to allow for changes in technology and in the marketplace;
- **an alignment of management styles and operational methods,** at least to the extent that they affect the underlying project (as in the case of a strategic alliance) or the management of the new company (as in the case of a formal joint venture); and
- **high levels of focus and leadership** from all key parties that are necessary to the success of *any* new venture or business enterprise.

CHAPTER ELEVEN PARTING COMPANY

Embarking on a search for a joint-venture partner is a bit like the search for an appropriate spouse. Take care to conduct a thorough review of prospective candidates and do extensive due diligence on the final few you consider. Develop a list of key objectives and goals to be achieved by the joint venture or licensing relationship, and compare this list with the benefits offered by your final list of candidates. Take the time to understand the corporate culture and decision-making process within each company. Consider the following issues: (1) How do each company's processes fit with your own? (2) What is each prospective partner's previous experience and track record with other joint-venture relationships? (3) Why did these previous relationships succeed or fail?

In many cases, small companies looking for joint-venture partners select a much larger Goliath offering a wide range of financial and non-financial resources that will allow the smaller company to achieve its growth plans. The motivating factor for the larger company is to get access and distribution rights to new technologies, products and services. In turn, the larger company offers access to pools of capital, research and development, personnel, distribution channels, and general contacts that the small company desperately needs.

But proceed carefully. Be sensitive to the politics, red tape and management practices in place at a large company that may be foreign to many small firms. Try to distinguish between what is being promised and what will actually be delivered. If the primary motivating force for the small firm is really only capital, then consider whether alternative (and perhaps less costly) sources of money have been thoroughly explored. Ideally, a large joint-venture partner will offer a lot more than money. If the primary motivating force is access to technical personnel, then consider whether it might be a better decision to purchase these resources separately, than to enter into a partnership in which you give up a certain measure of control. Also, consider whether strategic relationships or extended-payment terms with vendors and consultants can be arranged in lieu of the joint venture.

Consider the following key strategic issues before and during joint-venture or strategic-alliance negotiations:

- **Exactly what types of tangible and intangible assets** will be contributed to the joint venture by each party? Who will have ownership rights in the property contributed during the term of the joint venture and thereafter? Who will own property developed as a result of joint development efforts?
- **What covenants of nondisclosure or noncompetition** will be expected of each party during the term of the agreement and thereafter?
- **What timetables or performance quotas for completion** of the projects contemplated by the joint venture will be included in the agreement? What are the rights and remedies of each party if these performance standards are not met?
- **How will issues of management and control be addressed** in the agreement? What will be the respective voting rights of each party? What are the procedures in the event of a major disagreement or deadlock? What is the fallback plan?

Once you and your prospective joint-venture partner have discussed all of the preliminary issues, a formal joint-venture agreement or corporate shareholders' agreement should be prepared with the assistance of counsel. The precise terms of the agreement will naturally depend on the specific objectives of the parties.

Licensing

Licensing can be viewed as an exit strategy in that you are no longer directly responsible for the financial investment or day-to-day management needed to fuel future growth and expansion. Rather, this financial responsibility is shifted to the parties to whom you grant licenses to use your intellectual property. These licensees pay you initial license fees and royalties for the right to use your technology or brand name. Over time, this income stream can be a very valuable and lucrative asset around which to build an estate plan. Your transition from an active player to a passive one reduces the need for management and succession issues because over time the closely held company has only limited day-to-day operations and becomes a holding company that receives and distributes licensing fees.

Licensing is a contractual method of developing and exploiting intellectual property by transferring rights of use to third parties without the transfer of ownership. Virtually any proprietary product or service may be the subject of a license agreement, ranging from the licensing of the Mickey Mouse character by Walt Disney Studios in the 1930s to modern-day licensing of computer software and high technology. From a legal perspective, licensing involves complex issues of contract, tax, antitrust, international, tort and intellectual-property law. From a business perspective, licensing involves weighing the economic and strategic advantages of licensing against other methods of bringing the product or service to the marketplace, such as direct sales, distributorships or franchises.

Many of licensing's benefits to a growing company closely parallel the advantages of franchising, namely:

- **spreading the risk and cost of development** and distribution;
- **achieving more-rapid market penetration;**
- **earning initial license fees** and ongoing royalty income;
- **enhancing consumer loyalty** and goodwill;
- **preserving the capital** that would otherwise be required for internal growth and expansion;
- **testing new applications for existing** and proven technology; and
- **avoiding or settling litigation** regarding a dispute over ownership of the technology.

Licensing's disadvantages are also similar to those of franchising, such as:

- **a somewhat diminished ability to enforce quality-control** standards and specifications;
- **a greater risk of another party infringing** upon the licensor's intellectual property;
- **a dependence on the skills,** abilities and resources of the licensee as a source of revenue;
- **difficulty in recruiting, motivating** and retaining qualified and competent licensees;

- **the risk that the licensor's entire reputation** and goodwill may be damaged or destroyed by the acts of a single licensee; and
- **the administrative burden of monitoring** and supporting the operations of the network of licensees.

Failure to consider all of the costs and benefits of licensing could easily result in a poor strategic decision or getting stuck with the terms of an unprofitable license agreement. This could be due to either an underestimate of the licensee's need for technical assistance and support, or an overestimate of the market demand for your products and services. To avoid such problems, you should conduct a certain amount of due diligence prior to engaging in any serious negotiations with a prospective licensee. This preliminary investigation will generally include market research; legal steps to fully protect intellectual property; and an internal financial analysis of the technology with respect to pricing, profit margins and costs of production and distribution. It will also include a more specific analysis of the prospective licensee with respect to its financial strength, research and manufacturing capabilities, and reputation in the industry. Once the decision has been made to enter into more formal negotiations, the terms and conditions of the license agreement should be discussed. Naturally, these provisions will vary, depending on whether the license is for merchandising an entertainment property, exploiting a given technology or distributing a particular product to an original-equipment manufacturer or value-added reseller.

There are two principal types of licensing: (a) technology licensing, where the strategy is to find a licensee for exploitation of industrial and technological developments; and (b) merchandise and character licensing, where the strategy is to license a recognized trademark or copyright to a manufacturer of consumer goods in markets not currently served by the licensor.

Technology Licensing

The principal purpose behind technology transfer and licensing agreements is to make a marriage between the technology proprietor, as licensor, and the organization that possesses the resources to properly develop and market the technology, as licensee. This marriage is made between companies and inventors of all shapes and sizes. But it's often in the context of an entrepreneur that has the technology but lacks the resources to adequately penetrate the marketplace, as licensor, and the larger company, which has sufficient research-and-development, production, human resources and marketing capability to make the best use of the technology. The industrial and technological revolution has a history of very successful entrepreneurs who have relied on the resources of larger organizations to bring their products to market, such as Chester Carlson (xerography), Edwin Land (Polaroid cameras), Robert Goddard (rockets) and Willis Carrier (air conditioning). As the base for technological development becomes broader, large companies look not only to entrepreneurs and small businesses for new ideas and technologies, but also to each other, to foreign countries, to universities, and federal and state governments to serve as licensors of technology.

In a typical licensing arrangement, you, as the proprietor of intellectual-property rights (patents, trade secrets, trademarks and know-how) permit a licensee to make use of these rights, according to a set of specified conditions and circumstances set forth in a license agreement. Licensing agreements can be limited to a very narrow component of your intellectual-property rights, such as one specific application of a single patent, or be much broader in context, such as in a "technology-transfer" agreement, where an entire bundle of intellectual-property rights is transferred to the licensee in exchange for initial fees and royalties. The classic technology-transfer arrangement is actually closer to a "sale" of the intellectual property rights, with a right by the licensor to get the intellectual property back if the licensee fails to meet its obligations under the agreement. An example of this type of transaction might be bundling a proprietary environmental cleanup system together with technical support and training services to a master overseas licensee with reversionary rights in the event of a breach of the agreement or the failure to meet a set of performance standards. As a general rule, any well-drafted technology-license agreement should address the following topics:

SCOPE OF THE GRANT. The exact scope and subject matter of the license must be initially addressed and carefully defined in the license agreement. Any restrictions on the geographic scope, rights of use, permissible channels of trade, restrictions on sublicensing, limitations on assignability or exclusion of improvements to the technology (or expansion of the character line) covered by the agreement should be clearly set forth in this section.

TERM AND RENEWAL. The commencement date, duration, renewals and extensions, conditions to renewal, procedures for providing notice of intent to renew, grounds for termination, obligations upon termination, and your reversionary rights in the technology should all be included in this section.

PERFORMANCE STANDARDS AND QUOTAS. To the extent that the payments to you or your estate by the licensees will be dependent on royalty income, which will be calculated from the licensee's gross or net revenues, you may want to impose certain minimum levels of performance in terms of sales, advertising and promotional expenditures and human resources to be devoted to the exploitation of the technology. Naturally, the licensee will argue for a "best efforts" provision that is free from performance standards and quotas. In such cases, you may want to insist on a minimum royalty level that will be paid regardless of the licensee's actual performance.

PAYMENTS TO THE LICENSOR. Virtually every type of license agreement will include some form of initial payment and ongoing royalty to the licensor. Royalty formulas vary widely, however, and may be based upon gross sales, net sales, net profits, a fixed sum per product sold or a minimum payment to be made to you over a given period of time), or may include a sliding scale in order to provide some incentive to the licensee as a reward for performance.

QUALITY-CONTROL ASSURANCE AND PROTECTION. You must spell out quality-control standards and specifications for the production, marketing and distribution of the products and services covered by the license. In addition, include in the agreement procedures that allow you an opportunity to enforce these standards and specifications, such as a right to inspect the licensee's premises, a right to review, approve or reject samples produced by the licensee, and a right to review and approve any packaging, labeling or advertising materials to be used in connection with the exploitation of the products and services that are within the scope of the license.

INSURANCE AND INDEMNIFICATION. You should take all necessary and reasonable steps to ensure that the licensee has an obligation to protect and indemnify you against any claims or liabilities resulting from the licensee's exploitation of the products and services covered by the license.

ACCOUNTING, REPORTS AND AUDITS. You must impose certain reporting and record keeping procedures on the licensee in order to ensure an accurate accounting for periodic royalty payments. Further, you should reserve the right to audit the licensee's records in the event of a dispute or discrepancy, along with provisions as to who will be responsible for the cost of the audit in the event of an understatement.

DUTIES TO PRESERVE AND PROTECT INTELLECTUAL PROPERTY. The obligations of the licensee, its agents and employees to preserve and protect the confidential nature and acknowledge the ownership of the intellectual property being disclosed in connection with the license agreement must be carefully defined. Any required notices or legends that must be included on products or materials distributed in connection with the license agreement (such as those describing the status of the relationship or naming the owner of the intellectual property) are also described.

TECHNICAL ASSISTANCE, TRAINING AND SUPPORT. Your obligation (if any) to assist the licensee in the development or exploitation of the subject matter being licensed is included in this section of the agreement. The assistance may take the form of personal services or documents and records. Either way, any fees due to the licensor for such support services that are over and above the initial license and ongoing royalty fee must also be addressed.

WARRANTIES OF THE LICENSOR. A prospective licensee may demand that you provide certain representations and warranties in the license agreement. These may include warranties regarding the ownership of the technology, such as absence of any known infringements of the technology or restrictions on the ability to license the technology. They may warrant that the technology has the features, capabilities and characteristics previously represented in the negotiations.

INFRINGEMENTS. The license agreement should contain procedures under which the licensee must notify you of any known or suspected direct or indirect infringements of the subject matter being licensed. The responsibilities for the cost of protecting and defending the technology should also be specified in this section.

Merchandise- and Character-Licensing Agreements

The use of commonly recognized trademarks, brand names, sports teams, athletes, universities, television and film characters, musicians and designers who use their recognized names to promote their image and reputation as well as foster the sales of specific products and services are at the heart of today's merchandise- and character-licensing environment. Manufacturers and distributors of a wide range of products and services license these words, images and symbols, which are then applied to everything from clothing to housewares to toys to posters. Certain brand names and characters have withstood the test of time, while others are fads and fall prey to shifts in consumer preferences, the selection of subpar licensees and stiff competition.

The trademark and copyright owners of these properties and character images are motivated to license for a number of reasons. Aside from the obvious desire to earn royalty fees and profits, many manufacturers view this licensing strategy as a form of merchandising to promote the underlying prod-

CHAPTER ELEVEN PARTING COMPANY

uct or service. The licensing of a trademark for application on a line of clothing helps to establish and reinforce brand awareness at the consumer level. For example, when R.J. Reynolds Tobacco licensed a leisure-apparel manufacturer to produce a line of Camel wear, the hope was to sell more cigarettes, appeal to the lifestyle of their targeted consumers, maintain consumer awareness and enjoy the royalty income from the sale of the clothing line. Similar strategies have been adopted by manufacturers in order to revive a mature brand or failing product. In certain instances, the spinoff product that has been licensed has been almost as financially successful as the product that it was originally intended to promote, for example, the Harley-Davidson clothing and merchandise which nearly outsells the motorcycles!

Brand-name owners, celebrities and academic institutions must be very careful not to grant too many licenses too quickly. The financial rewards of a flow of royalty income from hundreds of different manufacturers can be quite seductive, but they must be weighed against the possible loss of quality control and dilution of the name, logo or character. The loyalty of the licensee network is also threatened when too many licenses are granted in closely competing products. Retailers will also become cautious when purchasing licensed goods from a licensee if there is a fear that quality has suffered or that the popularity of the licensed character, celebrity or image will be short-lived. This may result in smaller orders and an overall unwillingness to carry inventory. This is especially true in the toy industry, where purchasing decisions are being made by (or at least influenced by) the whims of a 5-year-old child who may strongly identify with a given television or movie character one week and then turn his or her attention to a different character the next week. It is incumbent on the manufacturers and licensees to develop advertising and media campaigns to hold the consumer's attention for an extended period of time. Only then will the retailer be convinced of the potential longevity of the product line. This will require balancing the risks and rewards between licensor and licensee in the character-licensing agreement, in the areas of compensation to the licensor, advertising expenditures by the licensee, scope of the exclusivity and quality-control standards and specifications.

In the merchandise-licensing community, the name, logo, symbol or character is typically referred to as the "property" and the specific product or product line (for example, the T-shirts, mugs or posters) is referred to as the "licensed product." This area of licensing offers opportunities and benefits to both the owners of the properties and the manufacturers of the licensed products. For the owner of the property, brand recognition, goodwill and royalty income are strengthened and expanded. For the manufacturer of the licensed products, there is an opportunity to leverage the goodwill of the property to improve sales of the licensed products. The manufacturer has an opportunity to "hit the ground running" in the sale of merchandise by gaining access to and use of an already established brand name or character image.

Naturally, each party should conduct due diligence on the other. From your perspective as licensor, the manufacturer of the licensed product as licensee should demonstrate an ability to meet and maintain quality standards, possess financial stability, and offer an aggressive and well-planned marketing and promotional strategy. From the licensee's perspective, you as the brand owner should display a certain level of integrity and commitment to quality, disclose your future plans for the property's promotion and be willing to participate and assist in the overall marketing of the licensed products. For example, if a star basketball player were unwilling to appear at promotional events designed to sell his own specially licensed line of basketball shoes, this would present a major problem and would likely lead to a premature termination of the licensing relationship.

There are several key areas that must be addressed in the preparation and negotiation of a merchandise-licensing agreement. These include:

- **scope of the territorial** and product exclusivity;
- **assignability** and sublicensing rights;
- **the definition of the property** and the licensed products;
- **quality control** and approval;
- **ownership of artwork** and designs;
- **term-renewal rights** and termination of the relationship;

- **initial license** and ongoing royalty fees;
- **performance criteria** for the licensee;
- **liability insurance;**
- **indemnification;**
- **duty to pursue trademark** and copyright infringement;
- **minimum advertising** and promotional requirements;
- **accounting and record keeping** of the licensee;
- **inspection and audit rights** of the licensor;
- **rights of first refusal** for expanded or revised characters and images;
- **limitations on licensee's distribution** to related or affiliated entities;
- **representations and warranties** of the licensor with respect to its rights to the property;
- **availability of the licensor** for technical and promotional assistance; and
- **miscellaneous provisions,** such as law to govern, nature of the relationship, and required notices.

Federal Agencies

U.S. Small Business Administration (SBA)
1100 Vermont Avenue, NW
Washington, DC 20416
(800) 827-5722
www.sba.gov
Offers a wide variety of financing programs, workshops and seminars, management and technical assistance, typically through its many district offices.

U.S. Department of Commerce (DOC)
Herbert C. Hoover Building
14th Street & Constitution Ave., NW
Washington, DC 20230
(800) 734-2235
www.doc.gov
Offers a wide variety of programs and services relating to economic development, international trade and minority business. The U.S. Patent and Trademark Office (800-786-9199) is a division of the DOC which processes federal patent and trademark applications and publishes various resources on the protection of intellectual property.

Internal Revenue Service
1111 Constitution Avenue, NW
Washington, DC 20224
(800) 829-1040
www.irs.ustreas.gov
Offers resources and assistance on estate tax issues and Internal Revenue Code clarifications.

State Agencies

A comprehensive state-by-state directory is beyond the scope of this directory. Virtually every state has at least one office or agency responsible for coordinating programs and assistance for small, closely held and minority-owned businesses. These various state programs offer a wide range of services, from technical assistance to advocacy to financial support. Each state "houses" the small business division in a slightly different place, but a safe place to start is with a call to the state's Department of Commerce or Department of Economic Development. A few states, such as California (916-324-1295), Connecticut (860-258-4200), Illinois (217-524-5856), and Minnesota (800-657-3858) have stand-alone Offices of Small Business. Many states offer training programs, seminars, publications, and even tax breaks to foster and encourage the growth of small businesses. The Chambers of Commerce in each state are also an excellent starting point for determining the availability and extent small business development programs in a given region.

Trade Associations

There are thousands of trade associations, networking groups, venture clubs, and other organizations that directly or indirectly focus on the needs of small business owners, entrepreneurs, growing companies, women-owned businesses, minority-owned businesses, importers and exporters, and virtually every other group that shares common interests. Some of the more established groups with a genuine nationwide presence and solid track record include:

U.S. Chamber of Commerce
1615 H Street, NW
Washington, DC 20062
(202-659-6000)
www.uschamber.org
The U.S. Chamber of Commerce represents 215,000 businesses, 3000 state and local chambers of commerce, 1200 trade and professional associations, and 72 American Chambers of Commerce abroad. It works with these groups to support national business

interests and includes a Small Business Center (202-463-5503).

Alliance of Independent Store Owners and Professionals (AISOP)
PO Box 2014 Loop Station
Minneapolis, MN 55402
(612) 340-1568
AISOP was organized to protect and promote fair postal and legislative policies for small business advertisers. Most of its more than 4,000 members are independent small businesses that rely on reasonable third-class mail rates to promote their businesses and contact customers in their trade areas.

American Entrepreneurs Association
2392 Morse Avenue,
Irvine, CA 92714
(800) 482-0973
The American Entrepreneurs Association was established to provide small business owners with benefits and discounts that are otherwise generally reserved for big businesses, such as express shipping, health insurance, long-distance telephone rates).

American Small Business Association (ASBA)
1800 North Kent Street
Suite 901
Arlington, VA 22209
(800) ASBA-911
www.asbaonline.org
ASBA's membership base consists of small business owners with 20 or fewer employees. ASBA members have access to the same advantages that larger corporations enjoy through member benefits and services.

National Association of Development Companies (NADCO)
4301 N. Fairfax Drive
Suite 860
Arlington, VA 22203
(703) 812-9000
www.nadco.org

NADCO is the trade group of community-based, non-profit organizations that promote small business expansion and job creation through the SBA's 504 loan program, known as Certified Development Companies (CDC).

National Association of Manufacturers (NAM)
1331 Pennsylvania Avenue, NW
Suite 1500 North
Washington, DC 20004
(202) 637-3000
www.nam.org
NAM serves as the voice of the manufacturing community and is active on all issues concerning manufacturing, including legal system reform, regulatory restraint, and tax reform.

National Association for the Self-Employed (NASE)
2121 Precinct Line Road
Hurst, TX 76054
(800) 232-6273
www.nase.org
NASE helps its members become more competitive by providing over 100 benefits that save money on services and equipment. NASE's members consists primarily of small business owners with few or no employees.

National Federation of Independent Business (NFIB)
53 Century Boulevard, Suite 300
Nashville, TN 37214

600 Maryland Avenue, SW, Suite 700
Washington, DC 20024
(800) 634-2669
(800) 552-6342
www.nfibonline.com
NFIB disseminates educational information about free enterprise, entrepreneurship, and small business. The organization represents more than 60,000 small and independent businesses before legislatures and government agencies at the federal and state level.

National Small Business United (NSBU)
1155 15th Street, NW
Suite 710
Washington, DC 20005
(202) 293-8830
www.nsbu.org
The NSBU is a membership-based association of business owners that presents small business's point of view to all levels of government and the Congress.

National Association of Women Business Owners (NAWBO)
1100 Wayne Avenue
Suite 830
Silver Spring, MD 20910
(800) 55-NAWBO
www.nawbo.org
NAWBO uses its collective influence to broaden opportunities for women in business, and is the only dues-based national organization representing the interests of all women entrepreneurs in all types of business.

National Center for Employee Ownership (NCEO)
1201 Martin Luther King, Jr. Way
Second Floor
Oakland, CA 94612
(510) 272-9461
www.nceo.org
NCEO is a private, non-profit membership and information organization. Supported by its members and services, NCEO serves as the leading source of accurate, unbiased information on ESOPs and other forms of employee ownership.

National Association for Female Executives (NAFE)
30 Irving Place
5th Floor
New York, NY 10003
(800) 285-NAFE
www.nafe.com
Through education and networking programs, NAFE helps

women share the resources and techniques needed to succeed in the competitive business world.

National Business League (NBL)
1511 K Street, NW
Suite 432
Washington, DC 20005
(202) 737-4430
www.thenbl.com
NBL is primarily involved in business development among African Americans and serves as a voice for black business on Capitol Hill and in the federal government.

U.S. Hispanic Chamber of Commerce
1030 15th Street, NW
Suite 206
Washington, DC 20005
(202) 842-1212
www.ushcc.com
The Hispanic Chamber advocates the business interests of Hispanics and develops minority business opportunities with major corporations and at all levels of government.

Colleges and Universities

There are also a wide variety of universities and other organizations that have established research centers that focus on family business and succession planning issues, including:

Tulane University Family Business Center
A.B. Freeman School of Business
7 McAlister Drive
New Orleans, LA 70118
(504) 865-5306
www.freeman.tulane.edu

Northeastern University's Center for Family Business
370 Common Street
Dedham, MA 02026

(617) 320-8015
www.fambic.com/orgs/necfb

University of Toledo Center for Family Business
College of Business
Toledo, OH 43606
(419) 530-4058

Kennesaw State University Family Enterprise Center
1000 Chastin
Kennesaw, GA 30144
(770) 423-6045
www.kennesaw.edu/fec

The Florida International University's Family Business Institute
FIU—University Park Campus
FBI—BA332
College of Business Administration
Miami, FL 33199
(305) 348-4237
www.fiu.edu

Baylor University Institute for Family Business
PO Box 98011
Waco, TX 76798
(817) 755-2265

Delaware Valley Family Business Center
1011 Cathill Road
Cellarsville, DE 18960
(800) 296-3832
www.dvfambus.com

University of Massachusetts Family Business Center
Division of Continuing Education
608 Goodell Building
Amherst, MA 01003
(413) 545-1537
www.umass.edu/fambiz

Loyola Center For Closely Held Firms
Loyola College
4501 North Charles Street
Baltimore, MD 21210
(800) 221-9107
www.loyola.edu/dept/chf/index.html

American University's Family Business Forum
American University
Kogod College of Business Administration
4400 Massachusetts Avenue, N.W.
Washington, DC 20016-8044
(202) 885-1897

The Partnership with Family Business
Weatherhead School of Management
Case Western Reserve University
10900 Euclid Avenue
Cleveland, OH 44106-7166
(216) 368-2041

The Cornell University Family Business Research Institute—Bronfenbrenner Life Course Center
102 MVR Hall
Cornell University
Ithaca, NY 14853-4401
(607) 255-2591

Creighton University Center for Family Business
College of Business Administration
Creighton University
2500 California Plaza
Omaha, NE 68178
(402) 280-5521

DePaul University Family Business Program
DePaul University
1 East Jackson Boulevard
Chicago, IL 60604

North Carolina Family Business Forum
Hartman Center, Fuqua School of Business
Duke University
Durham, NC 27708
(919) 660-7742

Family Business Forum
The George Rothman Institute of Entrepreneurial Studies
Fairleigh Dickinson University
285 Madison Avenue
Madison, NJ 07940
(201) 443-8842

Institute for Family Enterprise
1 Place Ville-Marie
Suite 3333
Montreal, Quebec, Canada H3B 3N2
(514) 877-6620

McMurray University Family Business Center
McMurray University
Fourteenth and Sayles Boulevard
Abilene, TX 79697
(915) 691-6430

Montana State University Family Business Program
College of Business
Montana State University—Bozeman
Bozeman, MT 59717-0304
(406) 994-6187
www.montana.edu/cob

The Jefferson Smurfit Center for Entrepreneurial Studies
School of Business Administration
Saint Louis University
221 North Grand Boulevard
St. Louis, MO 63103
(314) 977-3850
www.slu.edu/eweb/jsceshome.html

The Goering Center for Family/Private Business
University of Cincinnati
ML. 177
Cincinnati, OH 95221
(513) 556-7126

Family Business Program
School of Business Administration
University of Connecticut
Room 422B, U-41FB
368 Fairfield Road
Storrs, CT 06269-2041
(860) 486-4483
www.sba.uconn.edu/newcenters/fambus/index.html

The Family Business Center
College of Business and Public Administration
University of Louisville
Louisville, KY 40292
(502) 852-4792
www.cbpa.louisville.edu/fbc

The Family Business Forum
University of Memphis
Fogelman College of Business
Room 431
Memphis, TN 38152
(901) 678-4799

Family Business Institute
The University of San Diego
5998 Alcala Park
San Diego, CA 92110
(619) 260-4231

Center for Family Business
College of Business
University of Toledo
2801 West Bancroft Street

Toledo, OH 43606-3390
(419) 530-4058
www.utoledo.edu/mba/research.htm

Family Business Program
Marshall School of Business
University of Southern California
Bridge Hall One
Los Angeles, CA 90089-1421
(213) 740-0643

Australian Centre for Family Business
School of Business
Bond University
Gold Coast, Queensland, Australia
+61 (7)55-95-1161
www.bond.edu.au/bus

Institute for Family Enterprise
Bryant College Box A
1150 Douglas Pike
Smithfield, RI 02917-1284
(401) 232-6477

Austin Family Business Program at Oregon State University
201 Bexell Hall
College of Business
Corvallis, OR 97331-2603
(800) 859-7609
www.familybusinessonline.org

Industry-Specific Trade Associations and Foundations

The Family Firm Institute
221 North Beacon Street
Boston, MA 02135-1943

(617) 789-4200
www.ffi.org

Young Entrepreneurs' Organization (YEO)
1321 Duke Street
Suite 300
Alexandria, VA 22314
(703) 519-6700
www.yeo.org

National Foundation for Teaching Entrepreneurship to Handicapped and Disadvantaged Youth, Inc. (NFTE)
120 Wall Street, 29th Floor
New York, NY 10005
(800) FOR-NFTE
www.nfte.com

Council of Growing Companies
8260 Greensboro Drive
Suite 260
McLean, VA 22102
(800) 929-3165
www.ceolink.org

Opportunity International
360 W. Butterfield Road
Elmhurst, IL 60126
(708) 279-9300

American Electronics Association
1225 Eye Street, NW
Suite 950
Washington, DC 20005
(202) 682-9110
www.aeanet.org

American Farm Bureau Federation
225 W. Touhy Avenue
Park Ridge, IL 60068

(312) 399-5700
www.fb.com

American Society of Association Executives (ASAE)
1575 Eye Street, NW
Washington, DC 20005
(202) 626-2723

American Financial Services Association
919 18th Street, NW
Third Floor
Washington, DC 20006
(202) 296-5544
www.americanfinsvcs.com

National Retail Federation
325 Seventh Street, NW
Suite 1000
Washington, DC 20004
(800) NRF-HOW2
www.nrf.com

National Restaurant Association
1200 17th Street, NW
Washington, DC 20036
(800) 424-5156
www.restaurant.org

CEO Forums
Young President's Organization
Irving, TX
(800) 976-5556
www.ypo.org
150 chapters
MEMBERSHIP: 7,829 presidents and CEOs (39% family business) up to age 49, whose companies have more than 50 full-time employees.
MEETINGS: Monthly full-day meetings, half with outside speakers, half with private forum discussions.

ANNUAL DUES: National—$1,100. Chapter—varies.

Young Entrepreneurs' Organization
Alexandria, VA
(703) 519-6700
www.yeo.org
50 chapters
MEMBERSHIP: 1,200 members, no older than age 38; all are founders, co-founders, or controlling shareholders of a business with at least $1 million of sales.
MEETINGS: Two monthly meetings: a chapter education event plus a forum. Length varies.
ANNUAL DUES: National—$549 (plus 1-time $150 initiation fee). Chapter—$250 to $1,000.

Council of Growing Companies
McLean, VA
(800) 929-3165
20 chapters
MEMBERSHIP: 2,000 members in fast-growing businesses (half family owned) with $5 million to $1 billion of sales.
MEETINGS: Meet quarterly. National education and public policy meetings.
ANNUAL DUES: $1,000

Inc. Eagles CEO Program
Orlando, FL
(800) 900-4441
10 groups
MEMBERSHIP: 100 members (and growing) identified as the best CEOs in the market, based on financial performance, attitude, and aptitude.
MEETINGS: Meet 10 times a year for a day, focused on strategic issues. Preceded by one-on-one consultation with executive director to identify issues.
ANNUAL DUES: $7500 to $14,400 depending on size.

The Alternative Board
Denver, CO

(800) 219-7718
www.thealternativeboard.com
58 groups
MEMBERSHIP: 400 members with at least 10 employees and $750,000 sales; 60% are family businesses.
MEETINGS: Monthly meetings, 3 to 4 hours, directed at member issues, led by TAB-certified facilitator. No paid speakers.
ANNUAL DUES: $2,280 to $5,880 (depending on size and sophistication). Includes private consultations with TAB facilitator.

Entrepreneurs' Edge
San Diego, CA
(800) 274-2367
15 groups
MEMBERSHIP: 125 members. Must have 5 to 25 employees and sales of $750,000 to $3 million.
MEETINGS: Sponsored by TEC. Half-day monthly discussion meetings, plus quarterly meetings with paid speakers.
ANNUAL DUES: $5,400

Northeastern University Center for Family Business
Dedham, MA
(617) 320-8015
www.cba.neu.edu/alumni/fambiz.html
3 groups in Boston area
MEMBERSHIP: Members belong to 1 of 3 groups: leadership development; seniors' forum; women's forum.
MEETINGS: Bi-monthly meetings, 4 hours for leadership and seniors' groups; 2 hours for women's forum. Facilitated by the Center's executive director.
ANNUAL DUES: $2,200 Center dues per family, plus $475 for leadership and seniors' forums, $325 women's forum.

The Executive Committee
San Diego, CA
(800) 274-2367
275 groups
MEMBERSHIP: 4,000 members from companies with more than $3 million in sales; ⅓ to ½ are family businesses.

MEETINGS: Monthly all-day meeting. Half day paid outside speaker; half-day executive session devoted to members' discussions.
ANNUAL DUES: $8,700. Includes private consultation with TEC facilitator.

Small and Family Business Resources in Cyberspace

Hundreds of Web sites have been developed to provide resourceful support to family businesses, small-business owners and entrepreneurs. Here are some sites worth visiting that were up and running when this book went to press:

Small Business Advancement National Center
www.sbaer.uca.edu
Offers industry profiles, business plans, research articles, contact databases and loan information.

IdeaCafe
www.ideacafe.com/Welcome.html
Small-business meeting place.

Legaldocs
www.legaldocs.com
Low-cost legal forms.

eWeb
www.slu.edu/eweb
Information and resources for family and small businesses, including links to other Internet resources.

Venture Capital Institute
www.vcinstitute.org
Wide range of venture capital resources.

Small Business Resource Center
www.commnet.edu/nctc_sbrc
Offers dozens of tips to help make a small business a success.

Resource Directory

NetMarquee Family Business Net Center
www.fambiz.com
Offers articles and newsletters covering management issues of family-owned businesses.

Dun & Bradstreet Information
www.dnb.com
A comprehensive source of financial and demographic information.

Invest-O-Rama
www.investorama.com
Offers a directory of investment-related information such as the stock market, brokerage firms, mutual funds, and dividend and reinvestment plans.

The American Association of Individual Investors
www.aaii.org
Offers a basic guide to computerized investing and articles from the *AAII Journal* and *Computerized Investing*.

NETworth
www.quicken.com/investments
Offers information and links to mutual fund companies and online access to fund prospectuses.

EDGAR
www.sec.gov/edgarhp.htm
A database that contains all corporate annual and quarterly reports (and exhibits) filed with the Securities and Exchange Commission.

The Wall Street Journal's Interactive Edition
www.wsj.com
Allows users to access news and financial information about specified companies.

Center Court
www.centercourt.com

Offers extensive information on franchising and business opportunities.

Inc. Online
www.inc.com
Allows users to (1) build their own web sites; (2) read the current issue or browse through *Inc.* magazine's extensive archives; and (3) interact with other entrepreneurs, experts and *Inc.* editors.

Family Business Magazine
www.fambuspub.com
Selected articles from the print edition and other resources for family-business owners.

IFA Online
www.entremkt.com
Offers IFA's *Franchise Opportunities Guide*, *Franchising World*, bulletin boards, calendar of events and more for franchisors and franchisees.

Business Journal
www.amcity.com (home page)
Expert advice for small businesses on topics such as sales and marketing, technical, business financing, and tips on shopping for business products and services.

E-Span
http://www.espan.com
Used by human resource professionals to post jobs worldwide. Provides reference materials for human resource practitioners.

Monster Board
www.monster.com
Offers a variety of issues, from hiring to staffing to other related topics for human resource executives.

The Internet Mall
www.internetmall.com/career

Offers links to resume services, city job banks, career counseling and publications.

The Family Firm Institute
www.ffi.org
Offers a free directory of speakers and consultants as well as links to other family-business sites.

St. Louis University
www.slu.edu/eweb
An entrepreneurship-education site.

Austin Family Business Program at Oregon State University
www.familybusinessonline.org

Arthur Andersen Center for Family Business
www.arthurandersen.com/cfb

Family Business Roundtable
http://www.fbrinc.com

MassMutual Family Business Program
www.massmutual.com/fbn
Contains a discussion of the MassMutual/Gallup survey of family business owners and links to family business centers around the country.

Kaufman Center for Entrepreneurial Leadership
www.entreworld.org

Equity Financing Alternatives
There are a wide variety of resources available to identify possible sources of equity capital for growing a family business, which include:

Regional Investment Bankers Association (RIBA)
171 Church Street, Suite 260

Charleston, SC 29401
(803) 557-2000

Pratt's Guide to Venture Capital Firms
Published by Venture Economics (a subsidiary of Securities Data Publishing)
40 West 57th Street, Eleventh Floor
New York, NY 10019
(800) 455-5844

If you are considering the sale of your family or closely held business, the following resources may be useful:

International Business Brokers Association
11250 Roger Bacon Drive
Suite 8
Reston, VA 20190
(703) 437-4377
www.ibba.org

International Merger and Acquisition Professionals (IMAP)
3232 Cobb Parkway, Suite 437
Atlanta, GA 30339
(770) 319-7797
www.imap.com

Directory of M&A Intermediaries
c/o The Buyout Directories
40 West 57th Street
Eleventh Floor
New York, NY 10019
(212) 765-5311

Association for Corporate Growth
1926 Waukegan Road, Suite 100
Glenview, IL 60025
(800) 699-1331
www.acg.org

American Society of Appraisers (ASA)
555 Herndon Parkway, Suite 125
Herndon, VA 20170
(800) 272-8258
www.appraisers.org

APPENDIX | PARTING COMPANY

Legal Audit Checklist (Chapter 5)

Legal audits offer the small and growing company an inexpensive, yet comprehensive method of making sure that its plans and objectives are consistent with developments in the law. The process helps identify problem areas, maintain legal compliance, offer legal solutions and alternatives for the achievement of the company's short and long-term business objectives and forces a re-evaluation of the company's strategies in light of the legal costs, risks and problems that have been identified in the audit.

CORPORATE MATTERS

- **Under what form of ownership is the company operated?** When was this decision made? Does it still make sense? Why or why not?
- **Have all annual filings and related actions,** such as state corporate annual reports or required director and shareholder meetings been satisfied?
- **What are the company's capital requirements** in the next 12 months? How will this money be raised?
- **What alternatives are being considered?** What issues are triggered by these strategies?
- **Have applicable federal and state securities laws** been considered in connection with these proposed offerings?
- **Will key employees be offered equity** in the enterprise as an incentive for performance and loyalty? Is such equity available? Have the adoption of such plans been properly authorized? Will the plan be qualified or non-qualified? Up to what point?
- **Has anyone met with the key employees** to ascertain their goals and preferences?
- **Have all necessary stock option plans** and employment agreements been prepared and approved by the shareholders and directors of the corporation?
- **Will any of the founders of the company be retiring** or moving on to

other projects? How will this affect the current structure?
- **If the company is a corporation,** was an election under Subchapter S ever made? Why or why not If the entity is an S corporation, does it still qualify? Is such a choice unduly restrictive as the company grows (ability to attract foreign investment, taxation of undistributed earnings)?
- **If the entity is not a Subchapter S corporation,** could it still qualify? Is this a more sensible entity under the applicable tax laws? Or should a limited liability company (LLC) be considered as an alternative?
- **Have by-laws been prepared and carefully followed** in the operation and management of the corporation? Have annual meetings of shareholders and directors been properly held and conducted? Have the minutes of these meetings been properly and promptly entered into the corporate record book?
- **Have transactions "outside the regular course of business" been approved** or ratified by directors (or where required, by shareholder agreements or by laws) and resolutions recorded and entered into the corporate records?
- **Are there any "insider" transactions** or other matters that might constitute a conflict of interest? What "checks and balances" are in place to ensure that these transactions are properly handled?
- **Have quorum, notice, proxy and voting requirements** been met in each case under applicable state laws?
- **To what extent does the company's organizational** and management chart reflect reality?
- **Are customers and suppliers properly informed** of the limits of authority of the employees, officers or other agents of the company?

- **BUSINESS PLANNING MATTERS**
  - **Has a business and management plan been prepared?** Does it include information about the company's key personnel; strategic objectives; realistic and well documented financial statements; current and planned products and services; market data, strategy and evaluation of competition; capital structure and allocation of proceeds; capital formation needs; customer base; distribution network; sales and advertising strategies; facility and labor needs and risk factors?

Does it include realistic strategies and timetables for achieving objectives?
- **How and when was the business plan prepared?** Has it been reviewed and revised on a periodic basis, or is it merely collecting dust on a manager's bookshelf?
- **Has it been changed or supplemented** to reflect any changes in the company's strategic plans or objectives?
- **To whom has the plan been shown?** For what purposes? Have steps been taken to preserve the confidential nature of the document?
- **To what extent have federal and state securities laws** been reviewed to prevent violations from the misuse of the business plan as a disclosure document?

COMPLIANCE WITH GOVERNMENTAL AND EMPLOYMENT LAW REGULATIONS
- **Have all required federal and state tax forms been filed** (i.e., employer's quarterly and annual returns, federal and state unemployment tax contributions, etc.)?
- **Are federal and state recordkeeping requirements** being met for tax purposes?
- **Have all payroll and unemployment tax accounts** been established? Has the company been qualified to "do business" in each state where such filing is required?
- **Have all required local business permits** and licenses been obtained?
- **Are the company's operational policies in compliance** with OSHA, EEOC, NLRB and zoning requirements? Has the company ever had an external environmental law compliance audit performed?
- **Has the company developed policies and programs** related to smoking, substance-abuse testing, child labor laws, family leave or child care? Are these policies and programs in compliance with federal, state and local laws?
- **Have modifications been made to the workplace** in compliance with the Americans With Disabilities Act? Have steps been taken to ensure compliance with applicable laws regarding equal-employment opportunity, affirmative action, equal pay, wage and hours, immigration, employee benefit, and worker's compensation?
- **When did the company last consult these statutes** to ensure that

current practices are consistent with applicable laws?
- **Has an employment manual been prepared?** When was it last reviewed by qualified counsel?

EMPLOYEE BENEFIT PLANS
- **Has the company adopted a medical reimbursement plan?** Group life insurance? Retirement plans? Disability plans? If not, should they be adopted? If yes, have all amendments to the structure and ongoing manage-ment of these plans been made to maintain qualification?
- **Have annual reports been filed** with the U.S. Department of Treasury and U.S. Department of Labor for pension and profit-sharing plans?
- **Have there been any changes** in the administration of these plans? Have there been any recent transactions between the plan and the company, its trustees or its officers and directors?

CONTRACTUAL MATTERS
- **On which material contracts** is the company directly or indirectly bound? Were these agreements drafted in compliance with applicable laws, such as your state's version of the Uniform Commercial Code?
- **Is your company still able to meet its obligations** under these agreements? Is any party to these agreements in default? Why? What steps have been taken to enforce the company's rights or mitigate damages?
- **To what extent are contractual forms used** when selling company products and services? When were these forms last updated? Have these forms triggered any problems? What steps have been taken to resolve these problems?
- **Are employees who possess special skills** and experience under an employment agreement with the company? When was the last time the agreement was reviewed and revised? Are sales representatives of the company under some form of a written agree-ment and commission schedule? Has the scope of their authority been clearly defined and communicated to the third parties with whom they deal?
- **To what extent does the company hire independent contractors?** Have agreements been prepared with these parties? Have intellec-

tual-property considerations, such as "work for hire" provisions, been included in these agreements?

PROTECTION OF INTELLECTUAL PROPERTY
- **To what extent are trademarks, patents, copyrights** and trade secrets among the intangible assets of the business? What are the internal company procedures for these key assets?
- **What agreements** (such as ownership of inventions, nondisclosure and noncompete) have been struck with key employees who are exposed to the company's intellectual property?
- **What procedures are in place for receiving new ideas** and proposals from employees and other parties? What steps have been taken to protect the company's "trade dress," where applicable?
- **Have trademarks, patents and copyrights been registered?** What monitoring programs are in place to detect infringement and ensure proper usage by third parties?
- **Are documents properly stamped** with copyright and confidentiality notices?
- **Has counsel been contacted** to determine whether the new discovery is eligible for registration?
- **Does the company license any of its intellectual property** to third parties? Has experienced licensing and franchising counsel prepared the agreements and dis-closure documents?

RELATIONSHIPS WITH COMPETITORS
- **How competitive is your industry?** How aggressive is the company's approach towards its markets and competitors?
- **What incentives are offered** for attracting and retaining customers?
- **To what professional and trade associations** does the company belong? What type of information is exchanged?
- **Does the company engage in any type of communication** or have any cooperative agreement with a competitor regarding price, geographic territories or distribution channels that might constitute an antitrust violation or an act of unfair competition?
- **Has the company established an in-house program** in order to educate employees of the mechanics and pitfalls of antitrust violations?
- **Has an antitrust action ever been brought** or threatened by or

against the company? What were the surrounding facts? What was the outcome?
- **Have you recently hired a former employee of a competitor?** How was he or she recruited? Does this employee use skills or knowledge gained from the prior employer? To what extent has the prior employer been notified?
- **What steps are being taken to avoid a lawsuit** involving mis-appropriation of trade secrets and/or interference with contractual regulations?
- **Does the company engage in comparative advertising?** How are the products and services of the competitor generally treated?
- **Are any of your trademarks** or trade names similar to those of competitors? Have you been involved in any prior litigation with a competitor? Threatened litigation?

FINANCING MATTERS
- **What equity and debt financing have been obtained** in the past three years?
- **What continuing reporting obligations** or other affirmative/negative covenants remain in place? What triggers a default and what new rights are created to the investors or lenders upon default?
- **What security interests** remain outstanding?

MARKETING AND DISTRIBUTION ISSUES
- **Has the company clearly defined** the market for its products and services?
- **Who are the key competitors?** What are their respective market shares, strengths, weaknesses, strategies, and objectives?
- **What new players are entering this market?** What barriers exist to new entry?
- **What is the saturation point** of this market?
- **What are the key distribution channels** for bringing these products to the market? Have all necessary agreements and regulations affecting these channels been adequately addressed (i.e., labeling and warranty laws, consumer protection laws, pricing laws, distributorship agreements)
- **If the company is doing business abroad,** have all import/export regulations been carefully reviewed?

- **Has a system been established to ensure compliance** with the Foreign Corrupt Practices Act?

FRANCHISING STRATEGIES
- **Is the company considering franchising** as a method of marketing and distribution to expand market share?
- **To what extent can all key aspects** of the company's proven success be reduced to an operations manual and taught to others in a training program?
- **To what extent are competitors** engaged in franchising?
- **If franchising is appropriate** for distribution of the company's products or business, have all necessary offering documents and agreements been prepared by experienced franchise legal counsel?
- **What initial franchise fee will be charged?** Ongoing royalties? Are these fees competitive?
- **What ongoing programs and support are provided** to franchisees?
- **What products and services** must the franchisee buy from your company?
- **Under what conditions** may one franchise be terminated or transferred?
- **Are any alternatives to franchising** being considered? Has the company looked at dealer termination, multilevel marketing or pyramid laws?

Sample Shareholders' Agreement (Chapter 7)

THIS SHAREHOLDERS' AGREEMENT is made this [day] day of [month],[year] by and among [shareholder1], [shareholder2] and [shareholder3] (collectively referred to as the "Shareholders") and [company], a _____ corporation (the "Company").

Recitals:

Whereas, the Company has authorized capital stock consisting of _____ shares of Common Stock with a par value of _____ per share (the "Stock");

Whereas, the Shareholders are the record and beneficial owners of _____ (_____) shares of Stock of the Company as of the date hereof in the amounts set forth in Schedule 1 attached hereto and incorporated hereby;

Whereas, the Shareholders of the Company desire to provide continuity and effective management of the Company and to control the ownership of the Shares of the Company and thereby facilitate the operations and policies of the Company through certain provisions set forth hereunder;

Whereas, for purposes of this Agreement, any reference to "Shareholders" shall include only [shareholder1],[shareholder2], and [shareholder3]; and

Whereas, it is the intention of the Shareholders to restrict the transfer, encumbrance, pledge and assignment of the shares of Stock held by the Shareholders and to provide a market for the sale of such shares of Stock upon the death of a Shareholder and upon the occurrence of certain other events, as provided hereinafter in this Agreement.

Now, Therefore, in consideration of the mutual promises and agreements set forth herein, and for other good and valuable consideration, the receipt and sufficiency of which is hereby acknowledged, the parties hereto, intending to be legally bound, do hereby consent, promise and agree as follows:

Article I–Management

1.1 BOARD OF DIRECTORS. The Company's directors as of the date of this Agreement shall be the undersigned Shareholders. The Board of Directors (the "Board") shall take all corporate action deemed appropriate and necessary for the management of the Company.

1.2 OFFICERS. The following individuals shall serve as officers of the Company and shall continue to serve in such capacity at the discretion of the Board:

President _____

Vice President _____

Secretary _____

Treasurer _____

1.3 UNANIMOUS CONSENT REQUIRED. Subject to the requirements of applicable law, and until such time as the undersigned Shareholders are no longer the sole members of the Board, the affirmative vote of eighty percent (80%) of the issued and outstanding shares of the Company shall be required before any of the following actions set forth below may be taken by the Company:

(a) Amendment of the Articles of Organization and/or Bylaws of the Company or reconstitution or reclassification of the Board;

(b) Liquidation or dissolution of the Company; merger or consolidation involving the Company; or substantial alteration of the nature of the business conducted by the Company;

(c) The sale, lease, exchange, transfer, or disposition of all or substantially all of the assets or property of the Company or the purchase, lease, acquisition, sale, transfer, or disposition of personal property of the Company having a cost in excess of Two Hundred Fifty Thousand Dollars ($250,000);

(d) Borrowing, financing or refinancing (of any kind on any terms) or the lending of money on behalf of the Company reasonably expected to exceed Five Hundred Thousand Dollars ($500,000); and

(e) The execution of any contract, or series of contracts (including any mortgage, bond or lease) with any person or entity, and the performance, completion, assignment or rescission of any such contracts, in any instance where the consideration to be paid or received by the Company under any such contract(s) within a period of twelve (12) months is reasonably expected to exceed Five Hundred Thousand Dollars ($500,000).

1.4 EXECUTIVE COMMITTEE. _____ shall be allowed to hold himself out as Chairman of the Executive Committee during the term of this Agreement. This shall not be considered an officer position, unless approved by the Board, and shall be subject to the Board's redefining the goals of the Executive Committee, after good faith negotiation with _____, by way of an amendment to the Bylaws.

Article 2 – Transfer of Shares

2.1 TRANSFER RESTRICTIONS. No Shareholder shall sell, hypothecate, pledge, make a gift of, transfer, or otherwise dispose of any Stock (or any interest therein) owned by such Shareholder except in accordance with the provisions of this Agreement, or where the Company's Board has approved a merger, share exchange, consolidation, or other reorganization or recapitalization where the shares of Stock of the Company are in substantial part exchanged for or converted into securities of another corporation or cash (or both) or a debt restructuring requiring encumbrances on the Stock.

2.2 COMPANY/SHAREHOLDER OPTION. Each Shareholder and the Company hereby grants the other an option to purchase the Stock owned by such Shareholder, exercisable upon the occurrence of any of the events specified in Sections 2.3 and 2.4 below. The terms and conditions of the exercise of such option by a Shareholder is specified in Article 5; and the terms and conditions of the exercise of such option by the Company is specified in Articles 3 and 4 below.

2.3 RIGHT OF FIRST REFUSAL. Whenever a Shareholder receives from another person, who is neither a Permitted Transferee (as defined in Article 8) nor the Company, an offer to purchase shares of Stock (an "Offer") held by such Shareholder (the "Selling Shareholder"), and the Selling Shareholder is willing to accept such Offer (such offer to be in writing in a form legally enforceable against the Selling Shareholder and stating the potential transferee's name and address), the Selling Shareholder shall deliver to the Company a written notice stating the number of shares of Stock covered by the Offer and describing the disposition to be made, including the name of the person making the Offer (the "Offeror"), a full description of the purchase price therefor, and the other terms and conditions of the Offer. Upon receipt of such notice, the Company shall have the exclusive right and option to purchase all (but not less than all) of the shares of Stock described in the Selling Shareholder's notice for the same price and on the same other terms and conditions contained in the Offer. If either the Company or the other Shareholders do not exercise the option to purchase before expiration of the Option Period (as defined in Section 2.6 below), the Selling Shareholder shall have the right to transfer such shares of stock as provided in Article 7 hereof.

2.4 INVOLUNTARY TRANSFER. Whenever Stock owned by any Shareholder becomes subject to a right of involuntary transfer by operation of law such as (a) by a Shareholder becoming insolvent, (b) making a general assignment for the benefit of creditors or filing or having filed against him a petition in bankruptcy that is not dismissed within thirty (30) days from filing, (c) dying, or (d) being adjudicated incompetent; or upon the termination of such Shareholder's employ with the Company, either through his (i) termination by the Company, (ii) resignation or (iii) material failure to meet his obligations to the Company as such are reasonably determined by the Company's Board of Directors, the Company shall have the exclusive right and option to purchase all (but not less than all) of the shares of Stock owned by such Shareholder at the Purchase Price (defined in Section 3.3 below). A Shareholder subject to such an involuntary transfer shall be deemed a Selling Shareholder for purposes of this Agreement. Notwithstanding the foregoing sentence, if a Permitted Transferee holds shares of Stock due to an involuntary transfer by operation of law, such Permitted Transferee shall be free to hold such shares in accordance with the requirements of such involuntary transfer and neither the Company nor the other Shareholders shall have the purchase option described in this paragraph.

2.5 VOTING BY NON-INTERESTED SHAREHOLDERS AND DIRECTORS. A Selling Shareholder shall not be entitled to vote as a Shareholder or as a director, nor shall any nominee of such Selling Shareholder vote as a director, on the issue of whether the Company shall exercise its option to purchase shares of Stock owned by a Selling Shareholder and, if applicable, what the Purchase Price shall be therefor. In each such case, however, such Selling Shareholder or the directors nominated by the Selling Shareholder may, if present, be counted at any meeting for the purpose of establishing a quorum.

2.6 OPTION PERIOD. The "Option Period" shall be defined as a period of sixty (60) days following the day that the Company (i) receives from a Selling Shareholder a notice in compliance with Section 2.3 above; or (ii) receives actual notice of the existence of a right of involuntary transfer under Section 2.4 above; provided, however that the Option Period for exercise by a Shareholder shall commence on the earlier of the day that the Company's option expires or the Company declines or waives its option.

Article 3 – Option Exercise by the Company

3.1 EXERCISE OPTION AND NOTICE. Upon receipt by the Company of a notice of any event described in the preceding Article 2 (which creates an option to purchase shares of Stock), the Company shall have the exclusive right and option at any time before expiration of the Option Period to purchase all (but not less than all) of such shares of Stock at the Purchase Price (as defined in Section 3.3 below). The exercise of such option shall be effected by delivery of an exercise notice. Until the expiration or termination of the Option Period, no Shareholder shall have the right to take action, including any attempted disposition, with respect to the shares of Stock owned by the Selling Shareholder or subject to involuntary transfer.

3.2 COMPANY DESIGNEE. Whenever the Company shall exercise an option pursuant to Article 2 above, the Company shall have the right to designate, in the exercise notice, another person or persons to purchase all or part of the shares of Stock subject to such option. If it has not done so already, each designee shall execute and deliver to the Company a counterpart of this Agreement on or before the Closing Date. Notwithstanding any such designation, the Company shall have the primary obligation to perform all its obligations as the option holder and obligor hereunder and shall be discharged therefrom only to the extent that such designee renders due and timely performance of such obligations.

3.3 DEFINITION OF PURCHASE PRICE. "Purchase Price" shall mean (i) the price offered for the shares of Stock by an Offeror or (ii) the fair market value of the shares of Stock as of the date of the event triggering the sale or transfer of Stock as determined by the Board and the Selling Shareholder no later than the tenth (10th) day following notice of such event. In the event the Board cannot agree with the Selling Shareholder on the Purchase Price, the Purchase Price shall be determined by appraisal in accordance with the following provisions:

(a) The Board shall select an independent appraisal company ("Appraiser") to determine the value of the Company and the Stock; and
(b) In the event the Selling Shareholder disputes the Purchase Price established by the Board of Directors or the Appraiser, the

Selling Shareholder shall have the right (at his own expense) to have a second appraisal performed by an unrelated Appraiser. If the second appraisal is unacceptable to the Board, a third Appraiser shall be selected (and paid for mutually by the Board and the Selling Shareholder) whose appraisal shall be final.

Article 4 – Closing

Following the exercise of an option by the Company pursuant to the preceding Article 3, payment shall be made on the Closing Date at the office of the Company by certified or bank check payable to the order of the Selling Shareholder, in exchange for such Shareholder's delivery to the Company of a certificate or certificates representing the shares of Stock to be purchased (free and clear of any liens or encumbrances, registered in the name of such Selling Shareholder and duly endorsed in blank, or accompanied by a duly executed stock power in blank) with signature duly guaranteed and all requisite stock transfer stamps affixed. Failure to tender at the Closing Date a certificate or certificates in proper form for the shares of Stock to be purchased may (at the election of the Company) be excused, in which event any such missing or formally improper certificate or certificates shall be deemed surrendered and canceled and the Company shall pay the Purchase Price therefor by depositing and retaining such amount in trust for the benefit of such Shareholder to be paid and delivered to the Shareholder upon tender of such certificate in proper form or other documentary proof satisfactory to the Company.

Article 5 – Option Exercise by Shareholders

In the event that the Company declines, waives or fails to exercise an option pursuant to Article 2 hereof, the Shareholders shall have the right and option, at any time before expiration of the Option Period, to purchase all (but not less than all) of such shares of Stock at the Purchase Price. The exercise of such option shall be effected by delivery of an Exercise Notice. Until the expiration of the Option Period, no Selling Shareholder shall have the right to take action, including any attempted disposition, with respect to his or her shares of Stock. In the event that such Exercise Notice results in an oversubscription, then each subscribing Shareholder shall be entitled to purchase, on a pro rata basis, shares of Stock being offered by the Selling Shareholder, based upon each subscribing Shareholder's number of shares of Stock as compared with the aggregate number of shares of Stock held by all Shareholders who delivered an Exercise Notice. If the exercise of options by the Shareholder is under subscribed, the Shareholders that delivered an Exercise Notice shall be given a reasonable time (not to exceed fifteen (15) days) to increase their subscription to purchase all of the shares of Stock offered by the Selling Shareholder.

Article 6 – Other Agreements

The Company and either Shareholder may, at any time, agree in writing that all or any part of the Purchase Price for shares of Stock held by such Shareholder may be paid for in property having an agreed-upon value, which property may include notes or other debt securities of the Company. Any such agreement may provide that it is revocable by the Shareholder on notice to the Company at any time before the exercise date respecting such shares of Stock and, if not so revoked, shall be binding on the Company and such Shareholder upon the Company's exercise of its option hereunder respecting such shares of Stock.

Article 7 – Transfer of Stock Upon Non-Exercise of Options

A Selling Shareholder who has complied with Article 2 hereof shall be free to sell such shares to the Offeror for the price and on the terms and conditions contained in the Offer and communicated by written notice to the Company until sixty (60) days from the expiration or termination of the Option Period (the "Free Transfer Period"), provided that (a) the Company does not exercise either its option to purchase or its right to designate pursuant to Article 3 hereof before the end of the Option Period; or (b) the Company does exercise its option but the appropriate Purchase Price for the shares of Stock subject to such option is not paid on the Closing Date;

or (c) the other Shareholders do not exercise their option to purchase the shares of Stock subject to the option pursuant to Article 5 hereof before the end of the Option Period. All shares of Stock so disposed of during the Free Transfer Period shall be held by the transferee subject to the provisions of this Agreement and such transferee shall sign a counterpart of this Agreement and deliver it to the Company and all shares of Stock so transferred shall be represented by certificates bearing the legend set forth in Section 13.2 hereof. Any shares of Stock not disposed of by the Selling Shareholder before the end of the Free Transfer Period shall again become subject to the provisions of Article 2.

Article 8 – Transfers of Stock to Immediate Family

Notwithstanding any provision herein to the contrary, with the written consent of the Company (which consent shall not be unreasonably withheld), a Shareholder may sell, transfer or otherwise dispose of shares of Stock to members of such Shareholder's immediate family, which shall include his or her parents, spouse or children and grandchildren, or to a family trust (each a "Permitted Transferee"), provided, however, that prior to such transfer becoming effective, such Permitted Transferee shall sign a counterpart of this Agreement and deliver it to the Company and all shares of Stock so transferred shall be represented by the legend set forth in Section 13.2 hereof.

Article 9 – Sale of Control Shares

9.1 TRIGGER FOR TAG-ALONG RIGHTS. In the event that (a) a Selling Shareholder shall determine to make a transfer of Stock that will result in a transferee ("Control Transferee") controlling a majority of the voting shares of Stock of the Company; and (b) the Company does not exercise its rights under Article 2 hereof with respect to such sale, such sale or other disposition shall not be permitted unless the Selling Shareholder shall offer (or cause such transferee to offer) to the other Shareholders the right to elect to include (at the

Shareholders' sole option) their Stock in the sale or other disposition to such transferee.

9.2 TAG-ALONG NOTICES. The Selling Shareholder shall give notice to the other Shareholders describing the transaction(s) (the "Tag-Along Notice") and at any time within fifteen (15) days after the giving of the Tag-Along Notice, the other Shareholders may elect to include the same portion (but not less) of their issued and outstanding Stock in such a sale or other disposition as are being sold by the Selling Shareholder (e.g., if the Selling Shareholder, is selling three-fourths (3/4) of his holdings, the other Shareholders would also sell that amount) by giving written notice thereof to the Selling Shareholder and delivering to the designated representative of the Selling Shareholder, a stock certificate or certificates representing that Shareholder's Stock (the "Tag-Along Stock"), together with a limited power-of-attorney that authorizes the Selling Shareholder to sell or otherwise dispose of such Tag-Along Stock pursuant to the terms of the Control Transferee's offer.

9.3 IDENTICAL TERMS. The purchase from a Shareholder pursuant to this Article 9 shall be on the same terms and conditions, including the price per share and the date of sale or other disposition, as are received by the Selling Shareholder and stated in the Tag-Along Notice.

9.4 NOTICE OF SALE. Promptly (but in no event later than five (5) business days) after the consummation of the sale or other disposition of Stock to the Control Transferee pursuant to the Control Transferee's offer, the Selling Shareholder shall (i) notify the other Shareholders of the completion thereof; (ii) cause to be remitted to the other Shareholders the total sales price attributable to the Stock that the Selling Shareholder (on behalf of the other Shareholders) sold or otherwise disposed of pursuant thereto; and (iii) furnish such other evidence of the completion and time of completion of such sale or other disposition and the terms thereof as may be reasonable requested by the other Shareholders.

9.5 WAIVER OF TAG-ALONG ELECTION. If within fifteen (15) days after the Tag-Along Notice is given, the other Shareholders have not accepted the offer to sell their shares of Stock pursuant this Article 9, the other Shareholders shall be deemed to have waived any and all of their rights with respect to the sale or other disposition of shares described in the Tag-Along Notice. The Selling Shareholder may, during the Free Transfer Period after such fifteen (15) day period, sell or otherwise dispose of their Stock to the Control Transferee or any other person at a price and on terms not more favorable to the Selling Shareholder than were set forth in the Tag-Along Notice.

9.6 TERMINATION OF FREE TRANSFER PERIOD. If, at the end of the Free Transfer Period, the Selling Shareholder shall not have completed the sale of his Stock in accordance with the terms of the Tag-Along Notice, each of the restrictions on sale contained in this Agreement with respect to the Selling Shareholder's Stock shall again be in effect (unless such period is extended with the consent of the other Shareholders).

9.7 PERMITTED TRANSFERS. The rights provided in this Article 9 shall not be applicable to or restrict in any way: (i) any merger, share exchange, consolidation or other reorganization or recapitalization that involves the Company in which the shares of Stock of the Company are in substantial part exchanged for or converted into securities of another corporation or cash (or both); or (ii) any transfer of Stock by a Shareholder to a Permitted Transferee; provided that this Agreement shall continue to be applicable to the Stock after any such transfer to the Permitted Transferee and provided further that the Permitted Transferee shall have agreed in writing to be bound by the provisions of this Agreement affecting the Stock so transferred.

9.8 STOCK SUBJECT TO AGREEMENT. In the event that a sale of Stock is made to a Control Transferee pursuant to this Article, the Stock held by such Control Transferee shall remain subject to this Agreement in accordance with the provisions of Article 7 hereof.

Article 10 – Term and Termination

This Agreement shall be effective as of the date set forth above and shall terminate upon the first to occur of any of the events listed below, upon which all rights and obligations set forth in this Agreement shall cease:

(a) the parties hereto agree in writing to terminate this Agreement;
(b) the adjudication of the Company as a bankrupt, the execution by the Company of the assignment for the benefit of creditors or the appointment of a receiver for the Company;
(c) the voluntary dissolution of the Company;
(d) in the event that there shall be only one (1) Shareholder remaining of issued and outstanding shares of the Company;
(e) on the effective date of a registered public offering of Stock of the Company pursuant to the Securities Act of 1933, as amended; or
(f) in the event that the Shareholders no longer hold any of the Stock of the Company.

Article 11 – Specific Performance

The Stock of the Company cannot be readily purchased or sold in the open market, and for that reason (among others) the Company and the Shareholders will be irreparably damaged in the event that this Agreement is not specifically enforced. Should any controversy arise concerning a sale or disposition of any shares of Stock, an injunction may be issued restraining any sale or disposition pending the determination of such controversy, and the resolution thereof shall be enforceable in a court of equity by a decree of specific performance. Such remedy, however, shall be cumulative and not exclusive and shall be in addition to any other remedies which the parties may have.

Article 12 – Endorsement of Stock Certificates

Whenever any Shareholder acquires any additional Shares of the Company or any other "securities" of the Company other than the Shares owned at the time of the execution of this Agreement, such Stock or such other "securities" of the

Company so acquired shall be subject to all of the terms of this Agreement, and the certificates therefor shall be surrendered to the Company for legending as set forth below, unless they already so bear said legends.

The Securities represented by this Certificate have not been registered under the Securities Act of 1933 or any applicable state securities law. These Securities may not be sold or transferred in the absence of such registration or an exemption therefrom under such acts. In addition, the sale, transfer, assignment, pledge or encumbrance of the Securities represented by this Certificate are subject to the terms and conditions of a Shareholders' Agreement dated as of [date], among [Company], [Shareholder1], [Shareholder2], and [Shareholder3]. Copies of such Shareholders' Agreement may be obtained at no cost by written request made by the holder of record of this Certificate to the Secretary of [Company].

Article 13 – Key-Man Insurance

The Board may, but need not, insure the life of the Shareholders, with the Company as the beneficiary of such policies. The policies and net proceeds received thereunder shall be held by the Company in trust for the purposes of this Agreement. The Company shall have the right to take out additional insurance on the life of each Shareholder, whenever, in the opinion of the Board, additional insurance may be desirable to carry out the obligations under this Agreement. The Company shall pay all premiums on insurance policies taken out by it pursuant to this Agreement. The Company shall be the sole owner of all such policies and may apply to the payment of premiums, any dividends declared and paid on the policies. The proceeds of the policies insuring a life of a deceased Shareholder shall be paid by the Company to the successor of the decedent to the extent necessary and sufficient to discharge all or part of the Company's obligations hereunder. The Company reserves the right to cancel any policy, change the named beneficiary or the method of payment of the proceeds, or change the policy in any other manner, or assign the rights in it, as long as this Agreement remains in effect.

Article 14 – Deadlock

14.1 DEFINITION OF DEADLOCK. In the event of an interim vacancy or in the event the Board is unable to resolve matters pertaining to: (i) the consolidation, merger, transfer of assets or amendment of the Articles requiring shareholder approval under _____ law; (ii) the payment of dividends; (iii) the issuance of Stock or any security of the Company; (iv) the repurchase of any Stock of the Company; (v) the election of officers of the Company; or (vi) any transaction or action with respect to which the Company makes a payment or assumes a liability or obligation in an amount equal to or in excess of Five Hundred Thousand Dollars ($500,000), then the Board shall be considered in a "Deadlock" and the provisions of Section 14.2 below shall apply.

14.2 ARBITRATION. The resolution of a Deadlock (as described in Section 14.1 above) shall be determined solely and exclusively by arbitration under the rules of the American Arbitration Association. Upon the demand of any Director or a majority of Stock of the Shareholders, all Directors or their designated representatives, together with counsel to the Company, shall meet within two (2) weeks of the time the demand is made, unless the parties otherwise agree in writing. The Directors or their representatives and counsel shall agree upon a single arbitrator (the "Arbitrator"), who shall be a member of the American Bar Association in good standing for at least fifteen (15) years. If the Directors or their representatives and Company counsel are unable to agree, then the Company's counsel, in his sole discretion, shall select the Arbitrator. The Arbitrator shall hear the dispute within two (2) weeks of the date of the meeting of the representatives. Except as otherwise expressly provided by applicable state law or regulation, the Arbitrator shall hear the dispute in the State of _____ (or at such other location as may be designated by the Company counsel) and may properly consider any and all matters related thereto that would be admissible in a non-jury trial under applicable Federal Rules of Civil Procedure or Evidence. The Arbitrator's award shall be announced within seven (7) days of the hearing of the dispute. The Company shall pay for all fees, costs and attorneys' fees.

Article 15 – Prohibition Against Removal or Use of Company Information

15.1 NO REMOVAL OF COMPANY PROPERTY. Should the relationship between any Shareholder and the Company be terminated for any reason whatsoever, such Terminated Shareholder agrees and covenants that he shall not remove any files or information contained in files or otherwise pertaining to the business and/or the clients of the Company (such files and information to be deemed the property of the Company) without the express written consent of the Company, which in all events shall be considered the owner and possessor of all such files, documents and information. The Terminated Shareholder further agrees and covenants that such information shall in no way be utilized by him for his gain or advantage or to the detriment of the Company.

15.2 POST-TERMINATION CONFIDENTIALITY. The Terminated Shareholder further agrees that he will, at no time, except within the scope of his relationship with the Company, before or after termination of this Agreement, directly or indirectly, disclose to any person or entity, for any purpose, any matter of a secret, confidential or business nature relating to the Company, including, but not limited to, any information concerning the business operations or internal structure of the Company, financial condition of the Company, gross receipts, marketing techniques and plans, pricing mechanisms of the Company, or any or all of the information set forth herein, which he has learned by reason of his affiliation with the Company. The Terminated Shareholder further acknowledges that all information, knowledge and data connected with or related to the Company, not generally known to the public, that is created by or disclosed to the Terminated Shareholder as a consequence of its relationship with the Company, whether or not pursuant to this Agreement, including without limitation, all software, techniques, method systems, methodologies, facts, data or other information of whatever kind and whatever form concerning the Company or its business or affairs, are valuable, special and unique assets of the Company. The Company shall be entitled to an injunction by any court of competent jurisdiction to enjoin and restrain the unauthorized disclosure of any information specified herein.

Article 16–Trade and Business Secrets; Covenant Not to Compete

16.1 CONFIDENTIALITY DURING THE TERM OF THE AGREEMENT. During the period set forth in Section 16.2 below, a Shareholder shall not (i) on behalf of any person or entity other than the Company, directly or indirectly employ or solicit for employment, or advise or recommend for employment to such other person or entity, any person that is employed by the Company or who should be recommended or solicited for employment with the Company; or (ii) divulge, publish or otherwise reveal either directly or indirectly or through another, to any person, firm or corporation, any knowledge, information or any facts concerning any processes, methods, inventions, techniques, devices or trade secrets used by the Company in the operation of its business. Each Shareholder further agrees that during the period set forth in Section 16.2 below, the Shareholder will not divulge, publish or otherwise reveal either directly or indirectly or through another, to any person, firm or corporation (i) any secret, confidential or business information of any nature relating to the Company, including, but not limited to, any information concerning the business operations or internal structure of the Company, the financial condition of the Company, marketing techniques and plans, pricing mechanisms and customer lists; and (ii) any customized software techniques, method systems, methodologies, facts, data or other information of whatever kind and whatever form concerning the business of the Company.

16.2 COVENANT NOT TO COMPETE. For so long as each Shareholder (i) is employed by or under contract with the Company; or (ii) owns, holds or controls any shares of Stock of the Company, plus a three (3) year period after the date (A) his consulting relationship with the Company is terminated; or (B) he sells, transfers, disposes of or otherwise relinquishes control over all of his Stock, whichever event occurs later, such Shareholder shall not, without the prior written consent of the Company, engage in any activity in competition with, or directly or indirectly perform services (as principal, agent, employee, manager, consultant, independent contractor, officer, director, advisor or otherwise) for any business that engages in direct or indirect competition with the business conducted by the Company. For the purpose of this Agreement, the "business of the Company" shall be the development of a wide range of programs, services and resources for emerging growth companies.

16.3 BOUNDARIES. The restrictions contained in this Article 16 shall apply throughout the world, however, such restrictions do not prohibit the Shareholders from purchasing or holding stock or other securities of any corporation (regardless of its business) which shall have securities listed upon any recognized securities exchange or traded on a recognized market in the United States or Canada, provided that the Shareholders are not involved in the management of said Company.

16.4 INJUNCTIVE RELIEF. Each Shareholder acknowledges that the restrictions contained in this Article 16 in view of the nature of the business in which the Company is engaged, are reasonable and necessary in order to protect the legitimate interests of the Company, and that any violation thereof would result in irreparable and substantial harm to the Company for which the Company does not have an adequate remedy at law; each Shareholder acknowledges, therefore, that in the event of his violation of any of these restrictions, the Company shall be entitled to seek from any court of competent jurisdiction, temporary, preliminary and permanent injunctive relief as well as damages and an equitable accounting of all earnings, profits and other benefits arising from such violation, which rights shall be cumulative and in addition to any other rights or remedies to which the Company may be entitled.

16.5 ADJUDICATION. If any of the time periods or the geographical areas specified throughout this Article 16 should be adjudicated as unreasonable in any arbitration or judicial proceeding, then the time period shall be reduced by such number of months or the geographical area shall be reduced by the elimination of such portion thereof or both so that such restrictions may be enforced for such time period and in such geographical area as is adjudicated to be reasonable. If the Shareholders violates any of the restrictions contained in this Article 16, the restrictive period shall not run in favor of the violating Shareholder from the time of the commencement of any such violation until such time as such violation shall be cured by him to the satisfaction of the Company.

Article 17–Miscellaneous

17.1 NOTICES. Any and all notices, requests or other communications provided for herein shall be given in writing and sent by messenger, overnight delivery or by registered or certified mail, return receipt requested, with first-class postage prepaid; and such notices shall be addressed to the Company as follows:

Company
Address
Attn: President

and to each Shareholder at the address shown for each Shareholder in the corporate minute book of the Company unless notice of a change of address is furnished to the Company in the manner provided in this Section 17.1. Any notice which is required to be made within a stated period of time shall be considered timely if delivered or mailed before midnight of the last day of such period.

17.2 INVALID OR UNENFORCEABLE PROVISIONS. The invalidity or unenforceability of any particular provision of this Agreement shall not affect the other provisions hereof, and this Agreement shall be construed in all respects as if such invalid or unenforceable provision were omitted.

17.3 BENEFIT AND BURDEN. This Agreement shall inure to the benefit of, and shall be binding upon, the parties hereto and their legatees, distributees, estates, executors, administrators, personal representatives, successors and assigns, and other legal representatives. In the event that a shareholder transfers any of the shares of Stock to a third party designee, as and to the extent permitted pursuant to this Agreement, such designee shall take such shares subject to all of the terms and provisions of this Agreement.

17.4 CHANGES: WAIVER. No change or modification to this Agreement shall be valid unless the same is in writing and signed by all of the parties hereto. No waiver of any provision of this Agreement shall be valid unless in writing and signed by the person against whom it is sought to be enforced. The failure of any party at any time to insist upon strict performance of any condition, promise, agreement or understanding set forth herein shall not be construed as a waiver or relinquishment of the right to insist upon strict performance of the same or any other condition, promise, agreement or understanding at a future time.

17.5 ENTIRE AGREEMENT. This Agreement sets forth all of the promises, agreements, conditions, understandings, warranties and representations among the parties hereto. Any and all prior agreements among the parties hereto, including any prior shareholders' agreement involving any of the parties, are hereby revoked and this Agreement is, and is intended by the parties to be, an integration of any and all prior agreements or understandings, oral or written.

17.6 GOVERNING LAW. This Agreement shall be construed and enforced in accordance with the laws of the State of _____.

17.7 HEADINGS. The headings, subheadings and other captions of this Agreement are for convenience and reference only and shall not be used in interpreting, construing or enforcing any of the provisions of this Agreement.

17.8 CONSTRUCTION. All references in this Agreement to the singular apply to the plural where appropriate, and all references to the masculine include the feminine.

17.9 COUNTERPARTS. This Agreement may be executed in any number of counterparts, all of which together shall constitute one instrument.

IN WITNESS WHEREOF, the parties hereto have executed this Shareholders' Agreement as of the day and year first above written.

ATTEST:

The Company

_____
(COMPANY)

By:_____

Its:_____

Witness

By:_____
(SHAREHOLDER 1)

_____
(SHAREHOLDER 1), INDIVIDUALLY

By:_____
(SHAREHOLDER 2)

_____
(SHAREHOLDER 2), INDIVIDUALLY

By:_____
(SHAREHOLDER 3)

_____
(SHAREHOLDER 3), INDIVIDUALLY

SCHEDULE 1—Stockholders of the Company

NAME OF STOCKHOLDER	PERCENTAGE OF TOTAL AUTHORIZED SHARES
(SHAREHOLDER 1)	_____%
(SHAREHOLDER 2)	_____%
(SHAREHOLDER 3)	_____%

Sample Stock Option Plan (Chapter 8) GrowCo Enterprises, Inc. 1999 Stock Option Plan

Introduction

GrowCo Enterprises, Inc. a [state] corporation (hereinafter referred to as the "Corporation"), hereby establishes an incentive compensation plan to be known as the "GrowCo Enterprises, Inc., 1999 Stock Option Plan" (hereinafter referred to as the "Plan"), as set forth in this document. The Plan permits the grant of Non-Qualified Stock Options and Incentive Stock Options.

The Plan shall become effective on the date it is adopted by the Corporation's Board of Directors. However, it shall be rendered null and void and have no effect, and all Plan Awards granted hereunder shall be canceled, if the Plan is not approved by a majority vote of the Corporation's stockholders within twelve (12) months of the date the Plan is adopted by the Corporation's Board of Directors.

The purpose of the Plan is to promote the success and enhance the value of the Corporation by linking the personal interests of Participants to those of the Corporation's stockholders by providing Participants with an incentive for outstanding performance. The Plan is further intended to assist the Corporation in its ability to motivate, and retain the services of, Participants upon whose judgment, interest and special effort the successful conduct of its operations is largely dependent.

Definitions

For purposes of this Plan, the following terms shall be defined as follows unless the context clearly indicates otherwise:

(a) "Award Agreement" shall mean the written agreement, executed by an appropriate officer of the Corporation, pursuant to which a Plan Award is granted.

(b) "Board of Directors" shall mean the Board of Directors of the Corporation.

(c) "Code" shall mean the Internal Revenue Code of 1986, as amended, and the rules and regulations thereunder.

(d) "Committee" shall mean the Board of Directors of the Corporation or any committee of two or more persons designated by the Board of Directors to serve as the Committee.

(e) "Common Stock" shall mean the common stock, par value [$__] per share, of the Corporation.

(f) "Corporation" shall mean GrowCo Enterprises, Inc., a [state] corporation.

(g) "Disability" shall have the same meaning as the term "permanent and total disability" under Section 22(e)(3) of the Code.

(h) "Employee" shall mean a common-law employee of the Company or of any Subsidiary.

(i) "Exchange Act" shall mean the Securities Exchange Act of 1934, as amended, and the rules and regulations thereunder.

(j) "Fair Market Value" of the Corporation's Common Stock on a Trading Day shall mean the last reported sale price for Common Stock or, in case no such reported sale takes place on such Trading Day, the average of the closing bid and asked prices for the Common Stock for such Trading Day, in either case on the principal national securities exchange on which the Common Stock is listed or admitted to trading, or if the Common Stock is not listed or admitted to trading on any national securities exchange, but is traded in the over-the-counter market, the closing sale price of the Common Stock or, if no sale is publicly reported, the average of the closing bid and asked quotations for the Common Stock, as reported by the National Association of Securities Dealers Automated Quotation System ("NASDAQ") or any comparable system or, if the Common Stock is not listed on NASDAQ or a comparable system, the closing sale price of the Common Stock or, if no sale is publicly reported, the average of the closing bid and asked prices, as furnished by two members of the National Association of Securities Dealers, Inc. who make a market in the Common Stock selected from time to time by the Corporation for that purpose. In addition, for purposes of this definition, a "Trading Day" shall mean, if the Common Stock is listed on any national securities exchange, a business day during which such exchange was open for trading and at least one trade of Common Stock was effected on such exchange on such business day, or, if the Common Stock is not listed on any national securities exchange but is traded in the over-the-counter market, a business day during which the over-the-counter market was open for trading and at least one "eligible dealer" quoted both a bid and asked price for the Common Stock. An "eligible dealer" for any day shall include any broker-dealer who quoted both a bid and asked price for such day, but shall not include any broker-dealer who quoted only a bid or only an asked price for such day. In the event the Corporation's Common Stock is not publicly traded, the Fair Market Value of such Common Stock shall be determined by the Committee in good faith.

(k) "Good Cause" shall have the equivalent meaning set forth in the employment agreement between the Participant and the Corporation or Subsidiary or, in the absence of such agreement such term shall mean (i) a Participant's willful or gross misconduct or willful or gross negligence in the performance of his duties for the Corporation or for any Subsidiary after prior written notice of such misconduct or negligence and the continuance thereof for a period of thirty (30) days after receipt by such Participant of such notice, (ii) a Participant's intentional or habitual neglect of his duties for the Corporation or for any Subsidiary after prior written notice of such neglect, or (1) a Participant's theft or misappropriation of funds of the Corporation or of any Subsidiary or commission of a felony.

(l) "Incentive Stock Option" shall mean a stock option satisfying the requirements for tax-favored treatment under Section 422 of the Code.

(m) "Non-Qualified Option" shall mean a stock option which does not satisfy the requirements for, or which is not intended to be eligible for, tax-favored treatment under Section 422 of the Code.

(n) "Option" shall mean an Incentive Stock Option or a Non-Qualified Stock Option granted pursuant to the provisions of Section V hereof

(o) "Optionee" shall mean a Participant who is granted an Option under the terms of this Plan.

(p) "Participant" shall mean any Employee participating under the Plan.

(q) "Plan Award" shall mean an Option granted pursuant to the terms of this Plan.

(r) "Securities Act" shall mean the Securities Act of 1933, as amended, and the rules and regulations thereunder.
(s) "Subsidiary" shall mean a subsidiary corporation of the Corporation within the meaning of Section 424(f) of the Code.

II. *Administration*
The Plan shall be administered by the Committee. Subject to the provisions of the Plan, the Committee may establish from time to time such regulations, provisions, proceedings and conditions of awards which, in its sole opinion, may be advisable in the administration of the Plan. A majority of the Committee shall constitute a quorum, and, subject to the provisions of Section IV of the Plan, the acts of a majority of the members present at any meeting at which a quorum is present or acts approved in writing by a majority of the Committee, shall be the acts of the Committee as a whole.

III. *Shares Available*
Subject to the adjustments provided in Section VII of the Plan, the aggregate number of shares of the Common Stock which may be granted for all purposes under the Plan shall be [NUMBER OF SHARES] shares. Shares of Common Stock underlying awards of securities (derivative or not) shall be counted against the limitation set forth in the immediately preceding sentence and may be reused to the extent that the related Plan Award to any individual is settled in cash, expires, is terminated unexercised, or is forfeited. Common Stock granted to satisfy Plan Awards under the Plan may be authorized and unissued shares of the Common Stock, issued shares of such Common Stock held in the Corporation's treasury or shares of Common Stock acquired on the open market.

V. *Eligibility*
Offices and key employees of the Corporation, or of any Subsidiary, who are regularly employed on a salaried basis as common law employees shall be eligible to participate in the Plan.

V. Authority of Committee

The Plan shall be administered by, or under the direction of the Committee, which shall administer the Plan so as to comply at all times with Section 16 of the Exchange Act and the rules and regulations promulgated thereunder, to the extent such compliance is required, and shall otherwise have plenary authority to interpret the Plan and to make all determinations specified in or permitted by the Plan or deemed necessary or desirable for its administration or for the conduct of the Committee's business. Subject to the provisions of Section XI hereof, all interpretations and determinations of the Committee may be made on an individual or group basis and shall be final, conclusive and binding on all interested parties. Subject to the express provisions of the Plan, the Committee shall have authority, in its discretion, to determine the persons to whom Plan Awards shall be granted, the times when such Plan Awards shall be granted, the number of Plan Awards, the purchase price or exercise price of each Plan Award (if applicable), the period(s) during which a Plan Award shall be exercisable (whether in whole or in part), the restrictions to be applicable to Plan Awards and the other terms and provisions thereof (which need not be identical). In addition, the authority of the Committee shall include, without limitation, the following:

(a) Financing. The arrangement of temporary financing for an Optionee by registered broker-dealers, under the rules and regulations of the Federal Reserve Board, for the purpose of assisting an Optionee in the exercise of an Option, such authority to include the payment by the Corporation of the commissions of the broker-dealer,

(b) Procedures for Exercise Of Option. The establishment of procedures for an Optionee (i) to exercise an Option by payment of cash, (ii) to have withheld from the total number of shares of Common Stock to be acquired upon the exercise of an Option that number of shares having a Fair Market Value, which, together with such cash as shall be paid in respect of fractional shares, shall equal the Option exercise price of the total number of shares of Common Stock to be acquired, (iii) to exercise all or a portion of an Option by delivering that number of shares of

Common Stock already owned by him having a Fair Market Value which shall equal the Option exercise price for the portion exercised and, in cases where an Option is not exercised in its entirety, and subject to the requirements of the Code, to permit the Optionee to deliver the shares of Common Stock thus acquired by him in payment of shares of Common Stock to be received pursuant to the exercise of additional portions of such Option, the effect of which shall be that an Optionee can in sequence utilize such newly acquired shares of Common Stock in payment of the exercise price of the entire Option, together with such cash as shall be paid in respect of fractional shares and (iv) to engage in any form of "cashless" exercise.

(c) Withholding. The establishment of a procedure whereby a number of shares of Common Stock or other securities may be withheld from the total number of shares of Common Stock or other securities to be issued upon exercise of an Option or for the tender of shares of Common Stock owned by any Participant to meet any obligation of withholding for taxes incurred by the Participant upon such exercise.

IV. Stock Options

The Committee shall have the authority, in its discretion, to grant Incentive Stock Options or to grant Non-Qualified Stock Options or to grant both types of Options. Notwithstanding anything contained herein to the contrary, an Incentive Stock Option may be granted only to common law employees of the Corporation or of any Subsidiary now existing or hereafter formed or acquired, and not to any director or officer who is not also such a common law employee. The terms and conditions of the Options shall be determined from time to time by the Committee; provided, however that the Options granted under the Plan shall be subject to the following:

(a) Exercise Price. The Committee shall establish the exercise price at the time any Option is granted at such amount as the Committee shall determine; provided, however, that the exercise price for each share of Common Stock purchasable under any Incentive Stock Option granted hereunder shall be such amount as the Committee shall, in its best judgment, determine to be not less than one hundred percent (100%) of the Fair Market Value per share of Common Stock at the date the Option is granted; and provided, further, that in the case of an Incentive Stock Option granted to a person who, at the time such Incentive Stock Option is granted, owns shares of stock of the Corporation or of any Subsidiary which possess more than ten percent (10%) of the total combined voting power of all classes of shares of stock of the Corporation or of any Subsidiary, the exercise price for each share of Common Stock shall be such amount as the Committee, in its best judgment, shall determine to be not less than one hundred ten percent (110%) of the Fair Market Value per share of Common Stock at the date the Option is granted. The exercise price will be subject to adjustment in accordance with the provisions of Section VII of the Plan.

(b) Payment of Exercise Price. The price per share of Common Stock with respect to each Option shall be payable at the time the Option is exercised. Such price shall be payable in cash or pursuant to any of the methods set forth in Sections IV(a) or (b) hereof as determined by the Participant. Shares of Common Stock delivered to the Corporation in payment of the exercise price shall be valued at the Fair Market Value of the Common Stock on the date preceding the date of the exercise of the Option.

(c) Exercisability of Options. Except as provided in Section V(e) hereof, each Option shall be exercisable in whole or in installments, and at such time(s), and subject to the fulfillment of any conditions on, and to any limitations on, exercisability as may be determined by the Committee at the time of the grant of such Options. The right to purchase shares of Common Stock shall be cumulative so that when the right to purchase any shares of Common Stock has accrued such shares of Common Stock or any part thereof may be purchased at any time thereafter until the expiration or termination of the Option.

(d) Expiration of Options. No Incentive Stock Option by its terms shall be exercisable after the expiration of ten (10) years from the date of grant of the Option; provided, however, in the case of an Incentive Stock Option granted to a person who, at the time such Option is granted, owns shares of stock of the Corporation or of any Subsidiary possessing more than ten percent (10%) of the total combined voting power of all classes of shares of stock of the Corporation or of any Subsidiary, such Option shall not be exercisable after the expiration of five (5) years from the date such Option is granted.

(e) Exercise Upon Optionee's Termination of Employment. If the employment of an Optionee by the Corporation or by any Subsidiary is terminated for any reason other than death, any Incentive Stock Option granted to such Optionee may not be exercised later than three (3) months (one (1) year in the case of termination due to Disability) after the date of such termination of employment. For purposes of determining whether any Optionee has incurred a termination of employment an Optionee who is both an employee and a director of the Corporation and/or any Subsidiary shall (with respect to any Non-Qualified Option that may have been granted to him) be considered to have incurred a termination of employment only upon his termination of service both as an employee and as a director. Furthermore, (i) if an Optionee's employment is terminated by the Corporation or by any Subsidiary for Good Cause or (ii) if an Optionee voluntarily terminates his employment other than for Disability with the Corporation or with any Subsidiary without the written consent of the Committee, regardless of whether such Optionee continues to serve as a director of the Corporation or of any Subsidiary, then the Optionee shall, at the time of such termination of employment, forfeit his rights to exercise any and all of the outstanding Option(s) theretofore granted to him.

(f) Maximum Amount of Incentive Stock Options. Each Plan Award under which Incentive Stock Options are granted shall provide that to the extent the aggregate of the (i) Fair Market Value of the shares of Common Stock (determined as of the time of the grant of the Option) subject to such Incentive Stock Option and (ii) the fair market values (determined as of the date(s) of grant of the option(s) of all other shares of Common Stock subject to incentive stock options granted to an Optionee by the Corporation or any parent of the Corporation or any Subsidiary, which are exercisable for the first time by any person during any calendar year, exceed(s) one hundred thousand dollars ($100,000), such excess shares of Common Stock shall not be deemed to be purchased pursuant to Incentive Stock Options. The terms of the immediately preceding sentence shall be applied by taking all options, whether or not granted under this Plan, into account in the order in which they are granted.

(g) Dividend Equivalents for Outstanding Options. The Committee may, in its sole discretion, provide that amounts equivalent to dividends shall be payable with respect to one or more shares of Common Stock subject to vested but unexercised Option(s) granted to a Participant. Such amounts shall be credited to a suspense account, and shall be payable to the Participant in cash or in Common Stock, as set forth under the terms of the Plan Award, at such time as the related Option(s) are exercised.

VII. Adjustment of Shares; Merger or Consolidation, etc. of the Corporation

(a) Recapitalization, Etc. In the event there is any change in the Common Stock of the Corporation by reason of any reorganization, recapitalization, stock split, stock dividend or otherwise, there shall be substituted for or added to each share of Common Stock theretofore appropriated or thereafter subject, or which may become subject, to any Option, the number and kind of shares of stock or other securities into which each outstanding share of Common Stock shall be so changed or for which each such share shall be exchanged, or to which each such share be entitled, as the case may be, and the per share price thereof also shall be appropriately adjusted. Notwithstanding the foregoing, (i) each such adjustment with respect to an Incentive Stock Option shall comply with the rules of Section 424(a) of the Code and (ii) in no event shall any adjustment be made which would render any Incentive Stock Option granted hereunder to be other than an incentive stock option for purposes of Section 422 of the Code.

(b) Merger, Consolidation or Change in Control of Corporation. Upon (i) the merger or consolidation of the Corporation with or into another corporation (pursuant to which the stockholders of the Corporation immediately prior to such merger or consolidation will not, as of the date of such merger or consolidation, own a beneficial interest in shares of voting securities of the corporation surviving such merger or consolidation having at least a majority of the combined voting power of such corporation's then outstanding securities), if the agreement of merger or consolidation does not provide for (1) the continuance of the granted hereunder or (2) the substitution of new options for Options granted hereunder, or for the assumption of such Options by the surviving corporation, (ii) the dissolution, liquidation, or sale of all or substantially all the assets of the Corporation to a person unrelated to the Corporation or to a direct or indirect owner of a majority of the voting power of the Corporation's then outstanding voting securities (such sale of assets being referred to as an "Asset Sale") or (iii) the Change in Control of the Corporation, the holder of any such Option theretofore granted and still outstanding (and not otherwise expired) shall have the right immediately prior to the effective date of such merger, consolidation, dissolution, liquidation, Asset Sale or Change in Control of the Corporation to exercise such Option(s) in whole or in part without regard to any installment provision that may have been made part of the terms and conditions of such Option(s); provided that any conditions precedent to the exercise of such Option(s), other than the passage of time, have occurred. The Corporation, to the extent practicable, shall give advance notice to affected Optionees of such merger, consolidation, dissolution, liquidation, Asset Sale or Change in Control of the Corporation. All such Options and which are not so exercised shall be forfeited as of the effective time of such merger, consolidation, dissolution, liquidation or Asset Sale (but not in the case of a Change in Control of the Corporation).

(c) Definition of Change in Control of the Corporation. As used herein, a "Change in Control of the Corporation" shall be deemed to have occurred if any person (including any individual, firm, partnership or other entity) together with all Affiliates and Associates (as defined under Rule 12b-2 of the General Rules and Regulations promulgated under the Exchange Act) of such person (but excluding (i) a trustee or other fiduciary holding securities under an employee benefit plan of the Corporation or any subsidiary of the Corporation, (ii) a corporation owned, directly or indirectly, by the stockholders of the Corporation in substantially the same proportions as their ownership of the Corporation, (iii) the Corporation or any subsidiary of the Corporation or (iv) only as provided in the immediately following sentence, a Participant together with all Affiliates and Associates of the Participant) is or becomes the Beneficial Owner (as defined in Rule 13d-3 promulgated under the Exchange Act), directly or indirectly, of securities of the Corporation representing 40% of more of the combined voting power of the Corporation's then outstanding securities. The provisions of clause (iv) of the immediately preceding sentence shall apply only with respect to the Option(s) held by the Participant who, together with his Affiliates or Associates, if any, is or becomes the direct or indirect Beneficial Owner of the percentage of securities set forth in such clause.]

VIII. *Miscellaneous Provisions*

(a) Administrative Procedures. The Committee may establish any procedures determined by it to be appropriate in discharging its responsibilities under the Plan. Subject to the provisions of Section XI hereof, all actions and decisions of the Committee shall be final.

(b) Assignment or Transfer. No grant or award of any Plan Award (other than a Non-Qualified Option) or any rights or interests therein shall be assignable or transferable by a Participant except by will or the laws of descent and distribution or pursuant to a domestic relations order. During the lifetime of a Participant, Incentive Stock Options granted hereunder shall be exercisable only by the Participant.

(c) Investment Representation. In the case of Plan Awards paid in shares of Common Stock or other securities, or, with respect to shares of Common Stock received pursuant to the exercise of an Option, the Committee may require, as a condition of receiving such securities, that the Participant furnish to the Corporation such written representations and information as the Committee deems appropriate to permit the Corporation, in light of the existence or nonexistence of an effective registration statement under the Securities Act to deliver such securities in compliance with the provisions of the Securities Act.

(d) Withholding Taxes. The Corporation shall have the right to deduct from all cash payments hereunder any federal, state, local or foreign taxes required by law to be withheld with respect to such payments. In the case of the issuance or distribution of Common Stock or other securities hereunder, either directly or upon the exercise of or payment upon any Plan Award, the Corporation, as a condition of such issuance or distribution, may require the payment (through withholding from the Participant's salary, reduction of the number of shares of Common Stock or other securities to be issued, or otherwise) of any such taxes. Each Participant may satisfy the withholding obligations by paying to the Corporation a cash amount equal to the amount required to be withheld or by tendering to the Corporation a number of shares of Common Stock having a value equivalent to such cash amount, or by use of any available procedure as described under Section IV(c) hereof.

(e) Costs and Expenses. The costs and expenses of administering the Plan shall be borne by the Corporation and shall not be charged against any award nor to any employee receiving a Plan Award.

(f) Funding of Plan. The Plan shall be unfunded. The Corporation shall not be required to segregate any of its assets to assure the payment of any Plan Award under the Plan. Neither the Participants nor any other persons shall have any interest in any fund or in any specific asset or assets of the Corporation or any other entity by reason of any Plan Award, except to the extent expressly provided hereunder. The interests of each Participant and former Participant hereunder are unsecured and shall be subject to the general creditors of the Corporation.

(g) Other Incentive Plans. The adoption of the Plan does not preclude the adoption by appropriate means of any other incentive plan for employees.

(h) Plurals and Gender. Where appearing in the Plan, masculine gender shall include the feminine and neuter genders, and the singular shall include the plural, and vice versa, unless the context clearly indicates a different meaning.

(i) Headings. The headings and sub-headings in this Plan are inserted for the convenience of reference only and are to be ignored in any construction of the provisions hereof.

(j) Severability. In case any provision of this Plan shall be held illegal or void, such illegality or invalidity shall not affect the remaining provisions of this Plan, but shall be fully severable, and the Plan shall be construed and enforced as if said illegal or invalid provisions had never been inserted herein.

(k) Payments Due Missing Persons. The Corporation shall make a reasonable effort to locate all persons entitled to benefits under the Plan, however, notwithstanding any Provisions of this Plan to the contrary, it after a period of one (1) year from the date such benefits shall be due, any such persons entitled to benefits have not been located, their rights under the Plan shall stand suspended. Before this provision becomes operative, the Corporation shall send a certified letter to all such persons at their last known addresses advising them that their rights under the Plan shall be suspended. Subject to all applicable state laws, any such suspended amounts shall be held by the Corporation for a period of one (1) additional year and thereafter such amounts shall be forfeited and thereafter remain the property of the Corporation.

(l) Liability and Indemnification. (i) Neither the Corporation nor any Subsidiary shall be responsible in any way for any action or omission of the Committee, or any other fiduciaries in the performance of their duties and obligations as set forth in this Plan. Furthermore, neither the Corporation nor any Subsidiary shall be responsible for any act or omission of any of their agents, or with respect to reliance upon advice of their counsel provided that the Corporation and/or the appropriate Subsidiary relied in good faith upon the action of such agent or the advice of such counsel.

(ii) **Except for their own gross negligence or willful misconduct** regarding the performance of the duties specifically assigned to them under, or their willful breach of the terms of, this Plan, the Corporation, each Subsidiary and the Committee shall be held harmless by the Participants, former Participants, beneficiaries and their representatives against liability or losses occurring by reason of any act or omission. Neither the Corporation, any Subsidiary, the Committee, nor any agents, employees, officers, directors or shareholders of any of them, nor any other person shall have any liability or responsibility with respect to this Plan, except as expressly provided herein.

(m) Incapacity. If the Committee shall receive evidence satisfactory to it that a person entitled to receive payment of any Plan

Award is, at the time when such benefit becomes payable, a minor, or is physically or mentally incompetent to receive such Plan Award and to give a valid release thereof and that another person or an institution is then maintaining or has custody of such person and that no guardian, committee or other representative of the estate of such person shall have been duly appointed, the Committee may make payment of such Plan Award otherwise payable to such person to such other person or institution, including a custodian under a Uniform Gifts to Minors Act, or corresponding legislation (who shall be an adult a guardian of the minor or a trust company), and the release by such other person or institution shall be a valid and complete discharge for the payment of such Plan Award.

(n) Cooperation of Parties. All parties to this Plan and any person claiming any interest hereunder agree to perform any and all acts and execute any and all documents and papers which are necessary or desirable for carrying out this Plan or any of its provisions.

(o) Governing. All questions pertaining to the validity, construction and administration of the Plan shall be determined in accordance with the laws of the State of [ ].

(p) Nonguarantee of Employment. Nothing contained in this Plan shall be construed as a contract of employment between the Corporation (or any Subsidiary), and any employee or Participant, as a right of any employee or Participant to be continued in the employment of the Corporation (or any Subsidiary), or as a limitation on the right of the Corporation or any Subsidiary to discharge any of its employees, at any time, with or without cause.

(q) Notices. Each notice relating to this Plan shall be in writing and delivered in person or by certified mail to the proper address. All notices to the Corporation or the Committee shall be addressed to it at [ADDRESS], Attn: [TITLE]. All notices to Participants, former Participants, beneficiaries or other persons acting for or on behalf of such persons shall be addressed to such person at the last address for such person maintained in the Committee's records.

(r) Written Agreements. Each Plan Award shall be evidenced by a signed written agreement (the "Award Agreements") between the Corporation and the Participant containing the terms and conditions of the award.

IX. *Amendment or Termination of Plan*

The Board of Directors of the Corporation shall have the right to amend, suspend or terminate the Plan at any time, provided that no amendment shall be made which shall increase the total number of shares of the Common Stock of the Corporation which may be issued and sold pursuant to Incentive Stock Options, reduce the minimum exercise price in the case of an Incentive Stock Option or modify the provisions of the Plan relating to eligibility with respect to Incentive Stock Options unless such amendment is made by or with the approval of the stockholders within 12 months of the effective date of such amendment but only if such approval is required by any applicable provision of law. The Board of Directors of the Corporation shall also be authorized to amend the Plan and the Options granted thereunder to maintain qualification as "incentive stock options" within the meaning of Section 422 of the Code, if applicable. Except as otherwise provided herein, no amendment, suspension or termination of the Plan shall alter or impair any Plan Awards previously granted under the Plan without the consent of the holder thereof.

X. *Term Of Plan*

The Plan shall automatically terminate on the day immediately preceding the [__th -10th FOR ISOs] anniversary of the date the Plan was adopted by the Board of Directors of the Corporation, unless sooner terminated by such Board of Directors. No Plan Awards may be granted under the Plan subsequent to the termination of the Plan.

XI. *Claims Procedures*

(a) Denial. If any Participant, former Participant or beneficiary is denied any vested benefit to which he is, or reasonably believes he is, entitled under this Plan, either in total or in an amount less than the full vested benefit to which he would normally be entitled, the Committee shall advise such person in writing the specific reasons for the denial. The Committee shall also furnish such person at the time with a written notice containing (i) a specific reference to pertinent Plan provisions, (ii) a description of any additional material or information necessary for such person to perfect his claim, if possible, and an explanation of why such material or information is needed and (iii) an explanation of the Plan's claim review procedure.

(b) Written Request for Review. Within sixty (60) days of receipt of the information stated in subsection (a) above, such person shall, if he desires further review, file a written request for reconsideration with the Committee.

(c) Review of Document. So long as such person's request for review is pending (including the sixty (60) day period in subsection (b) above), such person or his duly authorized representative may review pertinent Plan documents and may submit issues and comments in writing to the Committee.

(d) Committee's Final and Binding Decision. A final and binding decision shall be made by the Committee within sixty (60) days of the filing by such person of this request for reconsideration; provided, however, that if the Committee, in its discretion, feels that a hearing with such person or his representative is necessary or desirable, this period shall be extended for an additional 60 days.

(e) Transmittal of Decision. The Committee's decision shall be conveyed to such person in writing and shall (i) include specific reasons for the decision, (ii) be written in a manner calculated to be understood by such person and (iii) set forth the specific references to the pertinent Plan provisions on which the decision is based.

(f) Limitation on Claims. Notwithstanding any provisions of this Plan to the contrary, no Participant (nor the estate or other beneficiary of a Participant) shall be entitled to assert a claim against the Corporation (or against any Subsidiary) more than three years after the date the Participant (or his estate or other beneficiary) initially is entitled to receive benefits hereunder.

Sample Letter of Intent (Chapter 9)

Ms. Prospective Seller
SellCo, Inc.
{address}

Re: Letter of Intent Between BuyCo, Inc. and SellCo, Inc.

Dear Ms. Prospective Seller:

This letter ("Letter Agreement") sets forth the terms by which BuyCo, Inc. ("BCI") agrees to purchase shares of a newly authorized class of convertible preferred stock of SellCo, Inc. (the "Company") in accordance with the terms set forth below. BCI and the Company are hereinafter collectively referred to as the "Parties."

Section I of this Letter Agreement summarizes the principal terms proposed in our earlier discussions and is not an agreement binding upon either of the Parties. These principal terms are subject to the execution and delivery by the Parties of a definitive Stock Purchase Agreement, Employment Agreement and other documents related to these transactions.

Section II of this Letter Agreement contains a number of covenants by the Parties, including BCI's funding commitment and the execution and delivery of a Promissory Note in consideration therefor, which shall be legally binding upon the execution of this Letter Agreement by the Parties. The binding terms in Section II below are enforceable against the Parties, regardless of whether or not the aforementioned agreements are executed or the reasons for non-execution.

Section I–Proposed Terms

1. STOCK PURCHASE. The Parties will execute a Stock Purchase Agreement, pursuant to which, BCI will purchase shares of a newly authorized class of convertible preferred stock of the

Company (the "Shares"), for a total purchase price of $_____.
The Company's Board will amend its articles of incorporation (and bylaws if necessary) and take any formal corporate action necessary to create and authorize this new class of stock. The Shares will constitute_____% of the total capitalization of the Company on a fully-diluted, post-transactional basis. The Shares will have no dividend or liquidation preferences to the Company's common stock ("Common Stock") and will be identical in every other way to the Common Stock except that each of the Shares will have_____votes compared to each share of Common Stock (which has one vote). The Shares will be automatically convertible into shares of Common Stock on a one-for-one basis upon the disposition of the Shares by BCI to any party not affiliated with BCI. Simultaneous to the issuance of the Shares to BCI, BCI will give limited revocable proxies to Prospective Seller ("Seller"), entitling her to vote 50% of the Shares issued to BCI, respectively, on any matters on which the shareholders of the Company are entitled to vote, except matters relating to an initial public offering by or a sale of the Company where the holders of a majority of the Common Stock have already approved such an action. The foregoing exception will not apply, however, where all of the holders of Common Stock have unanimously approved an initial public offering by or a sale of the Company, provided, however, that all the holders of any class of stock of the Company will receive the same rights under such a transaction. Additionally, the proxies will be subject at all times to automatic revocation at the time that the proxy holder is no longer employed by the Company.

2. EMPLOYMENT AGREEMENTS. Prior to closing, the Company will enter into an individual employment agreement with Seller for year-terms at the compensation levels set forth in the Company's business plan previously presented by the Company to BCI. The employment agreement will contain such other terms and conditions as are reasonable and customary in the type of transaction contemplated hereby.

3. BOARD OF DIRECTORS OF THE COMPANY AND BCI. Seller will be nominated to serve on the Board of Directors of BCI. BCI will be entitled to designate members to three of the eight seats on the Company's Board of Directors. The Company's Board (and its shareholders, if necessary) will undertake all necessary corporate action to ensure the proper size and make-up of the Company's Board. Any future borrowing by the Company will require approval by the Company's Board and any such borrowing not related to the Company's ordinary course of business will require the approval of 70% of the Company's Board of Directors.

4. CLOSING AND DOCUMENTATION. The Parties intend that a closing of the agreements shall occur on or before_____, 19___, at a time and place that is mutually acceptable to the Parties. BCI or its representatives will prepare and revise the initial and subsequent drafts of the necessary agreements.

Section II–Binding Terms

In consideration of the costs to be incurred by the Parties in undertaking actions toward the negotiation and consummation of the Stock Purchase Agreement and the related agreements, the Parties hereby agree to the following binding terms ("Binding Terms"):

5. REFUNDABLE DEPOSIT. BCI will pay a refundable deposit in the amount of $_____ to the Company at the time of the execution of this Letter Agreement, and will pay an additional $_____ no later than _____ days after the execution of this Letter Agreement. All sums paid hereunder shall be deductible from the purchase price to be paid for the Shares as described in Paragraph 1. In the event that BCI does not complete the purchase of the Shares, the sums payable hereunder shall be deemed an advance and subject to repayment to BCI _____ months from the date of execution of this Letter Agreement in a lump sum with interest at the rate of 1.5% above the highest U.S. prime rate published in The Wall Street Journal from the date of execution of this Letter Agreement to the date of repayment. In the event that the closing is delayed beyond _____ 2000, BCI will advance additional funds of $_____ on _____, 2000 and

$_____on_____, 2000. Each additional advance shall be repaid within six months of the date of the advance at the rate of 1.5% above the highest U.S. prime rate published in The Wall Street Journal from the date of advance to the date of repayment. The Company shall execute and deliver a Promissory Note in consideration of the advance of funds hereunder and pursuant to the terms stated above.

6. RIGHT OF FIRST REFUSAL FOR ADDITIONAL CAPITAL CONTRIBUTIONS. The Company agrees to grant BCI a right of first refusal for any future equity financing (except in the case of an initial public offering). Holders of Common Stock shall have a pre-emptive right, however, to contribute such proportionate share of any such equity financing in order to maintain their respective interests in the Company. In the event that a valuation cannot be agreed upon by the contributing parties hereunder, an independent appraisal of the Company shall be obtained from a qualified investment banker at the Company's expense.

7. DUE DILIGENCE. The directors, officers, shareholders, employees, agents and other representatives (collectively, the "Representatives") of the Company shall (a) grant to BCI and its Representatives full access to the Company's properties, personnel, facilities, books and records, financial and operating data, contracts and other documents; and (b) furnish all such books and records, financial and operating data, contracts and other documents or information as BCI or its Representatives may reasonably request.

8. NO MATERIAL CHANGES. The Company agrees that, from and after the execution of this Letter Agreement until the earlier of the termination of the Binding Terms in accordance with Paragraph 14 below or the execution and delivery of the agreements described herein, the Company's business and operations will be conducted in the ordinary course and in substantially the same manner as such business and operations have been conducted in the past and the Company will notify BCI of any extraordinary transactions, financing or business involving the Company or its affiliates.

9. NO-SHOP PROVISION. The Company agrees that, from and after the execution of this Letter Agreement until the termination of the Binding Terms in accordance with Paragraph 14 below, the Company will not initiate or conclude, through its Representatives or otherwise, any negotiations with any corporation, person or other entity regarding the establishment of a line of credit, the sale of substantially all of the assets of or the management of the Company. The Company will immediately notify the other Parties regarding any such contact described above.

10. LOCK-UP PROVISION. The Company agrees that, from and after the execution of this Letter Agreement until (a) the consummation of the transactions contemplated in Section I and the execution of definitive agreements thereby, or (b) in the event that definitive agreements are not executed, until the repayment of all amounts advanced hereunder, plus accrued interest, that without the prior written approval of BCI and subject to any anti-dilution provisions imposed hereunder, (x) no shares of any currently issued Common Stock of the Company shall be issued, sold, transferred or assigned to any party; (y) no such shares of Common Stock shall be pledged as security, hypothecated, or in any other way encumbered; and (z) the Company shall issue no additional shares of capital stock of any class, whether now or hereafter authorized.

11. CONFIDENTIALITY. Prior to Closing, neither Party nor any of their Representatives shall make any public statement or issue any press releases regarding the agreements, the proposed transactions described herein or this Letter Agreement without the prior written consent of the other Party, except as such disclosure may be required by law. If the law requires such disclosure, the disclosing party shall notify the other Party in advance and furnish to the other Party a copy of the proposed disclosure. Notwithstanding the foregoing, the Parties acknowledge that certain disclosures regarding the agreements, the proposed transactions or this Letter Agreement may be required to be made to each Party's representatives or certain of them, and to any other party whose consent or approval may be required to complete the agreements and the transactions provided for thereunder, and that such disclosures shall not require prior written consent. BCI and its employees, affiliates and associates will (a) treat all information received from the Company confidentially, (b) not disclose such information to third parties without the prior written consent of the Company, except as such disclosure may be required by law, (d) not use such information for any purpose other than the consideration of the matters contemplated by this Letter of Intent, including related due diligence, and (d) return to the Company any such information if this Letter Agreement terminates pursuant to Paragraph 14 below.

12. EXPENSES; FINDER'S FEE. The Parties are responsible for and will bear all of their own costs and expenses incurred at any time in connection with the transaction proposed hereunder up to $_____$. Any additional or extraordinary expenses above this amount shall be borne by BCI; provided, however, the Company shall be responsible for any finder's fees payable in connection with the transactions contemplated hereby.

13. BREAK-UP FEE. The Company agrees to pay BCI a break-up fee of $_____ in the event that the sale and purchase of the shares contemplated in Section I is not accomplished by _____, 2000 as a result of the Company's failure or refusal to close pursuant to the terms set forth above and not due to any refusal or delay on the part of BCI to close by that date.

14. EFFECTIVE DATE. The foregoing obligations of the Parties under Section II of this Letter Agreement shall be effective as of the date of execution by the Company, and shall terminate upon the completion of the transactions contemplated in Section I above or, if such transactions are not completed, then at such time as all of the obligations under this Section II have been satisfied, unless otherwise extended by all of the Parties or specifically extended by the terms of the foregoing provisions; provided, however, that such termination shall not relieve the Parties of liability for the breach of any obligation occurring prior to such termination.

Please indicate your agreement to the Binding Terms set forth in Section II above by executing and returning a copy of this letter to the undersigned no later than close of business on , 2000. Following receipt, we will instruct legal counsel to prepare the agreements contemplated herein. The Binding Terms shall become binding on the Company upon the advance of funds pursuant to Paragraph 5 and the execution of Promissory Note in consideration therefor.

Very truly yours,

/s/ Prospective Buyer_____
Prospective Buyer, President
BuyCo, Inc.

ACKNOWLEDGED AND ACCEPTED:
SellCo, Inc.

By: Prospective Seller, President

Dated:

INDEX

A

A.M. Best, 35
American Capital Strategies Inc., 114
Appraisals. *See also* Business appraisers
  appraisal reports, 16-17
  buy-sell agreement provisions, 88, 90-91
Appraised value definition, 21
Appraisers. *See* Business appraisers
Arbitration, 104
Asset-valuation method, 23-24
Attorneys
  as advisers, 127
  preparation of work schedule, 138, 140-142
Audits. *See* Legal audits

B

Best Ratings, 35
Book value definition, 21
Business appraisers. *See also* Appraisals
  determining strategic value of a business, 20-21
  guidelines for, 18-20
  methods of valuation, 21-25
  valuation reports, 27
Business due diligence, 128-129
Business heirs, 42
Business interest rate of return, 80
Business plans
  for family-owned businesses, 59-60
  issues to consider, 56-57
  outline, 57-59

Business valuation
  annual assessments, 101
  book value, 90-91
  buy-sell agreements and, 90-91
  choosing a method, 25-27
  determining strategic value, 20-21
  importance of, 15-17
  IRS guidelines, 26
  methods of valuation, 21-25
  multiple of earnings, 90-91
  for small and closely held companies, 17-18
  using professional business appraisers, 18-20
  valuation reports, 16, 27
Buy-back rights, 119
Buy-out agreements, 33
Buy-sell agreements
  advantages of, 89
  decision-making and governance procedures, 88-89
  life insurance and, 30
  non-family co-founders and, 87-90
  types of, 90

C

Calls on stock, 76
Capital-gains taxes, 108, 117
Cash-flow projections, 20
Cashless deductions, 110
Cash-value insurance, 31-32
Certified Public Accountants, 127
Character licensing, 171-174
Charitable Lead Trusts, 78-79

247

Cliff vesting, 109
Closely held companies. *See* Small and closely held companies
Co-founders. *See* Non-family co-founders
Collective management, 46-47
Common stock
 preferred-stock recapitalizations, 80-81
Comparable-worth valuation method, 22-23
Completion clauses, 77
Conditional puts, 76
Conditional value
 definition, 21
Conflicts of interest business
 appraisers and, 19-20
Consumer Federation of America Insurance Group, 35
Corporate structure, 54-55
Corporations
 advantages of, 82
 life insurance and, 33
 preferred-stock recapitalizations, 80-81
 trusts, 77
 voting and non-voting stock, 75-77, 79
Cost of reproduction/replacement, 23
Coverage test, 109
CPAs. *See* Certified Public Accountants
Cross-licensing agreements, 103
Cross-purchase agreements, 33, 90, 93

D

Deadlocks, 100
Death of owner
 family business exemption, 73
 non-family co-founders, 86-87
Deferred-compensation plans, 82
Definitive documents, 136-137
Dispute resolution, 94-104
Disqualifying dispositions, 117
Divorces

 benefits of trusts, 77
 buy-sell agreements and, 88
 shareholders' agreements and, 76-77
Due-diligence process, 128, 130, 146
Duff & Phelps, 35
Dynasty trusts, 79-80

E

Electing Small Business
 trusts, 78
Embezzlement, 96, 103
Employee stock ownership plans
 advantages of, 107-108
 coverage test, 109
 description, 106
 legal considerations, 109-112
 legal documents needed, 112-114
 leveraged ESOPs, 108
 non-leveraged ESOPs, 109
 raising equity capital for a transaction, 114
 risks involved, 108-109
 selling to an ESOP, 111
 stock-purchase agreements, 113
 structuring, 107-108
 valuation reports and, 16
Employment agreements, 102
Equalizing legacies, 29, 30
Equity capital for an ESOP
 transaction, 114
ESBT. *See* Electing Small Business trusts
ESOPs. *See* Employee stockownership plans
Estate freezes, 80-82
Estate planning
 compared with succession planning, 6
 determining needs, 53-54
 for non-family cofounders, 86-87
Estate taxes. *See also* Gift taxes; Gifting
 business valuation and, 17, 26
 credits and exemptions, 68-69

Index

dynasty trusts and, 80
family limited partnerships and, 83-84
life insurance and, 32, 78
minimizing, 5
Estate-and-gift-tax credit
accelerated taxable giving and, 70-72, 75
description, 68-69
family-business exemption and, 73
rate schedule, 71
Exchange Act, 150, 153
Exchange provisions, 76
Exit strategies. *See also* Succession planning; Transition management
franchising, 157-162
goals of, xx
importance of, 11-13
joint ventures, 163-165
licensing, 165-174
options, 155-157
selling to employees, 105-119
third-party sales, 121-142
Expected value definition, 21

F

Fair market value
buy-sell agreements and, 93
definition, 17, 21
determining, 15
IRS guidelines, 16
stock options, 117
Family Business Continuity Plan
business and financial planning, 56-60
components of, 60-61
importance of flexibility, 50-51
issues to consider, 62-63
legal impact of, 61-62
objectives of, 52-53
pre-planning process, 49-55
Family Business Council
policies and procedures, 44

Family Business Stock Index, 144
Family councils, 44-45
Family limited partnerships, 82-84
Family-owned businesses. *See also* Family Business Continuity Plan; Small and closely held companies
buy-sell agreements, 88
collective management, 46-47
continuity strategies, 74
corporate structure, 54-55
equalizing legacies, 29-30
estate freezes, 80-82
family business exemption, 73
family limited partnerships, 82-84
gifting, 69-77
importance of succession planning, 5
nontraditional succession planning strategies, 83
outside employment, 46
resource centers, 40
selling, 76
separating duty from opportunity, 45-46
shareholders' agreements, 75-77
succession issues to consider, 39-47
transfer of wealth, 1
trusts, 77-80
FBCP. *See* Family Business Continuity Plan
FBSI. *See* Family Business Stock Index
Federal Trade Commission, 162
Financial advisers, 127
Financial planning, 56-60
Financial recasting, 131
Financial performance
valuation method, 24-25
Formula pricing, 90, 91
Franchising
benefits of, 157
components of, 158
foundation for responsible franchising, 159-162
reasons for, 158-159
regulatory issues, 162
Fraud, 96, 103

249

G

GAAP. *See* Generally accepted accounting principles
Generally accepted accounting principles, 150
Generation-skipping tax exemptions, 77, 79-80
Gift taxes. *See also* Estate taxes annual exclusion, 70, 77
business valuation and, 17, 26
charitable deduction, 78-79
minimizing, 5
preferred-stock recapitalizations and, 80
trusts and, 77
Gifting
accelerated, taxable gifting, 70-75
benefits of, 69-70
completion clauses, 77
determining retirement needs, 54
irrevocable trusts, 76-77
issues to consider, 75-77
life insurance and, 29-30
preferred-stock recapitalizations and, 81
shareholders' agreements, 76-77
tax-free annual gifting, 70-75
Going concern value definition, 21
Going public. *See* Publicly held companies
Good-faith deposits, 136
Goodwill value, 23-24
Grantor trusts, 78

H

Heir financing, 30
Hybrid agreements, 90

I

Incentive stock options, 106, 116-118
Income taxes
life insurance and, 32-33, 78

Industry multipliers, 26
Initial public offerings, 16, 97, 144
Installment sales, 82
Insurance. *See* Life insurance
Intangible assets, 20, 23-24
Intellectual-property rights, 168
Interim agreements, 132
Internal rate of return analysis, 25
Internal Revenue Service. *See also* Tax issues business valuation guidelines, 26
fair market value guidelines, 16
family limited partnerships rulings, 83-84
gift-tax disputes, 17
Investment bankers
as advisers, 127
IPOs. *See* Initial public offerings
IRR. *See* Internal rate of return analysis
Irrevocable life insurance trusts, 78
Irrevocable trusts, 76-77
IRS. *See* Internal Revenue Service
ISOs. *See* Incentive stock options

J

Joint ventures, 103, 163-165

K

Key-person life insurance, 87, 93-94, 102

L

Legal audits, 54, 101, 126
Legal counsel
as adviser, 127
preparation of work schedule, 138, 140-142
Legal due diligence, 128
Letters of intent
advantages and disadvantages of, 134

Index

binding terms, 135-138
choosing a type, 132-133
due diligence and, 128
proposed terms, 135
Licensing
benefits of, 165-166
character licensing, 171-174
disadvantages of, 166-167
merchandise licensing, 171-174
technology licensing, 167-171
Life insurance
amount needed, 33-34
buy-out agreements, 33
buy-sell agreements and, 30
company ratings, 34-35
cross-purchase agreements, 33
equalizing legacies, 29-30
family limited partnerships and, 83
irrevocable life insurance trusts, 78
key person policies, 87, 93-94, 102
marital deduction, 32
partnerships and, 33
second-to-die life insurance, 78
for spouses, 34
taxes and, 32-33
types of policies, 31-32
Limited partnerships
family limited partnerships, 82-84
trusts, 77
Limited-liability companies, 33, 83-84
Liquidation value definition, 21
Litigation, 104
LLCs. *See* Limited liability companies

M

Management buyout transactions, 114
Management succession compared with ownership succession, 6
Family Business Continuity Plans and, 53
Marketability discounts, 80
MBOs. *See* Management buyout transactions
Mediation, 104
Merchandise licensing, 171-174

Minority-interest discounts, 80
Money-purchase pension plans, 110
Moody's Investors Service, 35

N

National Association of Securities Dealers (NASD), 152
Net present value analysis, 24-25
Net worth definition, 21
Non-family co-founders
avoiding disputes, 98-102
buy-sell agreements, 87-90
functions of, 85-86
key-person insurance, 93-94
managing breakups, 102-104
managing disputes, 94-98
planning issues for, 86-87
tax issues, 91-93
valuation and pricing issues, 90-91
Non-qualified stock options, 106, 117-118
Non-voting shares, 75-77, 79, 81
NPV. *See* Net present value analysis
NQSOs. *See* Non-qualified stock options

O

Offering memorandum, 128
Option fees, 136
Organization charts, 43
Ownership succession
compared with management succession, 6
Family Business Continuity Plans and, 53

P

Partnerships
dispute resolution, 94-104
family limited partnerships, 82-84
life insurance and, 33
preparing agreements, 101-102

trusts, 77
Preferred-stock recapitalizations, 80, 81
Preliminary agreements, 128
Pre-qualifying buyers, 131-132
Publicly held companies
   benefits of, 143-145
   comparable-worth valuation, 22-23
   disadvantages of, 145
   legal costs, 145-148
   negative factors, 149
   registration process, 151-152
   registration statements, 149-150, 151
   reporting and disclosure requirements, 153-154
   selecting an underwriter, 148-150
   Small Business Initiatives, 150-151

Q

Qualified Subchapter S trusts (QSST), 78

R

Rabbi Trusts, 82
Rates of return. *See* Internal rate of return analysis
Redemptions. *See* Stock redemption agreements
Registration statements, 149-150, 151
Registration states, 162
Reproduction/replacement costs, 23
Restricted stock program, 106
Retirement
   determining needs, 53-54
Return on investment ratio, 25
Revenue Ruling, 59-60, 26
Rights of first refusal, 88
ROI. *See* Return on investment ratio
Rule 436, 162

S

S corporations
   preferred-stock recapitalizations

and, 80
   tax issues, 83
   trusts, 77-78
   voting and non-voting stock, 75-77
Scheduled vesting, 109
Second to die life insurance, 78
Securities Act, 151-152
Securities and Exchange Commission (SEC)
   guidelines for public announcements, 137
   registration of initial public offerings, 144, 151-153
   regulations for public offerings, 145-147
   Small Business Initiatives, 150, 151
Seller's remorse, 129
Selling to employees
   employee stock ownership plans, 107-113
   gradual sale to key employees, 115
   issues to consider, 118-119
   stock bonus award plans, 116
   stock options, 116-118
   strategies, 105-106
Shareholders' agreements, 75-77, 101-102
Shomaker, Barbara, 59
Small and closely held companies. *See also* Family-owned businesses
   difficulties in determining valuation, 17-18
   methods of valuation, 21-25
   responsibilities of owners, 100
   using professional business appraisers, 18-20
Small Business Initiatives, 150-151
Sole proprietorships
   tax issues, 67-68
Spouses
   life insurance for, 34
   of non-family co-founders, 86
Standard & Poor, 35
Stock
   buy-back rights, 119
   buy-sell agreements and, 91-93
   calls on, 76
   preferred-stock recapitalizations, 80-81

stock bonus award plans, 116
stock options, 116-118
voting and non-voting shares, 75-77, 79, 81
Stock-redemption agreements, 76, 90, 93
Strategic reorganization, 81-82
Strategic values, 20-21
Strike price, 117
Substitute assets, 23-24
Succession planning. *See also* Exit strategies; Transition management
  business valuation, 15-27
  choosing a strategy, 11
  compared with estate planning, 6
  considerations for family owned business, 39-47
  elements of an effective plan, 4
  importance of, 5, 11-13
  issues to consider, 2-3, 6-11
  life insurance and, 29-35
  nontraditional strategies, 83
  options for, 10-11
  steps involved, 10
  tips for, 7
SWOT analyses, 60

T

Tax issues. *See also* Gifting buy-sell agreements and, 91-93
  capital-gains taxes, 108
  credits and exemptions, 68, 75-77
  employee stock ownership plans, 109-112
  family limited partnerships, 82-84
  family-business exemption, 73
  generation-skipping exemptions, 77, 79-80
  life insurance and, 32-33, 78
  S corporations, 83
  stock bonus awards, 116
  strategies for reducing taxes, 67-68
  tax brackets, 68
  trusts, 77
Technology licensing, 167-171
Technology-transfer agreements, 168
Term life insurance, 31

Termination conditions, 102
Third-party sales
  as alternative to gifting, 76
  buyer's motivations, 124
  common mistakes sellers make, 130-132
  dispute resolution, 97
  issues to consider, 122-123
  letters of intent, 132-138
  preparing to sell your business, 123-130
  reasons for, 121-122
  reasons for unsuccessful deals, 129
  seller's motivations, 124
  structuring deals, 139, 142
  team of advisers, 125-127
  valuation reports and, 16
  work schedules, 138, 140-141
Third-party financing, 30
Trademarks, licensing, 171-174
Training systems, 43
Transition management. *See also* Exit strategies; Succession planning
  advisers, 43-44
  characteristics of successful plans, xx
  communication channels, 45
  definition, xv
  establishing criteria, 45
  flow chart, 3
  governance and communications groups, 44-45
  importance of, 11-13
  organization charts, 43
  stepping down, 47
  training systems, 43
Triggering events, 87-88, 91
Trustees
  responsibilities of, 79
Trusts
  advantages of, 77
  Charitable Lead Trusts, 78-79
  dynasty trusts, 79, 80
  employee stock ownership plans and, 109
  irrevocable life insurance trusts, 78
  irrevocable trusts, 76-77
  S corporations and, 77-78
  trustee responsibilities, 79

U

Underwriters, 148, 150
Uniform Franchise Offering Circular (UFOC), 162

V

Valuation. *See* Business valuation
Valuation reports, 16, 27
Value
   definitions, 21
Vesting
   employee stock ownership plans, 109
Voting rights, 110
Voting shares, 75-77, 79, 81

W

Walk-away fees, 135
Weiss Research, 35
Whole-life insurance, 31-32
Wills
   succession planning and, 6
Work schedules, 138, 140-142